There is no group of people in the United States about whom less is known, than the undocumented aliens who come to North America to escape the poverty of their homelands. WITHOUT DOCUMENTS sets out to explode the innumerable myths which surround the undocumented aliens: that they go on welfare, that their children crowd into the schools, that they contribute to crime, that they send mythical amounts of money out of the country, that they have more children than United States citizens do, that they take jobs away from citizens.

But they are used: by employers, by politicians seeking to get their names in the headlines. Since most are young, unmarried males, their contributions help support not only schools and other services which they do not use, but the Social Security fund, from which they cannot collect benefits. They are abused: assaulted by the Border Patrol, unable to seek recourse for wages below the minimum, for hours which can run to as many as 60 a week.

This book sets the record straight, giving the history of immigration to the United States, and in particular the history of Mexican immigration, for it is from Mexico that the greatest percentage of immigrants comes. The author shows that the solution lies not in closing the borders—which is impossible—but in a cure to the economic problems of Mexico.

WITHOUT DOCUMENTS

by
DICK J. REAVIS

CONDOR

NEW YORK

WITHOUT DOCUMENTS

CONDOR

PRINTING HISTORY
CONDOR edition published June 1978

All Rights Reserved
Copyright © 1978 by Dick J. Reavis

ISBN 0-89516-035-8
Library of Congress Catalog Number: 78-53470

Printed in the United States of America

CONDOR PUBLISHING COMPANY, INC.
521 Fifth Avenue
New York, N.Y. 10017

For Foncho, Jorge, Reyna y Pedro, quienes me enseñaron más que los libros; for my parents, who are patient; y para Marti, quien me da anhelos de vivir.

CONTENTS

Dedication v
Acknowledgements ix
Foreword xi
Glossary of Terms xiii

Part I: The Human Subject 1
    Chapter 1   A Tale of Two Countries 3
    Chapter 2   Profile of *Sin Papeles* 7
    Chapter 3   *Sin Papeles* Made Good 11

Part II: The Historical Background 21
    Chapter 4   Statue of Liberty 23
    Chapter 5   In Time of Need 33
    Chapter 6   Operation Wetback 41
    Chapter 7   Closing the Door on *Braceros* 47
    Chapter 8   Closing the Door on *Inmigrants* 57

Part III: The Contemporary Subject—Dynamics of
    the Controversy 63
    Chapter 9   What it Takes to Immigrate 65
    Chapter 10   Deportation Blues 69
    Chapter 11   Why Mexicans Flee Home 76
    Chapter 12   Law and Reality 85
    Chapter 13   The Current Debate 89
    Chapter 14   Gen. Chapman's Smear Campaign .. 99
    Chapter 15   Inflating the Estimates 103
    Chapter 16   They're Stealing Our Jobs 109
    Chapter 17   Tax Evaders! Welfare Cheats! 117
    Chapter 18   Unemployment 127
    Chapter 19   Health, Education and Welfare 129
    Chapter 20   Balance of Exchange 133
    Chapter 21   The Breeder Myth 135

Chapter 22   The Chicano Movement 139
Chapter 23   The Carter Plan 145
Chapter 24   The European Parallel 153
Chapter 25   The States Get Into the Act 163
Chapter 26   Ku Klux Klan Diplomacy 167
Chapter 27   Is Leonel Castillo the Answer? 173
Chapter 28   UFW Dualism 181
Chapter 29   Inside the Border Patrol 183
Chapter 30   Life, Limb and Legality: The Civil
              Liberties Issue 195

Part IV: Case Histories 207
Chapter 31   The *Pollero* Game 209
Chapter 32   Crossing the Bridge 215
Chapter 33   River Jumpers 225
Chapter 34   Visa Jumper 233
Conclusion 239
Appendix A S.2252, the Carter plan bill 251
Appendix B Immigration Counseling Groups 256
Appendix C Statistical Tables 262
Index 271

ACKNOWLEDGMENT

Writers live on the forebearance and cooperation of friends and acquaintances. Those who write about public policy also take advantage of government, academic and newspaper researchers. This book owes its roots to dozens of people and agencies, among them: the Association for Critical Social Studies and Action, at the University of Michigan; to Mike McGrath, who wrote the chapters on European guestworkers and American civil liberties; to Kate Tweedy, who struggled to weed the passive voice out of my style; to *compañeros* Chon, Bernardo and Craig; to Jim Haskins, agent and friend; to Nenita; to Gilbert Cardenas at the University of Texas; to Congressman Jack Hightower's office, efficient Elaine at INS, and the honest researchers who did the Linton report; to my wife and parents; and above all, to the *sin papeles* themselves, whose suffering has not been lightened by all the controversy surrounding them.

FOREWORD

Undocumented immigration is one of the more complex issues facing Congress and the public today. As a controversy, its importance is relatively recent, and therefore, much study of the subject remains to be done. No single work can fill all the gaps in current information, nor can it explain the myriad aspects of the question. This work, however, should serve well as an introduction to the topic.

The design of the book attempts to accomplish several ends: (1) to humanize understanding of the subject, by introducing case histories of undocumented immigrants; (2) to retrace the historical background of the immigration controversy; (3) to analyze, from an economic point of view, the interests of the parties to the Congressional dispute over undocumented immigration; and (4) to sketch out ways in which the problem might be solved.

Much of the information presented represents a synthesis of points raised by labor unions, business lobbyists, Chicano organizations, and the government, each of which has depicted undocumented immigration, especially Mexican immigration, in a different light. Other information is original with this writing, for the newness of the subject forces original research on anyone seriously interested in it. Likewise, while some of the suggestions and commentaries presented are the products of academic scholarship, others are the fruit of imaginative activists and the author's own speculation.

For a variety of reasons, it is unlikely that Congress or federal agencies will do anything soon to resolve the question of undocumented immigration, or to alleviate the problems of immigrants themselves. Legislation currently pending in the Senate and House is largely of value for vote-getting purposes, and it is likely that undocumented immigration will continue to be an element in campaigning into the future. Therefore, this book should make important reading for a long time to come.

Glossary of Terms

Anglo—A Southwestern term for English-speaking persons of European ancestry. Generally speaking, Southwesterners classify themselves as Anglo, Black, or Chicano.

alambrista—(literally, a fence man); an undocumented immigrant who enters the U.S. by climbing or cutting a wire along the U.S.-Mexican border.

bracero—In Spanish, a day laborer. In Mexican and American usage, the term often refers to Mexicans brought to the U.S. as temporary workers under legal labor import programs.

Chicano—synonym for Mexican-American; sometimes, a native-born American of Mexican descent.

coyote—(literally, a coyote); a labor agent who contracts Mexicans to work in the U.S.

ejidos—Mexico's semi-collectivized farms.

gabachos—identical to *gringos.*

green-carders—*inmigrantes,* or "permanent resident aliens."

gringos—a disparaging term for Anglos or U.S. residents of non-Latin heritage.

Immigration—the Immigration and Naturalization Service or its police arm, the Border Patrol.

INS—The U.S. Immigration and Naturalization Service, a Justice Department division and parent agency of the Border Patrol.

inmigrante—a legal immigrant to the U.S.; in INS terms, a "permanent alien legal resident" or "green-carder."

La Migra—The Border Patrol or INS.

mojados—(literally, "wets"); the term most widely used by undocumented Mexican immigrants to describe themselves. In educated circles, *"mojado"* and *"mojados"* are regarded as disparaging terms.

el norte—(literally, the north). A Mexican term for the United States.

paisano—countryman.

pistolero—a gunman for large landowners in Mexico.

pochos—an insulting Mexican term for *inmigrantes* and Chicanos.

pollero—(literally, a poultryman); a smuggler of undocumented immigrants.

pollo—(literally, a chicken); an undocumented immigrant who is brought to the U.S. by a smuggler.

la raza—the people, or race. A Mexican and Chicano term for the Mexican and Mexican-American people; sometimes, a term for all the descendents of Spanish and native ancestry.

sin papeles—(literally, without papers); in the nominative, a Mexican term for undocumented immigrants, or a single undocumented immigrant.

tostón—a unit of Mexican money, the 50-centavo coin.

wetbacks—a disparaging Southwestern term for undocumented immigrants.

yanqui—literally yankee. A disparaging term for U.S. citizens.

PART I

The Human Subject

CHAPTER 1

A Tale of Two Countries

On the afternoon of May 26, 1976 Border Patrolman Kent Nyguarrd apprehended a Mexican citizen, Silverio Hernandez, inside the city dump at Eagle Pass, Tex., just yards away from the Rio Grande. Nyguarrd handcuffed Hernandez to an abandoned refrigerator and then chased off after other suspected *sin papeles* in the area. When he returned minutes later, his prisoner was gone. Hernandez had moved about 10 yards back down the riverbank, where he pushed himself and the refrigerator over a 5-foot mudbank, off into the depths of the Rio Grande. His apparent plan was to use the rusting appliance as a raft to carry himself back to the Mexican shore. Instead, it took in water and dragged him down. This is the story Border Patrolmen told newsmen.

Hernandez, 24, was a resident of Piedras Negras, the Mexican town across the Rio Grande from Eagle Pass. His friends say that he had no reason to flee from custody, and that he must have known from its very weightiness that he could not raft the refrigerator across the river. They think he was pushed in to drown. Yet no grand jury was called to investigate the death of Silverio Hernandez, nor were any charges filed. Nyguarrd was reportedly transferred to another Border Patrol station within weeks after the May 26 incident.

3

The bizarre death of Silverio Hernandez is perhaps an atypical listing in the daily reports of the Border Patrol, but his desperate bid to enter the U.S. is increasingly common. Each year, hundreds of thousands of undocumented Mexican immigrants come to the U.S. and succeed in their attempts to get a toehold on survival. Though many are apprehended and returned to Mexico, most of them return to the U.S.—illegally—in a matter of weeks.

Had Silverio Hernandez survived, he would have been returned home, one of nearly a million Mexicans now turned back annually in a rising wave of deportations which has swollen to 10 times the crest reached in 1964, following the cancellation of seasonal labor import programs with Mexico. The influx of undocumented immigrants has created a carryover population estimated as high as 8 million, but probably much lower. The rising number of *sin papeles*—which former Immigration Service Commissioner Leonard F. Chapman called a "silent invasion"—is predominantly Spanish-speaking. Chapman estimated that 5 million of America's undocumented immigrants are Mexican nationals, with Central and South Americans accounting for another million or more. Of the Mexican majority, nearly 90 per cent come to the United States without any immigration documents whatever, chiefly by crossing the dry California desert or the wet Rio Grande undetected.

The fate of Silverio Hernandez and that of thousands who cross the Mexican border successfully each month is no longer a question of regional significance alone. For four generations, undocumented Mexican immigrants have made Southwestern harvests profitable, and today, the destinations they stake out before leaving home run as far north as Seattle, Salt Lake City and Chicago. The arrest of some 80 Mexican illegals at the Belmont race track in New York, the deportation of others found working as janitors at INS headquarters in Washington, D.C., are indicators that the *scope* of undocumented immigration—if not its *base*—is widening eastward.

Whether he heads for San Diego or Detroit, the aim of the *sin papeles* is to get a job and hold it, either to work up a nest egg for survival on return to Mexico, or to establish himself in America. As simple and constructive as that goal may be, the *sin papeles* finds himself in a hostile environment. He is the hunted species of the Border Patrol, the police agency of the Immigration and Naturalization Service (INS)—which itself is a branch of the federal Justice Department. The *sin papeles* is an object of dislike inside the Spanish-speaking community where he settles, for he is seen as a job competitor. Outside, the *sin papeles* is viewed as a disposable source of cheap labor, as a welfare chiseler and tax evader, as a carrier of dreaded diseases and of poverty—in short, he is seen as a character to fit nearly every role of shame. The *sin papeles* as "illegal alien" is the subject of politicians' speeches and the object of racial discrimination, the stowaway in the Statue of Liberty. He is, in a word, an unwelcomed immigrant, but also an immigrant without any choice, for he cannot turn back to Mexico, whose myriad crises mount higher daily with no amelioration in sight. The *sin papeles* is forced by hunger in his homeland to seek out the status of a social outcast in America.

Since 1970, the presence of *sin papeles* in the United States has been developed into a public issue of major importance. Popular fears of a "Mexican invasion" have already lead several state legislatures—and one city government—to pass laws prohibiting the hiring of undocumented workers. Congress is again on the brink of passing anti-alien measures, including a proposal which would require all Americans to prove their citizenship when applying for work, or welfare, or even admission to hospital emergency rooms. The ultimate effect of these laws may be to lead us nearer to a police state, libertarians say—and Chicano leaders without exception predict that passage of the bills will intensify discrimination against the Spanish-speaking minority.

America today is in the breach of a historic decision, which in long-range terms is reducible to but two alternatives: Latinization or xenophobia. For the near future, the choice is one between welcoming Mexican immigrants and erecting an electronic wall, buttressed by armed guards, along nearly 2,000 miles of borderland. The course Congress and the people will chose is presumably based on the truth of the information brought to light, on realism in assessing the present. The task of this work, then, is to dig out the basis for claims that America should hail or repel the millions of poor who are banging on the doors of our southern border.

CHAPTER 2

———— ▶◀ ◀▶ ▶◀ ————

Profile of Sin Papeles

A Labor Department study released in 1975 provides a statistical profile of undocumented immigrants. The study, by Linton and Company, shows that Mexicans account for both the majority and the poorest segment of America's undocumented millions. The study divided seven hundred ninety-three undocumented immigrants it interviewed into three categories: Mexicans, other Western Hemisphere (WH) people, and Eastern Hemisphere natives. Of the 481 Mexicans interviewed, 90 per cent said they came to the U.S. to find a job, compared to 60 per cent of the WH immigrants and only 23 per cent of the Europeans. The Mexicans averaged but 4.9 years of schooling, the WH respondents 8.7 years, and the Europeans 11.9 years, a figure close to the U.S. norm. In their homelands, the Mexicans were most likely to have been farmworkers—49 per cent were—and least likely to have held white collar jobs; only 6.8 per cent. Nearly 48 per cent of the Europeans were office workers in their homelands, as were 34 per cent of the Western Hemisphere immigrants interviewed.

Once in the U.S., the Mexicans continued to be the poorest among undocumented immigrants. The average wage of those interviewed for the study was $2.34 an hour, compared to $4.08 for Europeans and $3.05 for the

Western Hemisphere sample. These wages compared to an average of $4.47 for American labor as a whole in 1976.

All of those interviewed by the Linton teams had worked two weeks or more in the U.S. Data from the study indicates that undocumented workers, on the whole, are younger than most workers in the domestic labor force. The average age of Mexicans interviewed for the study was 27.6 years; the average age of American workers is 39 years. This contention—that undocumented labor is youthful labor—is further buttressed by the finding that 46 per cent of the Mexicans in the sample were between 16 and 24 years old. In the U.S. work force, only 23 per cent fit into that age category. Not only were the Mexicans younger than most American workers, they were younger than the Europeans in the study group, who averaged 30.7 years of age, and younger than the Western Hemisphere aliens, whose average age was 30.

Mexicans were found to have the largest family obligation. On the average, Mexican *sin papeles* reported 5.4 dependents in their home country, compared to 3.6 for the WH group, and 1.8 for the European sample, again, a figure close to the U.S. norm.

The Linton study found that 48% of the Mexicans and WH immigrants were married, compared to 30% of the EH group.

Marriage characteristics differed sharply from those of the American population at large. Only 55 per cent of the undocumented immigrants age 25 to 34 were married, compared to some 80 per cent of the population as a whole. More than a third of those in this age group were never married, compared to only 15 per cent of the U.S. population. Of those undocumented immigrants questioned, 39 per cent had spouses in the U.S.. Of 135 married aliens questioned, 82 indicated that their spouses were also undocumented. While there is some dispute about sex ratios among undocumented immigrants, 90 per cent of those interviewed by the Linton study were males; the INS estimates that less than 10 per cent of the nation's *sin papeles* are women.

The picture of the Mexican *sin papeles* which emerges from the Linton study is one of a young peasant, married and with children, uneducated and unemployed before coming to the U.S., poor by American standards even after his arrival, and separated from his family while he is here. The typical *sin papeles* hardly fits the description signalled by two words Congressmen and Border Patrolmen frequently use—the words, "alien invader." Instead, undocumented Mexicans resemble the European "poor, hungry, wretched masses" once welcomed to Ellis Island.

CHAPTER 3

———— ◦◦ ◅━━━▸ ◦◦ ————

Sin Papeles Made Good

The problems of undocumented Mexican immigration were unstudied as late as five years ago. Since then, scholars and social planners have produced more than two dozen volumes in separate attempts to find ways of preventing unauthorized immigration, or adjusting to it. Though several recent studies have turned up details of statistical relevance, only a few have begun where public policy investigations must being to be successful: with the human subjects to whom any new policy would apply. For obvious reasons, *sin papeles* who have established themselves are difficult to reach and untalkative. Therefore, most sociologists have interviewed *sin papeles* in Border Patrol custody. This circumstance has lead to the creation of a statistical profile of only the *sin papeles* who *fail* in their bids to advance themselves by coming here.

The story which follows is the true account of a successful *sin papeles*, whose last name is abbreviated with the letter "T" to protect his identity. Quotes are translated from the Spanish.

Martin T., 29, now lives in the Texas Panhandle town of Dalhart (pop. 7,000). Today this former *sin papeles* is a citizen, a union member, and an officer in the local Knights of Columbus chapter. He has proved to himself that the American dream can still come true: for today, in addition to being a homeowner, he is also a small-time landlord. Martin has succeeded where most men with his background of poverty—even native-born citizens—have failed.

Martin does not speak English with the ease of a native. He sometimes confuses "he" and "she," and also indulges a tendency to assign gender to all nouns as Spanish does: "See the hammer, he is over there," Martin might say. His style of dress is also reminiscent of Mexico, pointed toe cowboy boots, plaid western shirts, with Presley-style hair, combed back and oiled. Some of Martin's friends wear metal tips over the toes of their cowboy boots, a sure sign that they are from south of the Rio Grande.

Martin comes from a farm community near Meoqui, in the Mexican state of Chihuahua. Meoqui lies about 150 miles south through the desertland from El Paso, Tex. It is but a village, no larger than Dalhart, and intensely poor, because Mexico is a desperately poor country and the parched fields of Chihuahua produce little without irrigation. Like most *sin papeles*, Martin comes from a large family; he was the second son born to parents who had six children. He first came to the U.S. in 1968, at the age of 19. In his own words, Martin describes what he left behind.

"Before I came to the United States, my father owned a little piece of land, but the family couldn't make much of a living from it. In Mexico, you have to go to school for six years, and I went. It was hard for me sometimes, because I didn't always have shoes, and the other kids laughed at me. When I finished school—I guess I was about 14—I went to work in the fields other people owned."

When work was available, Martin earned about $1.15 per day: "I would work several days for one farmer, then be without work for a few days. Then I would find somebody else who needed help and work again as long as he needed me. I don't think I ever worked on the same farm for more than a month, because there never was enough work to do, and there were always other people looking for jobs, too."

The family home was a 4-room adobe dwelling with dirt floors. In each room, a light bulb hung from a single strand of wire. There was no indoor plumbing; younger members of the family brought water from a hand-operated pump about fifteen yards outside the house. Martin says the family's diet was far below standards for even the poorest Americans.

"Mainly we ate beans and tortillas, with a little salt and some peppers for seasoning. For a few months after each harvest, we would have meat maybe once a month. But we had chicken every week, because we owned chickens ourselves. A lot of people around Meoqui were not as lucky as we were, and never had chicken or eggs."

Like most peasant families, Martin's family believed that the way out of poverty lay in renting more land, or buying it. However, the family had no money for land acquisition. Emigration was not favored as a solution by anybody, because it would mean the separation of the family. Martin's father would not go the U.S., for if he were jailed or injured there, no one would be left to care for the family. When Alberto, Martin's older brother, reached the age of 20, however, he volunteered to go to *el norte*.

"It was about 1965 when Alberto came to the U.S. for the first time. He began sending money back to us, which we used for necessary things. But most of what he sent, we put in the bank to buy land. Finally, about 1970 or 1971, he and my dad leased some land and bought a tractor to farm it. Now the family is doing alright," Martin says.

Alberto did not come back to Meoqui for visits during the years he spent in the U.S. But early in 1968, he wrote home advising that Martin come north to join him. Inside his letter was a money order for $75 and instructions for dealing with Paco, a *"pollero"* or alien smuggler, who operates in Meoqui.

Paco is a native-born American citizen whose parents settled in the U.S. some 60 years ago during the last Mexican revolution. Weekdays, Paco works at an industrial job in the Texas Panhandle. Every other weekend he visits Meoqui to check into the accounts of a taxi service he owns there, and to make arrangements with the *sin papeles* whom he carries with him on return trips. Through employees of the taxi company, Martin secured an appointment with Paco, who drove by Pedro's house to pick him up the following day, a Sunday.

"When Paco came by the house, he had two other men with him, Ramon and Chelito. I already knew Ramon, because we had gone to school together. Paco drove us up to the border, and then took us down to a little shack on the Mexican side. He told us to wait until nightfall, then to cross the river and walk up to the first highway. He said he would flash his turn indicators as he drove along the highway and that we should come out of the bushes when we saw him. Then he took our money and left."

About two hours later, at sundown, a Border Patrol jeep passed by on the opposite bank of the Rio Grande, about 100 yards away. Sensing, or seeing—perhaps knowing— that the four men were waiting to cross, the jeep moved upriver about a quarter mile, then doubled back, crossing the point opposite them and going downriver several hundred yards. The jeep continued patrolling back and forth along the spot where Martin and his companions had hoped to touch American soil. Darkness came, and still the Border Patrol jeep made its rounds, at times flashing a spotlight on the river below. Martin and his companions knew well that there are hundreds of "safe houses" along the Rio Grande, too many for constant Border Patrol vigilance of them all. They concluded that someone had tipped off the American agents to their plan. After several hours of waiting, during which time the green jeep did not cease to rove the area, Martin, Ramon and Chelito decided to give up. They began walking back towards home, a journey of nearly three days.

Two weeks later, Martin drove the three men, along with Hector, another Meoqui area farmworker, to the cover house again. No additional payment was made by the three men who had already been there two weeks ago: the rule in dealing with "polleros" is payment in advance, but for successful crossings only. Since Martin, Chelito and Ramon had paid two weeks earlier, Paco now owed them a crossing. This time, the procedure was uncomplicated.

"The river was deep enough that I had to take my pants off, but nothing more. It was like wading across a flooded street," Martin says.

When the four men reached the highway on the U.S. side of the river, Paco was waiting with his car. The course he set out drove them over isolated ranch roads, away from Border Patrol checkpoints. "We weren't in danger of the Border Patrol there, but on some of those roads early in the morning I saw sheep and deer jumping out on the road in front of the car. I thought we might hit one of them," Martin recalls. By sunup, they were in Odessa, where Paco left the other three men with a "*coyote*," or labor contractor. Paco drove Martin on to Alberto's house on a ranch about 20 miles outside of Dalhart. It was nearly noon when they arrived.

Several days later, a Chicano ranch hand took Martin into Dalhart to apply for a Social Security card. The Chicano translated questions on the application form to Martin, who answered all the questions truthfully: in the pre-Nixon era, there was no requirement that card applicants prove legal residency. The clerk in the Social Security station did not ask Martin about his immigration status, either, nor did she call policemen to investigate. *Sin papeles* are common in towns like Dalhart, so much so that they are almost an unquestioned institution. In West Texas, and across most of the Southwest, few people see any reason why Mexican immigration should be halted.

It was nearly six weeks before Martin's Social Security card came in the mail. In the interval, he helped the ranch crew replace fence posts, and was paid a gratuity by Alberto's employer. When the card arrived, through relatives of Chicano workers on the ranch, Martin found a job in Dalhart as a cement worker with a construction company. He was pleased with his new circumstances.

"A lot of places, they pay 'wetbacks' less than other people, sometimes as little as $5 a day. But my checks came out the same as the other guys on the job. The company either thought I was legal here, or they decided to treat me fair anyway. Nobody ever asked if I was 'wet', and I never said anything about it. All the foremen but one were Chicanos, so I didn't have any trouble communicating in Spanish."

Martin moved away from the ranch house into Dalhart, closer to his job. There he shared an apartment with a

Chicano co-worker. After spending his first paychecks on clothing, he began saving.

"I wanted to send money home to my family, and someday, to buy a new car. I tried to save all I could, but you know, it gets kind of lonely when you don't know anyone, so I did go to the dances. It was the only luxury I had."

In a period of six months, Martin saved some $1,800.

The dances Martin attended were sponsored by Chicano and Catholic church organizations in the area. They usually featured *ranchera* music, the same genre which Martin and nearly all Mexican peasants prefer in their homeland. At the dances, Martin met young Chicanos his own age, and even several acquaintances from Meoque, as well. Like him, many of the Mexicans he met were *sin papeles*. But there was no reason to fear, because by long local tradition, lawmen did not inquire into the immigration status of anyone who otherwise stayed within the law. From time to time, there were fights at the dances, usually between men who were legal residents. *Sin papeles* as a rule backed down from bullies, and were careful not to drink in excess: arrest for them could mean deportation.

Late one Saturday night as Martin and his roommate, who owned a car, returned from a dance, they were stopped by a city policeman on patrol. The left headlight on their car was burned out, and Martin's roommate smelled of beer. "The cop had both of us come down to the police station, where they gave my roommate a ticket for driving the car with the headlight out. They also asked him about immigration papers. Since he could speak English, he didn't have any trouble. Then they asked me.

"I really didn't understand the question, so my friend translated for me. Everybody had told me that if I lied, *La Migra* might rough me up. So I told the cop in Spanish that I didn't have any papers, and my roommate translated what I said. Then the cops let him go, but they kept me there for Immigration."

Two days later, Border Patrolmen came to Dalhart to question Martin. He again confessed that he had no documents. The Border Patrolmen asked if he would pay his passage back to Mexico, and Martin agreed: "The way people had told me, you don't get in much trouble if you pay your own way back."

The Patrolmen locked him in a van with other *sin papeles* rounded up in the area, and drove him to a jail in Lubbock, some three hours to the south. The following morning, all of them were put on a green and white Border Patrol bus, with bars on the windows. The bus headed south towards Mexico. A single Border Patrolman rode in it as guard.

The bus stopped at Marfa, Texas, on its way south. There, Martin and the other prisoners were processed through a deportation center. Border Patrolmen interrogated them, noting information on white index cards. The deportees were fingerprinted, and those who had money, paid $26 for the trip from Lubbock. After the brief processing stop, they were reboarded and taken to the Mexican side of the border. With Border Patrolmen and Mexican police watching, all of the men were boarded onto a train bound for Chihuahua, capital of the state of that name. A Mexican guard accompanied them, but he did nothing when several of the deportees jumped off the train as it pulled out of the station; these men were planning to make a quick return to the U.S. Martin rode with the others to Chihuahua, where all of them were released from custody. From the capital, Martin caught a bus to Meoque.

"I was afraid that when I got back people would laugh at me. But nothing like that happened. It was almost Christmas, and everybody was glad I could be home for the holidays."

His deportation did not alter Martin's plans to make a new life for himself in Texas. In Dalhart he had left behind a brother, a good job—and a fiancée.

His fiancée, Teresa, was a senior at Dalhart High School, a Chicana whom Martin had met at a dance some six months earlier. The young *sin papeles* knew that marriage to Teresa would open the door to permanent legal residency in the U.S., but he had not set a wedding date; Teresa wanted to graduate from school before marrying, and Martin, for his part, wanted to save up enough money to establish a household with her. He had been back in Meoque about 10 days when a letter came from Teresa, urging him to come back to Dalhart for an immediate marriage. In effect, Martin's deportation served as a catalyst to the couple's plans.

Martin again made arrangements to see Paco. But this time, the *pollero*'s fee was higher.

"Paco wanted $100 instead of $70 like before. He told me that he charged me less the first time just to help me set myself up in Texas. I argued with him, but finally I had to pay what he asked. It's always that way in Mexico; if people know you have money, they're going to make sure they get their share of it."

Martin's return to Dalhart was uneventful, but once there, he encountered new problems.

"I couldn't go back to my old apartment, except to get my things out, because once people know you've been deported, a lot of things are different. People are afraid to live with you, because they don't want *La Migra* coming around. And then there are always some people, especially among the Chicanos, who will turn you in if they see you. Every community has its informers for the Immigration."

After taking his belongings out of his old apartment, Martin took them to his brother Alberto's place on the ranch. Then he went to Teresa's house to plan for the wedding.

"We had wanted a big wedding, with a dance afterwards and everything else that is traditional. But both Teresa and I were afraid that Immigration would get me again, so we decided not to tell anyone else that I was back in town. Her parents didn't like the way we had to do it, but there was no choice. We didn't even send out wedding invitations for fear somebody would denounce me.

"We decided to have the little ceremony the following Saturday, six days away. I had to be careful, so I went back to my brother's house and stayed there all week. I only went out of the house twice, once to get the blood test, and once to sign the marriage license."

Teresa's relatives and Alberto were present at the bride's home that Saturday afternoon, when the couple was wed. After the brief Catholic ceremony, Martin moved his belongings to a bedroom in Teresa's family home.

"We would have rented a place of our own, but both of

us wanted to save up some money for putting my papers in order. I figured that if I went back to work and saved, we could hire a lawyer within a couple months.

"I went back to my old job. Everybody there knew that I had been deported, but nobody cared anyway. I was a good worker, and in this country, that's what is important. Here, they don't care who you are or what family you come from. All they care about is how hard you work."

But six weeks after he returned to work, Martin was picked up again.

"Two Border Patrolmen came out to the job we were working on, looking for another 'wetback' who worked with us. This particular guy was in a restroom across the street from our job, and nobody told the *Migras* anything. They looked around for awhile, and when they couldn't find him, they started questioning me because I was the only other Mexican around. I told them I was married to a citizen, but it didn't do any good. One of them argued with the other that I should be given a delayed deportation order. But the other one of them, who must have been the chief, didn't want to."

Martin pleaded with the Border Patrolmen for a chance to say good-bye to Teresa, and they relented. Both agents waited at the curbside while Martin went in to bid her farewell. He gave Teresa the money he carried, except for the fee he knew he would be asked to pay for transportation home. Teresa and her mother wept, for it was clear now that the wedding had been hurried for no good purpose, and once again, they feared Martin was in danger. He assured them that the Border Patrolmen were courteous, and that he had no fears about being deported. Teresa promised to meet him the following week in Meoqui, and Martin left. Once again he was taken to Lubbock, to Marfa, and back to Chihuahua. Three days later he was home in Meoqui again.

Marriage to an American citizen does not confer automatic immigration rights to Mexicans. The "beneficiary," or prospective immigrant, must provide documentation of several kinds. Martin's first task was to journey to Mexico City, 24 hours away, the only place in his homeland where Mexican citizens are issued passports. When Teresa came, she brought a document saying that Martin had not been convicted of any offenses in Texas, as well as a letter from his employer, saying that his job was waiting for him. Some three weeks after Martin's deportation, he and Teresa presented themselves at the U.S. Consulate in Chihuahua.

Martin saw an irony in the requirements: "You have to have money to get all the paperwork done, and you have to have a job in the U.S. to get in. The only way to get those things, at least for most of us in Mexico, is to go to the U.S. Or in other words, you have to break the immigration laws before you can ever make yourself legal."

The irony was deepened when Martin told the consul officer that he had been deported twice. "They said if I had been deported, it would take special permission for me to get it legally. So we waited nearly a month for them to check up on my deportations. When it was all done, they said they could find no record of them, so no special permission was needed." What actually happened, as Martin learned, was that his deportations were what the Immigration Services calls "voluntary departures." Normally, no criminal charges are filed against deportees who admit their illegal status and pay their fares home. Instead, these deportees, far and away the majority, are classified as "voluntary returns." The "voluntary return" process saves the Immigration Service the costs of long-term jailings and court actions. It saves the deportee from prejudicing his future, because records of "voluntary departures" are not indexed as criminal records in Justice Department files. The consulate was unable to find any record for Martin as a deportee, because technically, he never was. Finding his "voluntary departure" records would not have barred him from legal immigration, and therefore, no check of these records was made.

By the time his forms were processed and ready, Martin and Teresa had spent two months waiting. It was then too late for Teresa to make up lost weeks in school. She never graduated, but neither she nor Martin were embittered, for at last they had legalized their future. Martin succeeded where most *sin papeles* fail.

PART II

————————◆◆◆————————

The
Historical
Background

CHAPTER 4

Statue of Liberty

Give me your tired, your poor,
Your huddled masses yearning to breathe free,
The wretched refuse of your teeming shore.
Send these, the homeless, tempest-toss'd to me,
I lift my lamp beside the golden door.
    —The words of Emma Lazarus,
      inscribed at the base of the
      Statue of Liberty

The obstacles Martin T. encountered in establishing himself as an American are not new ones. Immigration law, over a period of two centuries, has grown increasingly restrictive and hostile. Today, the means to legal immigration are for practical purposes out of reach of the world's poor.

American immigration policy developed on the assumption that no distinction need be drawn between members of the work force and members of society. Aliens came here to find jobs or farmland, and to seek business opportunity. When they arrived, they automatically acquired the right to permanent residency, the right to participate in economic and social life, and the right to become naturalized citizens. During America's first 50 years, immigration restrictions were practically non-existent: the government did not begin listing the names of immigrants at seaboard ports until 1820, and not until nearly a century afterwards was a head-count taken as immigrants crossed the southern and northern borders.

The open door policy, however, was limited by one unwritten assumption. Slaves, whether native-born or imported, acquired no rights by virtue of their membership in the workforce. The first general bar to immigration, made law in 1820, was a prohibition against the importation of slaves. With the enactment of that first anti-slavery clause, illegal immigration got its start. Between 1820 and the outbreak of the Civil War forty years later, an estimated quarter-million slaves of African descent were brought into America as contraband.

Mexican immigration to the U.S. was practically unknown in the early 19th Century, accounting for only one listing in 1820, for example. At the time, Mexico had ample room for population growth in its vast northern territories, which today make up the American Southwest. Efforts by the Mexican government to colonize its northern frontiers brought little success; what they brought instead was a horde of English-speaking American settlers, many of whom were given land grants by the Mexican government. Grantees were required to affirm loyalty to Mexico and the Catholic faith. Once they took an oath of loyalty, they became Mexican citizens.

Immigrants were most numerous in Texas, where by 1830 there were 25,000 English-speaking inhabitants, compared to 2,000 native Spanish-speakers. Many of the American newcomers brought slaves with them, a practice which disturbed the Mexican government, though not for moral reasons. The U.S. Congress was embroiled in debates over slavery, and as a result of legislative action, forbade the extension of slavery into new U.S. territories. Slaveholders, however, believed that they could bring Texas into the Union as a slave state, thereby increasing their representation in the Senate. The Mexican government feared that slaveholders in Dixie would finance a Texas revolt. Therefore, in 1830, the Mexican congress passed a law which prohibited the importation of slaves into Mexico. The law, its makers believed, would reduce the attractiveness Texas held for the slaveocracy. Customs stations and military outposts were established on the borders between northern Mexico and the U.S., to make the new anti-slavery legislation effective. Nevertheless, Americans brought slaves in by stealth, and slavery inside Texas continued under color of law.

Mexico at the time was beset with internal difficulties. Advocates of a strong central government prevailed over federalists in a bitter political feud which led to open revolt in 1834, when centralists assumed office in the Mexican government. A group of Texans, both naturalized and native Mexicans, joined in the federalist rebellion, whose aim was to restore the Mexican constitution of 1824, a move which would have deprived centralists of power. But by early 1836, shifts in the ethnic balance and political leanings of the Texas rebel movement led to a new and historic step—the declaration of complete independence. Both the Mexican government and American Abolitionists saw in the new revolt the expansionist designs of southern planters. Once Texas was independent, they warned, there would be moves to bring it into the Union as a slave state.

By mid-year, Texas rebels had captured Mexican commander Santa Anna, and won their independence in exchange for his release. Efforts to have Texas annexed to the Union began, but collapsed under pressure from free states and the Abolitionist movement in the north. Texas became an independent nation in which slavery flourished. But it did not establish a border guard to halt immigration; indeed, there were no barriers to the movement of Mexicans north.

Bandits from both sides of the Rio Grande took advantage of the absence of border guards. Sweeping in from Mexico, they would raid settlements in Texas, then fade off below the border; or coming down from Texas, they would prey on Mexicans, running north to escape soldiers and police. With some justification, each government accused the other of backing the bandit gangs; police forces from Mexican and Texas towns frequently exchanged shots across the borders, keeping the state of tension that had brought on revolution alive throughout the 10-year trajectory of the Republic of Texas.

The Mexican government was already in debt and behind schedule on payments to the U.S. Now she was subjected to diplomatic pressures to sell New Mexico and

California to satisfy American claims. The purchase offers alarmed the Mexican government, which saw in them the signs of more serious expansionist aims. In 1845, the U.S. annexed Texas, despite Mexican protests. A year later, General Zachary Taylor invaded Mexico with the aim of securing a treaty which would cede the rest of the Southwest to the U.S. The annexation of Texas, the Mexicans saw, had been merely a preparation for war.

Brutality characterized the American invasion as much as success. General Winfield Scott complained that the troops, "committed atrocities to make Heaven weep and every American of Christian morals blush for his country. Murder, robbery and rape of mothers and daughters in the presence of tied-up males of the families have been common."

Anti-Catholic sentiment in the U.S., exemplified in the founding of the Native American Party in 1845, had heavily influenced many of the volunteers. American troops frequently desecrated Catholic shrines in Mexico, and anti-Papalism was so intense inside the ranks of the American army that some 250 soldiers, mostly Catholics, deserted and joined the Mexicans. Eighty members of this group, known as the San Patricio batallion, were executed when Mexico City fell.

The conflict was swiftly settled. General Taylor captured Montcrey in Mexico's north, while the Marines moved in at the Gulf port of Veracruz, in Mexico's south. Within six months the southern invasion force had reached Mexico City, where some 100 military school cadets, known in Mexico as the "The Heroic Youths of Chapultepec" fought valiantly to their deaths. They were the capital city's last defense. In commemoration of the conquest and the victory over the Chapultepec cadets, the Marine Corps added a red stripe down the pantslegs of dress uniforms.

While Mexico was embattled, American troops commanded by Colonel Stephen Kearny secured New Mexico and moved on to California to reinforce the Bear Flag rebels, who like the Texans before them, had declared independence. By late 1846, the Southwest was under United States control. Two years later, the treaty of Guadalupe Hidalgo was signed by both the Mexican and American governments, formally ending the hostilities. The terms of the treaty gave the U.S. the territories which form the states of Arizona, California, New Mexico, Nevada, and half of Colorado. Furthermore, the U.S. won undisputed title to Texas. In all, Mexico lost over half her national territory, more than a million square miles. The U.S. paid Mexico $15 million in exchange.

Within weeks after indebted Mexico ratified the Treaty of Guadalupe Hidalgo, gold was discovered in the isolated northern foothills of California. Miners converged from everywhere: native Californians, both Anglo and Mexican-American, moved north, where they were joined by Americans of German, French and Irish descent. Foreigners of several nationalities, including Peruvians and Mexican, also descended on the gold fields. But by mid 1849, Anglo vigilante groups had organized to drive "foreigners of several nationalities, including Peruvian and lantes did not differentiate between Spanish-speaking *californios*, who were American citizens, and Spanish-speaking immigrants. The drive to exclude alien labor was augmented by a legislative act requiring foreign miners to pay an occupational tax.

In 1850, vigilantes set blazes in the town of Sonora, where *californios* and Mexicans lived, and roamed through its ruins, shooting and lynching male survivors. This and similar violent attacks intimidated Spanish-speaking miners, and put an Anglo seal on gold exploitation. The hysteria of 1849-50 also provided a beginning, in sentiment and law, for future exclusionist movements in California.

The Treaty of Guadalupe Hidalgo gave Mexican citizens in the newly-acquired territories a year in which to assume American citizenship or to move south below the new borders. Some 80,000 stayed on, while only 2,000 moved to Mexico, most of them to protect landholdings there. From 1849 until the early 20th century, the comings and goings of Mexicans in the Southwest were a matter of official and popular indifference—except in California.

Anglos along the West Coast resented the Chinese perhaps more than the Mexicans, and Orientals became the next target of exclusionism. This time the thrust came from organized labor, which saw the Chinese as wage competitors. Under labor's influence, in 1882 Congress prohibited the immigration of all Chinese. The Chinese Exclusion Act, like previous limits on immigration, gave rise to undocumented entries. No longer able to come to America freely, as Europeans did, the Chinese first entered Mexico, crossing northward into the U.S. the way *sin papeles* do today.

The labor movement for the next 20 years sought to close gaps in enforcement of the Chinese Exclusion Act, and to bar entry of other Orientals as well. Samuel Gompers, secretary of the American Federation of Labor, led the way. In 1901 the Resolutions Committee of the AFL convention declared that the Chinese were propagators of "vice and sexual immorality." Opponents of Asian exclusion, Gompers told the convention, were "dilettante sentimentalists," "profit hungry businessmen" and "degenerate politicians." The following year, with Herman Gutstadt of San Francisco, Gompers co-authored a pamphlet entitled *Some Reasons For Chinese Exclusion: Meat Vs. Rice, American Manhood Vs. Chinese Coolie-ism*. This racist tract was later reprinted by the Asiatic Exclusion Society, a West Coast version of the segregationist societies prevalent in anti-labor Dixie.

At the behest of Gompers and the exclusionist movement, the U.S. Bureau of Immigration— until then largely a head-counting agency—in 1903 established a border guard along the southern frontier. The guard, forerunner of today's Border Patrol, was instructed not to impede Mexican immigration. Instead, its task was that of catching the Chinese, whom the Bureau called "the most resourceful of alien peoples."

At the request of American diplomats, in 1907 the Japanese stopped issuing passports to ordinary citizens. This "gentlemen's agreement" put an end to legal immigration from another sector of the Orient, and gave the border guard heightened authority. Records from the era are insufficient to establish the contention conclusively, but given the debility of civil liberties organizations and widespread xenophobia, it is likely that Koreans and other Asians were also denied entry to American borders and shores. Nevertheless, undocumented Asian immigrants, especially

Chinese, continued to arrive, using Oriental communities—like El Paso's Chinatown—as conduits to the north.

While the border guard kept its eyes peeled for Asians, Mexicans crossed into the U.S. in record numbers. Mexico was swaying under the weight of a dictatorship which had deprived thousands of their lands, and which by encouraging inflationary policies and uncontrolled foreign investment, had impoverished its industrial workers. Political refugees from the Díaz regime began grouping in American border cities as early as 1904, and by 1910, the U.S. was the center for Mexican revolutionary conspirators and gun-runners. Mexico's revolution began in 1910 when Francisco Madero, soon to be President, left San Antonio to oversee fighting south of the border. But lines of allegiance and the ultimate goals of the revolution were not clearly established at its onset. What began as a quick-victory rebellion, wore on, in intermittent peace and warfare, for fully seven years. During the chaos, more than a million Mexicans are estimated to have fled to the U.S., many to stay permanently. Their immigration established the base for today's Chicano population.

World War I created new opportunities for Mexican newcomers. U.S. aid to the European conflict and ultimately military intervention took the slack out of the labor market. With Oriental immigration proscribed, European immigration blocked by Atlantic warfare, and many Americans in uniform, industry ran short of workers to meet stepped-up wartime production schedules. Mexicans supplied much of the need. For the first time, Mexican laborers in number began working outside of the Southwest. Spanish-speaking communities sprang up in Chicago, Milwaukee, Philadelphia and other cities distant from the border. By war's end, there were some 700,000 Mexicans in the U.S., 10 per cent of them east of the Mississippi River.

The mood of American leaders at war's end was one of isolation and fear. The Bolshevik revolution in late 1917 was taken as a warning that radicalism was everywhere a danger, and in America, most radicals were foreign-born. Exclusionists took advantage of the new atmosphere. Southern and Eastern European immigrants, who had earlier been depicted as mental incompetents, were now styled in propaganda as the authors of a vast and insidious anarcho-socialist plot. The Italian anarchists Bartolomeo Sacco and Nicolá Vanzetti were subjected to a show trial which ended in death verdicts for both. On the West Coast, the Mexican exiles Ricardo and Enrique Flores-Magon were imprisoned on sedition charges. The Swedish immigrant Joe Hill, a songwriter for the radical Industrial Workers of the World, was executed on murder charges which even at the time were regarded as transparent. On Jan. 2, 1920, across 70 cities, mainly in the northeast, socialist meetings were broken up, homes were raided, and some 10,000 radicals, most of them foreign-born, were jailed. Deportation proceedings were begun.

Though many of the accused were ultimately freed, the so-called Palmer raids—named for the then U.S. Attorney General—had more lasting effects for another reason. They were planned by a young justice department investigator, J. Edgar Hoover, who coined the word "dragnet" to describe them—and rose to national prominence as a result of the publicity they drew.

A series of Congressional acts passed between 1917 and 1921 reflected exclusionism's advance and its racial and political motivations. Asians not already excluded were barred from legal entry to the U.S. For the first time, limits were set on European immigration. The new quota system put into effect favored Western Europeans over Eastern and Southern Europeans, whom the exclusionists most identified with radicalism. Moves were made to subject Western hemisphere immigration to limits as well—but agricultural, mining and railroad interests intervened. Two measures passed for all immigrants, a literacy requirement and a head tax, were quickly suspended for Mexican laborers at the request of Southwestern employers. While immigration from across the Atlantic slowed, Mexican immigration continued almost as freely as before, and became the principal target for exclusionists.

In 1924, the California Federation of Labor spearheaded a public campaign for exclusion. A call in Congress to pass a Mexican quota was repelled, but compromise brought about the creation of the Border Patrol, with an initial force of 450 men, nine times more than the number assigned to the old border guard. Though its tactics were modeled on those of the old border guard, the new Border Patrol was authorized to detain Mexicans as well as Chinese. The Labor Department administered the new police agency, and in a 1923 bulletin described its task in these words:

> When Chinese smuggling was rampant on this border, a force at least approximating that required to cope with the situation was available. There were river guards to apprehend, if possible, the aliens and smugglers in the act of illegal entry; mounted men to pursue if the aliens eluded the vigilance of the officers at the points of crossing and proceeded overland by wagon or automobile; men to open and inspect freight cars before they left the border towns, and men to inspect all passenger trains leaving such towns. All these constituted the first line of defense. The second line of defense consisted of inspectors at strategical interior points on all railroads running north from the border. . . . The officers at the points, likewise, covered the highways for Chinese travelling afoot, by wagon, or in automobiles. . . . It was found that smugglers accompanying aliens from the border unloaded them from trains —both passenger and freight—and detoured them around the inspection points. Third and even fourth lines of defense were therefore established on some railroads at points farther removed from the border.

The United States by the mid-twenties had gone from a position of encouraging immigration to one in which officials talked about "defense" of the nation from immigrants. The Border Patrol was created to "defend" the nation against what it today calls "the illegal alien invasion"—a concept foreshadowed in the 1923 Labor Department report. But the Border Patrol's transformation from a relatively weak frontier guard into a national police force did not come about overnight. In its first years of operation, the Border Patrol barely exceeded 5,000 deportations per year. This modest record did not please exclusionists, who continued to campaign for restrictive legislation, now with more vehemence towards Mexicans. In a 1928 Congressional speech in favor of a Western Hemisphere immigration quota, Representative John Box described Mexican immigrants as the exclusionists saw them:

The Mexican peon is a mixture of Mediterranean-blooded Spanish peasants with low-grade Indians who did not fight to extinction but submitted and multiplied as serfs. Into this was fused much negro slave blood. This blend of low grade Spaniard, peonized Indian and negro slave mixed with negroes, mullatoes and other mongrels, and some sorry whites, already here. The prevention of such mongrelization and the degradation it causes is one of the purposes of our laws which the admission of these people will tend to defeat.

No Mexican quota was approved, but in 1929 Congress made new concessions to exclusionists: it made unauthorized entry to the U.S. a felony offense. Prosecutions, however, soon became unnecessary. The Great Depression drove Mexicans home. Between 1930 and 1940, unemployment touched more than 25 per cent of the labor force, and workers who kept their jobs often were forced to accept wage cuts as steep as 25 per cent. Public works projects were established for the jobless, but in states where the exclusionist movement was most powerful—California, for example—legislatures passed provisions to deny both relief and public employment to aliens. Industrial unemployment had already driven uncounted thousands back to near-peonage in rural Mexico, and deportations sent even more back. Half the Mexican population of Michigan, Indiana and Illinois was repatriated. Border Patrol activity shifted from concentration on the border—where crossings were decreasing—and into Mexican settlements in the Southwest. Deportations and voluntary returns of Mexicans over the decade created a pattern of "reverse migration"—there were 226,000 less Mexicans in the U.S. in 1940 than there had been in 1930. Subsequent studies indicate that of the 100,000 presumed Mexicans who were deported, as many as half were U.S.-born persons of Mexican descent.

CHAPTER 5

In Time of Need. . . .

The modern history of Mexican immigration, and the controversy before Congress today, has its kernel in the *bracero* program of the World War II years. *Bracero* ("hand" or "day laborer") is a Spanish term which refers to laborers, especially fieldworkers. In modern American usage, it refers to the more than 4 million Mexican workers who were legally brought to the U.S. between 1942 and 1965 to supplement the labor force.

"Reverse immigration" during the Depression depleted a reserve of cheap labor, but did not solve the problem of mass unemployment. Joblessness continued to plague the work force until the months immediately prior to America's entry into World War II, in December 1941. Once war preparations were underway, the military draft and enlistments took the slack out of the labor market. At the same time, war production orders stimulated industry. A manpower shortage rapidly developed, and employers began looking for operatives outside the usual pool of workers.

As younger workers went into uniform, a new generation of migrants filled their posts. Poor whites and blacks, most of them from the rural South, flooded into northern industrial cities to take vacated factory jobs. Women, who had previously been excluded from most industrial tasks, also met a part of the labor shortage. To satisfy the needs of agriculture and the railroads, Mexicans were brought in. The *bracero* program was created to bring them to the U.S. legally.

As early as 1926, the Mexican government had sought a labor export agreement with the U.S. When World War II opened, Mexicans leaders sensed that opportunity had come. In June, 1942 Mexico declared war on the Axis, a formality intended to please Uncle Sam. Negotiations to bring Mexican laborers to the U.S. were called at the request of the Mexican government and California sugar beet growers. In July, 1942 the *bracero* agreement was signed by the governments of both countries. Under its terms, some 150,000 Mexican workers would be imported over the next 5-year period.

By terms of the agreement, workers were to be recruited in Mexico and transported to jobs in the U.S. at the expense of the American government. *Braceros* were granted health and accident insurance, and the right to quit their jobs and return home at any time. The Mexican government was to be remitted 10 per cent of the earnings of each individual *bracero*, to hold in trust for him until his return home; this provision was a guarantee that *braceros* would, indeed, return. The bilateral agreement which set up the program stipulated that Mexican workers were not to be used to compete with American labor, or to lower wage rates. It also contained an agreement allowing Mexican labor officials to inspect *bracero* worksites and living quarters as a means of insuring that wage and health protections were not abused. The program was to be administered by the Farm Security Administration.

The announcement that jobs were waiting in *el norte* created near-pandemonium in Mexico. Twenty would-be *braceros* were killed in a stampede of first-day registrants in Mexico City. According to the system set up by the *bracero* pact, prospective workers were to be given numbers, and then selected by lot in a drawing conducted by Mexican officials. In practice, however, bribery became the way to *bracero* status. Desperate workers paid uncounted thousands of pesos to functionaries, each of whom owed a part of his take to superiors. Ultimately, corruption in the selection process was exposed, and three members of Mexico's Chamber of Deputies, along with hundreds of minor officials, were indicted.

The *braceros* who came to work in the U.S. were not permitted to bring their families with them, nor were they permitted to change occupations or make arrangements for permanent jobs. They were usually quartered in labor camps, and the cost of food and shelter provided them was deducted from their paychecks. Many complained that their quarters were unsanitary, that food costs were exorbitant, or that their fare was either poorly prepared or suited only to *yanqui tastes*. Many also charged that they were cheated out of fair wages. There was no minimum earnings guaranteed for railroad workers, and in 1943, at the request of California growers, the War Food Administration set a ceiling on *bracero* earnings in fields where asparagus, tomatoes, grapes, and cotton were grown. Despite these flaws, however, *braceros* were generally content with the opportunity offered them; 70 per cent of the returnees signed up to work in the U.S. again.

Though it gave thousands of Mexican workers a legal means to enter the U.S., the *bracero* program did not halt undocumented immigration; indeed, it stimulated it. The lottery system by which *braceros* were selected did not make winners of them all, and often, lottery selections were rigged by bribery. Those prospective *braceros* who lost out were often enticed to come to the U.S. by small-time employers or outright exploiters who did not want to guarantee the wages or conditions required for legal workers under the *bracero* program. Further, employers who hired *braceros* for harvest labor customarily made offers for year-round employment to the most industrious *braceros* brought to them. More than anything else, the exclusion of Texas from the *bracero* plan set up a labor vacuum into which undocumented workers flowed.

Segregation of blacks was the universal practice across Texas at the time, and whites in many communities extended the color bar to Mexicans and Chicanos as well. In west and south Texas especially, Mexicans and Chicanos were denied access to restaurants, theatres, barbershops, and other public facilities—even cemeteries. The Spanish-speaking population was frequently victimized by callous lawmen, and by the anti-Catholic Ku Klux Klan. Complaints from Texas had been so numerous that in June, 1943, Roberto Medellin of the Mexican Ministry of Labor announced that *braceros* would no longer be sent there "because of the number of cases of extreme, intolerable racial discrimination."

Officials in Texas reacted immediately with a series of shallow reforms. In early 1943 Governor Coke Stevenson went on a goodwill tour of Mexico, and on his return, established a Good Neighbor Commission, charged with promoting ethnic harmony. He also declared a state holiday on Sept. 16, Mexican Independence Day. A measure of the success of Good Neighbor politics was given the Mexicans on Sept. 13, when the Mexican consul at Houston was denied service at the Blue Moon Café in New Gulf, where he had gone to officiate in Independence Day ceremonies. On the same day, a Mexican army sergeant was arrested at Sugarland, Texas, for demanding access to public facilities. The Mexicans were not impressed by Stevenson's gestures, and demanded that stronger measures be taken to promote Anglo-Latin harmony.

In response, the Texas Legislature in May of 1944 passed the Caucasian Race Resolution, which urged desegregation of public facilities, as regards the Mexican and Chicano people. It did not suggest the integration of Texas as regards blacks. Significantly, the resolution did not contain any penalty provisions or enforcement section; it was a resolution, a statement of legislative consensus, not a binding law. Mexican officials considered the measure too weak, and refused to certify Texas for the *bracero* program in 1944 and 1945. Again in response to their demands, in the spring of 1945 a measure was introduced in the legislature to force the desegreation of restaurants to Mexicans and Chicanos. It did not pass, and Texas remained on Mexico's blacklist.

Nevertheless, Texas did not go without Mexican labor during the war. Instead, employers in agriculture—and in industry as well—hired undocumented immigrants who came to be called "wetbacks." "Wetback" is a term with clearly Texan origins; it refers to Mexicans who presumably waded the Rio Grande on their way north. The extensive nature of unauthorized immigration and the dominant role Texas played in spurring it on is still evident in Mexican slang: today, undocumented Mexican immigrants who enter the U.S. at points in New Mexico, Arizona and California, where there is no river to mark the international boundary, nevertheless call themselves *"mojados"*, or "wets."

It cannot be concluded, however, that Texas was the settling point or entry point for all undocumented immigrants of the period, or that all *sin papeles* came from Mexico's northern borderlands. The *bracero* program itself, by introducing Mexicans to the U.S. and its job market, encouraged the desertion of *braceros,* or their return to the U.S. as *sin papeles* after they had completed a contract period and collected remittances in Mexico. Nor could *bracero* program regulations prevent imported workers from marrying in the U.S. and thereby acquiring a claim to residency status. In practice, many *braceros* used the program as a stepping stone to a more permanent status as settlers. Legal immigration to the U.S. during the war doubled in comparison to the preceding five years, partly as a result of successful attempts by *braceros* to legalize themselves as permanent residents.

It is technically illegal for a Mexican citizen to leave his country without first obtaining a passport—and passports are issued only in Mexico City. When undocumented immigration to Texas became a noticeable phenomenon, Mexican officials in the capital called for enforcement of passport laws. As they saw it, undocumented immigration undermined the campaign to force Texas to end discrimination against Hispanics, and provided employers with a means of evading the wage and health guarantees of the *bracero* program. Labor leaders in Mexico joined with those in the U.S. in condemning undocumented immigration on grounds that it created a sub-class of workers who could not be protected against exploitation.

But regionalism in Mexican politics barred the enforcement of passport laws along the northern border, where the undocumented made their crossings. Mexican officials in border states argued—and still argue—that the restriction of passport issuance to a single Mexico City office works a hardship on border state residents, who must travel 18 to 30 hours by bus to reach the capital. During the wartime period, *bracero* recruiting centers were also concentrated around Mexico City, far from the border. The sentiment was, and still is, that if central Mexico is to be favored in arrangements for legal emigration, northern Mexico will accept the advantage its geography provides—the advantage of proximity to the border and extensive commercial relations with the U.S. Border region residents risk less in crossing illegally, and because many have relatives in the U.S., establish themselves more easily.

By mid-1945 the end of the war was in sight. Labor, government and industrial economists began planning for the return of soldiers to the civilian labor market. Women who had taken industrial jobs during the war were generally laid off as veterans came back to work. The *bracero* program in agriculture and the rail industry was slated to expire, a measure which would have provided 80,000 jobs for railroad workers alone. But the *bracero* program did not expire. Lobbyists for the affected industries demanded and got extensions. The AFL, which represented unionized railroad workers, but did not include *braceros* in its ranks, campaigned vigorously for their repatriation. Not until April, 1946, was the last *bracero* railroad worker sent home.

The labor movement, unable to persuade Congress to terminate the *bracero* program in agriculture, concentrated instead on seeking an administrative way to repatriate the Mexicans. Its spokesmen encouraged deportations, which began to mount as the war wound down. Between June 1944 and June 1945, a total of 63,602 aliens, mostly Mexicans, were deported, four times as many as in the previous record year, 1933. In fiscal 1946 the figure rose to a new record of 91,456—and it doubled the following year. Since *braceros* could not be deported, the wave of Border Patrol apprehensions hit hardest in Texas, where the largest population of *sin papeles* was to be found.

At the insistence of government and labor leaders, the *bracero* program was terminated on the last day of 1946. But its demise was a phyrric victory for *bracero* program opponents. A month later, a new labor pact was signed with Mexico. By its terms, most of the protections formerly given *braceros* were eliminated, and a system of private contracting was authorized. Under the new agreement, contractors were allowed to bring in Mexican farm laborers to Texas, provided that a minimum wage of 25 cents an hour be paid them—a salary far below the established rates for American workers. Instead of ending alien competition with American labor, the new agreement legalized such competition. Instead of bringing about an increase in agricultural wages, it encouraged wage-cutting: for where Mexican labor could be cheaply hired, employers were reluctant to pay rates for native labor. In its assault on the *bracero* program, the AFL had sought to create conditions for unionizing American field hands. Instead, the campaign backfired.

The agreement of 1947 also contained a novel provision which established amnesty through deportation. Under its terms, undocumented Mexicans who were sent back across the border could return to the U.S. as temporary contract laborers; during the life of their contracts, they could not be again deported. In practice, employers often called Border Patrol stations to report their own undocumented employees, who were returned, momentarily, to border cities in Mexico, where they signed labor contracts with the same employers who had denounced them. This process became known as "drying out wetbacks" or "storm and drag immigration." "Drying out" provided a deportation-proof source of cheap seasonal labor. Between 1947 and 1949, some 142,000 Mexican workers were legalized by the "storm and drag" method, which continued in use through 1951. In addition, contract laborers brought from the interior of Mexico to the U.S. numbered some 74,600 in 1947 alone. Like the *bracero* program, the new contract law and "storm and drag" amnesty stimulated undocumented immigration. *Sin papeles* began crossing the border in hopes that they, too, could be apprehended and "dried out." Deportations during the period rose, partly as a reflex of increased undocumented immigration, and in part because, for perhaps the first time, employers co-operated with the Border Patrol, in order to "dry out" their work forces. In 1950 and 1951 a total of nearly 100,000 undocumented immigrants were repatriated, many for the purpose of "drying out."

Despite an agreement generally favorable to the interests of growers, the immediate postwar period was also marked by conflict between Texas employers and the Mexican government. Mexican officials resented the 25-cent minimum wage paid in Texas, and suspended labor contracts for that state during the last quarter of 1947—until growers in Texas agreed to raise the minimum agricultural wage to 40 cents hourly. Again, in the fall of 1948, contracts were suspended. Growers in Texas, who generally paid cotton harvesters a rate of $3 per hundred pounds, had offered only $2.50 to Mexican contract workers. The Mexican government responded with cancellation of the contract program—and sent 7,000 troops to its northern border to keep *sin papeles* from crossing without authorization. But in response to pressure from growers, the Immigration Service opened the International Bridge at El Paso to Mexican laborers. *Sin papeles* who came across were "arrested" by Border Patrolmen for unauthorized entry, and then "paroled" to local centers of the United States Employment Service. At the employment centers, labor agents of cotton growers loaded the "parolees" into trucks and drove them off to labor camps for the harvest. Inflamed, the Mexican government cancelled its labor contract agreement with the United States, a measure which affected growers in several Southern and Southwestern states. But six months later, a new agreement was penned, similar to the one in effect earlier in the year.

"Storm and drag" immigration transformed the role of the Border Patrol. Its task became not so much that of shutting off undocumented immigration as one of regulating it. The object was to make available cheap labor in agriculture without aggravating the problems of domestic unemployment in other sectors of industry. The President's Commission on Immigration at the end of the "storm and drag" period in 1951 pointed out that:

> The border could be effectively closed to wetbacks— nearly all Inspectors agree to that. But it cannot be closed without strong support and backing of their efforts on either the state or national level and at least a minimum of co-operation from local people. The role of the Border Patrol at present is like that of a balance wheel. They let in enough wetbacks to do the local work quickly and cheaply; but they send out enough to prevent serious overcrowding.

CHAPTER 6

Operation Wetback

The conflict of interests between unions and agribusiness over imported labor rose again in Congress during the Korean War. "Storm and drag" immigration was ended in 1951 in a manner satisfactory to the agricultural interests: in its place, a new *bracero* program was created by a measure known as Public Law 78. The new act authorized a labor import program similar to the *bracero* plan of World War II, but initially limited to the duration of the Korean War, which had begun in 1950.

Labor was halted in a drive to defeat Public Law 78, but won a minor consolation with passage of Public Law 283, which for the first time made smuggling or harboring undocumented aliens a federal offense. Under the law, first-time offenders are liable for a six-month jail term and a fine of up to $500; repeat offenders may be sentenced to two years in prison, and fined as much as $1,000. Public Law 283 became the weapon for prosecuting *coyotes*, the contractor-smugglers of *sin papeles*. As originally proposed to Congress, it would also have made knowing employment of undocumented aliens a punishable offense. However, a loophole, known as the "Texas proviso," was inserted into the language of the bill by farm state Senators. The "Texas proviso" stipulates that employing *sin papeles* is not to be construed as harboring them, or to be

41

otherwise taken as an offense under Public Law 283. The intent of the bill was further weakened by deletion of a proposed section which would have provided for the confiscation of autos used in smuggling *sin papeles*. Nevertheless, Public Law 283 remains the basis for prosecutions of *coyotes* today.

By the time the new *bracero* program created by Public Law 78 was passed, Cold War hysteria had overcome most Americans, especially those in positions of leadership. It was an era of xenophobia and gullibility, of "Americanism" and the belief that foreign plots endangered the nation; an era of showcase spy trials and the restriction of civil liberties. It was not an era marked by tolerance of dissenters or immigrants. The labor movement was the target of special legislation aimed at radical and foreign-born leaders, largely in the militant unions of the Congress of Industrial Organizations. Noteworthy were deportation proceedings against Harry Bridges, an accused Communist, a leader of the International Longshoremens' and Warehousemens' Union, and an Australian by birth. Bridges won his bid to remain in the U.S. after a series of court appeals which lasted nearly a decade and cost some $150,000. But other immigrants who were neither so fortunate nor so renowned lost their residency rights. Hundreds were returned to "homelands" they had not seen since infancy. Among them were many who spoke no language other than English. The majority of these deportees were of European parentage, not of Mexican descent. Nevertheless, the McCarthy era deportations had consequences for Mexicans in the U.S. They strengthened the power of exclusionist groups like the American Legion, and thinned out immigrant leadership in labor and civic organizations. The Cold War revived the alliance between the AFL and exclusionist groups which had counted as a political force in the 30's, and gave rise to the demands to restrict immigration which are current today. When the exclusionist lobby was unable to halt passage of Public Law 78, it sought friends in the administrative branch of government. The effort succeeded in producing a program which by today's standards may rightfully be called a terror: Operation Wetback.

The stimulus of prior labor import programs and the

pull of American prosperity, matched with the push of Mexican poverty, had by 1954 created a significant population of undocumented immigrants. Many were former *braceros* from the World War II era who had since brought their families from Mexico. Thousands had a basis for future claims to residency status because they had borne children on U.S. soil. Most of the *sin papeles* were employed at poorly-paid jobs in Southwestern agriculture, and few were interested in politics, Mexican or American, subversive or patriotic. Most could barely read the Spanish language, and only a small fraction had mastered English. If the popular image of the subversive European was overblown and dubious, the transference of that image to Mexicans was doubly false. Nevertheless, Attorney General Herbert Brownwell, Jr., cited "national security" as his reason for ordering the mass deportation drive known as Operation Wetback. General Joseph May Swing, newly-appointed Commissioner of the Immigration and Naturalization Service, headed up the effort and gave it the tactics and rhetoric of a military campaign. Operation Wetback began on June 17, 1954 with the concentration of 800 Border Patrol officers along the California border at El Centro and Chula Vista. According to an account by the INS:

> The operation was divided into two task forces which, in turn, were divided into command units, consisting of 12 men headed by a Senior Patrol Inspector and equipped with trucks, jeeps, and automobiles. Radio-equipped vehicles formed a communications link between the unit and Patrol aircraft and the task force headquarters. The aircraft pilot and observer were used to locate alien groups and direct ground units to them.

> When the task force went into action they [sic] used a system of blocking off an area and mopping it up. Gradually they enlarged the operation until it embraced the industrial and agricultural areas of the entire State of California.

Sin papeles netted in the California raids were bussed to Nogales, Arizona, where Border Patrolmen turned them over to the custody of Mexican officials. The Mexican immigration authorities, by special arrangement with the

Border Patrol, placed deportees on trains bound for the interior of Mexico. The object was to drop off *sin papeles* in cities far from the U.S. border, in hopes that their return to *el norte* would be delayed by the added distance. This tactic, since repeated by the INS, was apparently successful. A 1954 annual report notes that ". . . largely as the result of the excellent cooperation of the Mexican officials, very few were able to escape the trip to the interior."

By mid-July, General Swing's command had swung into action in South Texas, and by fall, was hitting industrial targets in cities as distant from the border as Spokann, Chicago, St. Louis and Kansas City. Operation Wetback signaled the Border Patrol's transformation from a mere frontier guard to a national police force. But the northern reach of Operation Wetback was comparatively unproductive: only 20,000 *sin papeles* were found. Nevertheless, the grand "mopping up" operations of 1954 set an all-time record high for deportations: 1,075,168 aliens, mostly Mexicans, were apprehended and sent home. Moreover, as the INS later noted, "As news of the operation of the Special Force spread, unknown thousands left the country voluntarily to avoid arrest and transfer to the interior of Mexico." "Reverse migration" became a fact of American life for the first time since the Great Depression, and the Border Patrol repudiated—if only momentarily—the role of regulator, assuming instead the duty of sealing off the southern border.

In assessing the importance of Operation Wetback, the INS in its 1954 annual report said:

> These aliens who entered the United States illegally are responsible for 75 per cent of all crimes committed in some Southern California and Texas counties. . . . Even more serious is the possibility that among the 'wetbacks' who seek employment there may be those whose entry would be detrimental to our national security.

The claim that *sin papeles* were exceptionally lawless, like the claim that many were "subversives," was not supportable by evidence. In Texas and California border counties, the most commonly reported crime during harvest seasons *is* undocumented entry, and therefore, it is technically true that "aliens who entered the United States illegally are responsible for 75 per cent of all crimes committed in some Southern California and Texas counties." But during most months, hot checking and drunk driving are the offenses which land most people in jail. No statistics have ever been shown to support the claim that *sin papeles* engage in robbery, vandalism or acts of violence more frequently than citizens do.

Admirers of Operation Wetback frequently cite deportation statistics for subsequent years as evidence that "mopping up" was effective. Deportations fell from 1 million to 72,000 in 1955, the year following Operation Wetback. Over the next five years, the number of *sin papeles* apprehended declined steadily to a low point of 29,651 in 1960, less than three per cent of the record figure for 1954. Indeed, General Swing cited Operation Wetback's success as the cause of decreased deportations. In 1955, he wrote:

The decline in the number of wetbacks found in the United States, even after concentrated efforts were pursued throughout the year, reveals that this is no longer, as in the past, a problem in border control. *The border has been secured.*

CHAPTER 7

———————•◆•———————

Closing the Door on Braceros

Operation Wetback placed *sin papeles* and their employers on notice. It was a warning and a demonstration that undocumented immigration would not be allowed to mushroom. But it did not result in a decrease in total Mexican immigration, as exclusionists had hoped. During World War II and the immediate postwar years, immigration without documents had become a convenience for many. When Operation Wetback made legalization necessary, deported *sin papeles* got documents as immigrants. The process was, by today's standards, relatively easy: anyone who had a valid offer of permanent employment in the U.S. was presumed eligible for permanent residence. In the five years between 1955 and 1960, the wake of Operation Wetback, legal immigration rose to pre-Depression levels. A total of 214,746 Mexicans were admitted as permanent residents, compared to only 78,723 in the five preceeding years. Operation Wetback slowed undocumented entries but stimulated legal immigration.

The *bracero* program authorized by Public Law 78 continued, bringing in an average of some 400,000 Mexican laborers yearly. It peaked in 1956, when 445,000 temporary workers were imported for tasks in California, Texas, New Mexico, Arizona, Arkansas, Colorado and Michigan. Throughout the 50's *bracero* labor accounted for about 25 per cent of the Southwestern farm work force. The *bracero* program, though unpopular with labor, was protected by the influence of a coalition of farm state Republicans and Dixiecrats. It was extended for two years in 1954, 1956, and 1958 despite labor and exclusionist calls for its termination. In 1959, 444,418 *braceros* were admitted to the U.S., nearly one-eighth of rural Mexico's economically active population.

Public Law 78 ran into determined opposition when it again came up for renewal in 1960. Liberals and labor, led by Congressman (later Senator) George McGovern, coalesced to stop its extension. Included in the anti-*bracero* lobby were the National Council of Churches, Americans for Democratic Action, the National Farmers Union, and the Agricultural Workers Organizing Committee (AWOC) of the AFL-CIO. Defending Public Law 78 were an array of agribusiness groups, headed by the American Association of Agricultural Employers. Debate over seven months culminated in a Congressional compromise favorable to opponents of Public Law 78: an extension was granted, but for six months only. At the end of its grace period, however, Public Law 78 was granted new reprieves, and in 1963 came up for extension again. The move was defeated, and the *bracero* program finally expired in December, 1964.

The *bracero* program has not been resurrected principally because its opponents are adamant and powerful. The objections raised to *bracero* importation are essentially of two types, humanitarian and unionist.

Humanitarian objections to labor importation have historically taken as starting points the separation of the *bracero* from his family, and his disenfranchisement in the U.S. *Braceros* could not vote, nor could they join unions. Therefore, they could not use the legislative process to influence the conditions under which they worked or the standards by which they were paid. Nor could they lobby effectively with administrative agencies for enforcement of protections granted them under laws which governed the *bracero* programs. In practice, the *bracero's* chief representative in the U.S. was the nearest Mexican consul, and his chief lobbyist, the government of Mexico. But by reason of its own poverty and dependence on the U.S., the

Mexican government was, and is, in no position to bargain with strength regarding the terms of *bracero* importation. In a phrase, *braceros* were subjected to the dictum, "America, Love It or Leave It." The only realistic alternative to accepting the conditions under which the workplace presented itself was to go home.

The conditions under which *braceros* lived during the lifespan of Public Law 78 on the whole compared poorly to those in American jails. Most *braceros* were quartered in dilapidated barracks-style buildings, often with three or four bunks to a tier. Though some employers issued blankets to them, sheets were a rarity in *bracero* camps, as were laundry machines. As often as not, sanitary facilities were inadequate and as many as 30 *braceros* cooked from a common stove. Thousands survived on a diet of potatoes and vegetables picked up in the fields, both in order to maximize their savings, and also because many worksites did not provide food; those which did usually served a fare of the cheapest sort. Since they did not have transportation of their own, nor was any guaranteed them during their stay in the U.S. *braceros* were rarely given an opportunity to make purchases in the towns near their worksites. Television was unknown in the *bracero* camps, and lack of mobility isolated them from other ordinary diversions. Most *braceros* came to the U.S., worked and went home without so much as seeing a movie or attending a Saturday night dance.

Work conditions were also far from ideal. During irrigation season, *braceros* worked around the clock; those on night shifts went into the chilly air without flashlights, and usually, without mudboots or jackets. Employers pushed them to the limits in tasks that involved lifting, digging, and other hard manual work; 12-hour days were the exception, not the rule where *bracero* labor was employed. Thousands were exposed to pesticides, some which contained cancer-causing substances. Today most of those *braceros* who were victimized by chemicals are in Mexico, far from access to knowledge of the causes of the ailments they may suffer, far from the courts of law which could in some cases compensate them for their disabilities.

Perhaps most notorious of all, *braceros* were almost universally subjected to the domination of overseers who had little regard for their workers. *Braceros* were overworked, humiliated, and abused by foremen, sometimes purely for perverse pleasure. Often those who complained were sent home. To endure, *braceros* ignored the present in favor of daydreams about buying land at home.

Though the *bracero* program probably benefitted the Mexican economy by providing a source of foreign exchange, the question was never thoroughly studied on either side of the border. There is some evidence to indicate that individual *braceros* imported under Public Law 78 gained little, if anything, from their venture into *el norte*.

A 1959 survey by the University of California at Berkeley revealed that the earnings of many temporary workers were cancelled out by the costs of being a *bracero*. Customarily, fees for food, shelter and insurance were deducted from the paychecks of *braceros*. The net earnings of most ranged from $10 to $29 dollars per week, depending on weather conditions and other variables. The median net income figure reported for 425 *braceros* in the Berkeley study was $19 per week. *Braceros* with family obligations reported a median cost of $9.52 weekly for maintaining their dependents in Mexico. In addition, the *braceros* interviewed in the study reported average weekly expenses of $4 while in the U.S., mainly for soft drinks, cigarettes, and food items not supplied by work gang cafeterias. After deductions, family expenses and incidental spending were figured out, average net earnings came to but $5.48 a week.

Given the living costs which prevailed in Mexico during the 50's, net earnings of $5.48 might have been a sufficient reward, had it not been for the indebtedness most *braceros* incurred during their wait for work in *el norte*. Those questioned by the Berkeley study team reported that on the average, three weeks passed between the day they applied for certification and the day they began work in the U.S. For most of them, waiting for certification meant waiting in a town other than their own, a town where a *bracero* recruiting center was located. Most *braceros* waited a week or more for certification, then waited another week or more for labor contractors to show up to carry them to *el norte*. Nearly all reported that in order to be certified, they had to pay bribes to Mexican officials.

The combined costs of waiting and bribe-paying were estimated at about $85 per *bracero*. Money for his expenses was often borrowed from loansharks in Mexico whose usual interest rate was 10 per cent per month. Labor Department statistics for the period show that *braceros* averaged about 13 weeks in the U.S. per contract. Certification costs, excluding interests on loans, therefore averaged about $6.50 per week, a figure in excess of the net weekly earnings reported by the Berkeley study. For many *braceros*, the study indicated, coming to the U.S. was a venture which ended in indebtedness, not gain.

The Berkeley study, however, confirmed two points which spoke in favor of continuing the *bracero* plan. First, it showed that single men could benefit somewhat by working in the U.S., though the net gain amounted to less than $5 weekly; 76 per cent of *braceros* were unmarried. More importantly, 93.7 per cent of those *braceros* interviewed for the study said that on return to Mexico they planned to again seek contracts for work in the U.S. In Senate testimony given in 1961, Dr. Henry Anderson summed up the conclusions of the Berkeley study:

> . . . the Mexican national progam is the equivalent of a lottery for the average bracero who participates in it. Some are winners: enough to keep the system going. Some are losers: so hopelessly entangled in financial obligations they cannot meet that their lives, and the lives of their families, are ruined. For the majority, the bracero system consists of running desperately hard to maintain one's present place, motivated by fear of the consequences if one stops running. For all, the system is a gamble, since no bracero has foreknowledge of his situation in the United States.

Mexican peasants preferred the *bracero* gamble to staying at home because peasant life in Mexico was, and is, difficult and embittering. If the barracks *braceros* were given in the U.S. were uncomfortable, so too were their adobe and palm huts at home. If there were no sheets on their bunks in America, there also were none on their cots and in their hammocks in Mexico. The absence of meat in their diet was nothing new, nor was isolation from city life; most rural communities in Mexico lack even postal service. If there were no laundry machines in the barracks, at least there was running water, a near-luxury in Mexico's countryside. Belligerent overseers were also far from foreign. In Mexico, millions of peasants live as their forefathers did, in mortal fear of *pistoleros*, armed guards hired by big landowners to supervise their estates. The greatest single difficulty experienced by *braceros* in the U.S. but not by peasants in Mexico was family separation. But in the U.S., *braceros*, though paid little, were paid something; in the Mexican countryside, laborers were fortunate to earn as much as 75 cents a day. Even today, peasants in Mexico rarely earn as much as $3 a day, and jobs are always scarce.

Humanitarian objections to labor import programs are essentially objections about the *way* in which the *bracero* programs of the past were managed. Most of these objections could ostensibly be satisfied in future programs by legislation and enforcement of standards to protect imported workers. Labor's objections to *bracero* programs, however, are not satisfiable except by the abolition of such programs, for what labor wants is unionization of the domestic workforce.

Organizing unions has always been a difficult and sometimes dangerous task, doubly so in agriculture. Modern industry aids the formation of unions by bringing hundreds of workers under one roof. These industrial workers have closely-identified common interests and can pay the costs of forming and maintaining a union organization. But since the end of the Civil War, American agriculture, has been characterized by small-scale enterprises. Most American farms employ less than a dozen workers, an insufficient number for union-organizing purposes. Most small commercial enterprises are unorganized, and like them, most farms are unsuited to unionization.

However, since the turn of the century, vegetable, fruit and cotton production in California has been characterized by large corporate enterprises employing 50 or more workers each. These farms have been the targets of unionizing efforts since 1903, when some one thousand Japanese and Mexican-American sugar beet pickers walked out of fields at Ventura.

However, California corporate farming did not do away

with another great obstacle to agricultural unionism: the seasonality of work. Irrigation and harvest have normally called for a tripling and quadrupling of the regular workforce—a circumstance conducive to use of migrant labor. Migrants are notoriously difficult to organize because the time in which organizing can be done is limited by the work season. No sooner are migrants organized in one location than they must move on to another farm.

The task of organizing in California fields has also been complicated by social history. The first laborers hired for West Coast corporate farms were Chinese. When exclusion shut off Chinese immigration in 1892, Japanese laborers were imported. In 1907, however, they too were barred from entry. In their places came Mexicans, Mexican-Americans (or Chicanos) and "Oakies" (Anglo-Protestant refugees from the Midwestern dust bowl). Today, harvests in California are carried out largely by workers of Mexican and Philippine descent. The Mexican-descent workers, however, are divided four ways by immigration status: there are Chicanos, who are citizens; so-called "green-carders," Mexican citizens with U.S. residency rights who still live in Mexico but commute to work; resident Mexican immigrants; and *sin papeles*.

Organizing was even tougher before the expiration of the *bracero* agreement because *braceros,* more than any other group, lived at the bidding of their employers. *Braceros* were not eligible for unionization, and when brought into harvests alongside domestic workers, they were often reluctant to affiliate with unions for fear of deportation. Most importantly, throughout the period of labor import programs, *braceros* were used as strikebreakers.

In 1961 hearings on the effects of labor importation, labor spokesmen cited more than 20 instances in which *braceros* were used as strikebreakers. Among the cases cited:

1. DiGiorgio Fruit Corporation, Arvin, Calif., 1947-49. The National Farm Labor Union sought recognition. Government officials openly escorted *braceros* through picket lines to perform critical irrigation tasks.
2. San Joaquin and Stanislaus Counties, Calif., 1950. Some 2,000 *braceros* were accompanied by highway

patrolmen and private guards as they crossed picket lines, breaking a 2-month strike by tomato workers.

3. Imperial Valley, Calif., April, 1951. The National Farm Labor Union organized cantaloupe workers to demand union recognition, wage hikes, and deportation of undocumented immigrants in the area. Deportations followed, but deportees were replaced on the job by *braceros*, not by union members.

4. Imperial Valley, May-June, 1952. Cantaloupe pickers struck again, this time against wage cuts. Growers brought in *braceros* who accepted the lowered wage rates and broke the strike.

5. Between 1954 and 1961, more than a dozen strikes of the National Agricultural Workers Union and the United Packinghouse Workers Union, AFL-CIO, were broken by *braceros*. Organization work was set back in asparagus, tomato, peach, cantaloupe, lettuce, carrot, celery and strawberry fields.

6. Braceros worked behind picket lines of the Agricultural Workers Organizing Committee, AFL-CIO, during the fall of 1960 at the tomato plantations of the Cochran Company in San Joaquin county; and at the Bowers peach ranch, in Butte county.

7. The Imperial Valley lettuce harvest of 1961 was picketed by members of two unions, but again broken by *braceros* despite demands from the Mexican government that strikebreaking *braceros* be sent home.

The standpoint of Mexican labor unions has always been one of discouraging *braceros* from strike-breaking; however, few *braceros* were union members in Mexico. Instances in which *braceros* refused to cross American picket lines were rare, no doubt because most of them were in debt for certification expenses before they reached the job sites being picketed. Their poverty in Mexico and the difficulties they might encounter if they became known to certification officials as labor sympathizers, persuaded most *braceros* to cross picket lines rather than go home empty-handed. Even had *braceros* religiously honored picket lines, however, it is doubtful that labor lobbyists would have withdrawn demands for termination of labor import programs. As labor economics work, a shortage of workers creates a favorable bargaining position; a surplus, whatever its source, weakens collective strength. So long as unemployment is an unresolved domestic problem, labor spokesmen will find grounds to argue that labor importation undermines unionization and the living standards of American workers.

CHAPTER 8

Closing the Door on Inmigrants

With the *bracero* question settled, in early 1965 Congress turned attention to the rest of immigration law. No major revisions had been made in policy since the passage of the Immigration and Nationality Act of 1952. The 1952 statute ended the half-century-old policy of Oriental exclusion, and set forth a system of priorities for assigning immigration visas which gave preference to skilled workers and relatives of U.S. citizens. It also replaced the system of national quotas in effect for the Eastern Hemisphere with a general limit of 170,000 immigrant visas per year. Under the new system, no Eastern Hemisphere nation was to be allocated more than 20,000 immigrant visas annually. However, the 1952 act did not set numerical limits on Western Hemisphere immigration to the U.S.

The debate over a new immigration policy, begun in 1965, continued until early 1968. During this period, a series of amendments to the Immigration and Nationality Act were passed, two of which were to have a profound impact upon the Latin American future. First, a numerical quota of 120,000 visas per year was established for Western Hemisphere immigrants. As with the system already in force for Eastern Hemisphere immigrants, each nation was limited to a maximum of 20,000 visas annually. The second critical revision dealt with procedures for the admission of immigrants by work papers. Traditionally, American policy had facilitated the immigration of anyone who could indicate usefulness to the economy. Workers who presented a letter promising permanent employment in the U.S. were presumed admissible as immigrants unless their acceptance was challenged by the Labor Department officials who reviewed visa applications. In practice, work letters were rarely challenged. Under new rules put into effect in December, 1968, the procedure was reversed: workers were presumed ineligible for admittance. The visa applicant was required to show that the job he had been promised was listed by the Labor Department as one which could not be filled by American labor.

Under the 1968 revision, which is still in effect, a shoe manufacturer in Los Angeles, for example, who wants to hire a bootmaker from Tijuana must file an immigration petition on behalf of the bootmaker. If the employer wants to hire several foreign employees, he must file a petition in the name of each. A job description is sent to Labor Department officials, who inquire at unemployment centers across the country for workers of the same trade. If the New York employment commission happens to list a bootmaker on its jobless rolls, certification may be denied—even though the Los Angeles jobsite is closer to Tijuana than to New York. The Labor Department under this system is not required to supply an employee for the job, nor to guarantee that any prospective employees will apply for it. Instead, it must merely report that workers are available somewhere in the U.S. The process eliminates most applicants whom employers would bring here to work. In 1974, for example, only .35 per cent of those who immigrated legally, or 14,183 immigrants out of a total of 394,861, were admitted on the basis of a work certification.

The effects of the new work-papers procedure are controversial. Agriculture spokesmen complain that few Americans have come forth to take the jobs *braceros* and worker-immigrants have been denied. Their viewpoint has been voiced in Congressional hearings by Richard C. White, a representative from a ranching district in Texas:

> The realities of the present indicate there is very little unskilled labor available in this country. . . . A

higher minimum wage for agricultural workers has been enacted, but other programs such as welfare and food stamps—as important as they are for those who need them—have helped to create a group of indolent persons who are able, but not willing, to accept certain types of employment. . . . Such is the situation all along the United States-Mexico border. You can go to the town square. You will see the people sitting around there, people who appear to be able bodied, and you will ask them if they would like to do some of this type of work, agricultural work, and they will say no, no, because they are drawing enough to sustain themselves in their standard of living at the time. . . . The farmers and ranchers must consequently look elsewhere for the unskilled work force necessary for such a livelihood. The available source has been from Mexico, from workers who are eager to accept such employment.

The case against the current system of work-letter certification is simply that it deprives the economy of needed workers. Farm spokesmen say that Americans no longer want to do rural work, and that given the availability of welfare and unemployment benefits, few Americans need to accept farm work in order to survive.

However, this claim cannot be accepted at face value. What agribusiness lobbyists do not point out is that, aside from the food stamp program, most adults of working age who are on welfare are female family heads. The agriculture industry has not distinguished itself by any willingness to provide on-the-job daycare, a condition which would allow women on welfare to take field jobs. During World War II, when many industrial plants did provide jobsite daycare for children of women workers, housewives were employed at traditionally-male tasks. Female welfare clients might be brought into the agricultural workforce today by the same reform, but agribusiness lobbyists do not speak for it. As during World War II, the farm industry prefers a predominantly male workforce of *sin papeles* or *braceros* to a labor pool composed mostly of mothers.

The argument for preserving the present system of labor certification usually comes, in veiled form, from union spokesmen, who regard the pre-1968 procedure as merely a formalized method of importing cheap labor. AFL-CIO lobbyists believe that little will be gained by excluding *braceros* if the means for legal immigration are readily available to Mexicans. This posture is essentially exclusionist, because it argues against the admission of all immigrants who are not privileged by professional standing or blood line to American citizens. It is also an argument to bar the admission of most members of foreign unions which have fraternal ties with the AFL-CIO. In order to avoid offending its Latin American affiliates, the AFL-CIO refrains from openly endorsing exclusionism. Nonetheless, its standpoint is evident from time to time in statements like the following, published in 1974 in the *Federationist*, the official journal of the labor congress:

> U.S. geographical sprawl makes the immigrant almost unnoticeable except in large urban centers. But immigrants are here and in great numbers, coming out of desire to escape economic and social deprivation in their homelands. Often, particularly in the past, immigrants came to escape political or religious persecution and their stories are woven into American folklore, with that image contributing to a certain extent to hiding the realities of present day immigration to the United States.

After citing statistics for legal immigration in 1973, the *Federationist* went on to say:

> These figures, lifted from expressionless tables in the 1973 Annual Report of the Immigration and Nationalization Service, may prove mildly interesting only to those highly motivated or to those whose curiosity for the trivial is boundless. In fact, these numbers don't hint that immigrants pose a problem in the United States, a problem whose dimensions are unknown simply because sheer numbers make it next to impossible to ascribe limits. . . . It is a story of human misery that affects the cross section of American life directly, deprives Americans of job opportunities, bleeds the welfare rolls. . . .

Diplomatically-worded statements of this sort perhaps require analysis. To say that "immigrants pose a problem" and that immigration "deprives Americans of job opportunities" is to say that even legal immigration should be halted or drastically limited. This, historically, has been the exclusionist stance, and has been the stance of the

AFL since the late 19th century, when it led the drive for Chinese exclusion.

The other major provision passed between 1965 and 1968, pertaining to the numerical limit for Western Hemisphere immigrants, has also been a source of continuing debate. While most testimony brought in Congress has favored a limit of some sort, several speakers have urged that Mexico and Canada be exempted from the 20,000 visas-per-year limit. The basis on which the argument is made is that since Mexico and Canada share frontiers with the U.S., their relations with the U.S. are more extensive than those of countries more distant. Immigration ceilings, proponents of change say, should reflect this closeness.

No major changes in U.S. immigration policy towards Latin America or Mexico have been legislated since the revisions of 1968. However, one important change has been wrought as the result of a ruling by a Chicago federal appeals court. Cuban refugees are admitted to the U.S. on special terms, as "parolees." "Parolees" are not required to satisfy visa standards—like labor certification or family status—as a condition for entering the U.S. Once here, they may adjust their status to that of "alien permanent residents," the status under which other immigrants must enter, and for which visa ceilings have been set. Cubans who adjust their immigration status were until 1977 charged against the visa ceiling for the Western Hemisphere. Several organizations, including the bar association of New York City, questioned this practice in congressional testimony, on grounds that "Cubans coming into the United States for the last several years . . . were not, for the most part, refugees but rather were persons coming for economic betterment . . . Cuban refugees utilize a disproportionate share of the total Western Hemisphere visa numbers." But Congress did not alter the policy; instead, it was challenged by attorneys representing Mexican immigrants in Chicago. In 1977, a federal appeals court upheld the Chicago suit, and ordered immigration officials to exempt Cubans from the Hemispheric visa ceiling.

PART III

The Contemporary Subject—Dynamics of the Controversy

CHAPTER 9

———◆————◆————◆———

What it Takes to Immigrate

The 1965-68 immigration law restrictions have put legal entry to the U.S. beyond the reach of most Mexicans, and most working people. Would-be immigrants must be the immediate relatives of citizens or legal residents, or members of one of the preferred professions, engineering, medicine, or the clergy, for example. Immediate relatives of U.S. citizens are admitted outside quota restrictions, and therefore do not usually have to wait for immigration papers to be approved, though delays of as much as six months are common in some consular offices. Parents, children and spouses of citizens are included in the category of immediate relation, but siblings and more distant relations are not.

Those with less-than-direct blood or marriage ties to citizens must wait for quota numbers to come up. Waiting with them are applicants with direct ties to legal residents, i.e., applicants related to *immigrantes* already in the U.S. Also in line are members of the preferred professions. The waiting list in Mexico and across Latin America is about two years long. Mexicans who do not have relatives in the U.S. nor employers who will sponsor them may apply for immigrant status, but for practical purposes, have no hopes of getting a spot on the waiting list. Few attempt to do so, because the costs of applying are considerable.

Applications for immigrant status must be accompanied by certain documents, among them: two certified copies of a birth or baptismal record, and of marriage and divorce certificates; a Mexican passport; a statement from the police authorities in each town where the applicant has resided, stating that he or she has no felony arrest record; and the report of a medical examiner, affirming that the applicant is of sound mind and free from communicable diseases. Further, the "sponsor" who requests immigration on behalf of the Mexican applicant or "beneficiary" must file a certified copy of his or her last income tax report, along with a sworn statement guaranteeing financial support of the "beneficiary" for five years. These documents are filed with immigration petitions supplied by the State Department at its consulates and embassy, or by the Immigration Service in the U.S. When filing petitions, the "sponsors" and "beneficiaries" are required to pay fees for the costs of processing them.

Applicants who are granted immigrant status are given "green cards," photo identification cards which entitle them to reside permanently in the U.S. These legal residents or *inmigrantes* are not citizens, however. Legal residents may apply for naturalization after three years, if they are married to citizens, or after five years in other cases. Applicants for citizenship must prove good moral character, proficiency in English, and a general knowledge of the U.S. Constitution. It is noteworthy that many native-born Americans could not satisfy the standards for naturalization, especially in regard to its morals section. The citizenship application form asks, for example, if the applicant has ever committed adultery. Applicants who answer "yes" are then required to list the dates, persons and places connected with each adulterous act. Citizenship may not be granted to Communists or to "habitual drunkards." These standards, immigration lawyers say, amount to a statement that "the prospective citizen must be cleaner than the house he's coming into."

The differences between residency and citizenship are significant. Residents may not vote, but must pay taxes. When the military draft was active, *inmigrantes* were draftable. Legal residents may own property as citizens may do, and they may engage in civic debate, so long as the topics concern such items as public school, roads, taxes or police protection. But they may not join political parties, engage in electioneering, or hold elective or appointive offices. Violation of these rules is punishable by immediate deportation. Significantly, residents are eligible for welfare benefits, but only after they have passed five years on American soil.

Visas given tourists and students are not considered as immigrant visas, and therefore, may be issued without numerical limitations. In the past, many Latin Americans who wanted to settle permanently in the U.S., but could not qualify as resident immigrants, instead took out nonimmigrant visas. In this way, they entered the U.S. legally, and afterwards, simply hid from immigration and Border Patrol investigators. Today, however, administrative standards for issuing nonimmigrant visas have also been tightened.

Tourists coming to the U.S. from Mexico, for example, are usually required to present, along with a visa application medical report, passport, etc. a two-way bus or train ticket. Additionally they must show proof of ability to spend money while here. The requirement of spending money was once satisfiable by showing cash. However, many applicants borrowed or actually rented a sum of money to show at the U.S. embassy or consulate where tourist visas are issued. Today, many embassy and consular officials require prospective tourists to present a bankbook showing a balance of as much as $2,000, deposited as long as six months prior to the date of visa application. These tighter rules, a product of the Nixon administration years, have made it virtually impossible for ordinary Mexican citizens to visit the interior of the U.S.

Student visas are also difficult to obtain. Formerly, students who were admitted to an American institution were usually granted visas. Since 1970, however, consular and embassy officials have required proof of financial self-sufficience as well. Self-sufficience is proved by a letter from a bank stating that it has been named to administer an educational trust fund for the applicant, and will send $300 or more to the student each month. Visa regulations prohibit students from accepting any employment not offered by the college, university or other school they attend, and further prohibit students from carrying less than a full course load. As a result, foreign students cannot work part-time, and study part-time, as many American college students do. The visa tightening rules have made it difficult for foreign students to work—or for foreign workers to study.

Though there are perhaps many arguments to justify the tighter requirements in effect for visas today, there is nevertheless an indisputable argument against them, especially in regards to the tourist visa. American tourist restrictions are the strictest in the hemisphere. The United States citizen who wants to vacation in Mexico need not show a passport, bus or plane ticket, bankbooks—nor any document other than a voter registration card. Mexican tourist visas are normally issued for 180 days; American visas, for 7 to 60 days. Mexican tourist visas are issued without delay; applicants for American visas usually wait a week or more. Mexico encourages tourism. The U.S., despite the perennial speeches of our leaders about Good Neighbor Policy, discourages visits from foreigners, especially foreigners of moderate means.

and further graded students from earning less than a 50
penalty. No, the 3 result, able to relocate career level

CHAPTER 10

———•◄─══─►•———

Deportation Blues

Most undocumented immigrants cross our borders and arrive in the interior undetected. Nobody, however, knows what percentage of those who cross are picked up by the Border Patrol over any given period of time. Former INS Commissioner Chapman estimated that his agents apprehend 25 to 33 per cent of the Mexicans who cross the southern border without documents, and case histories by *sin papeles* bear out the estimate. Apprehensions, however, are countable. Since the decade opened, arrests have numbered:

1970—420,126
1971—387,713
1972—467,193
1973—584,847
1974—737,564
1975—766,000
1976—900,000 (INS estimate)

When undocumented aliens are apprehended they are deported. The process is a simple one along the border, where the Border Patrol maintains its own jails and booking facilities. The apprehended alien is first searched and fingerprinted. He is told that he has violated a law of the

69

United States by having made an illegal entry, and that he has two choices: he may deny the charge, or voluntarily go back to Mexico. Undocumented aliens rarely deny their guilt. Once they have admitted it, Border Patrolmen transfer information the aliens give onto forms which record biographical data and the circumstances under which apprehension was made. Following this interrogation, the alien is escorted to the nearest crossing point or international bridge, where he is released. The process of "voluntary return" ordinarily takes less than two hours. Often, the returnee walks into Mexico and doubles back, hours or minutes later, to the American side. Border Patrolmen frequently catch and deport the same individual twice during a single 8-hour tour of duty.

If an alien is apprehended by other law enforcement agencies, Border Patrolmen come to interrogate him and then process him as they would any other undocumented alien. In the interior of the United States, local lawmen make most alien arrests, usually in connection with drunk driving or disturbance investigations. Local authorities customarily turn undocumented aliens over to the Border Patrol, rather than bring them to trial on minor charges. When an undocumented immigrant is captured in the interior, he or she is usually transported to one of 47 regional booking offices in the interior, where the procedures for "voluntary return" are carried out. However, deportation from the interior involves bus or plane fare. During an informal hearing the suspect is told that if he chooses voluntary return and will pay his own fare back to Mexico, his apprehension will not prejudice future dealings with the Immigration Service. Otherwise, a file will be opened which notes that he was "required to depart." Being "required to depart" is not as serious a step as formal deportation, but it is a grade higher than "voluntary return," and therefore, those undocumented aliens who can pay their fare back to Mexico ordinarily do so. A guard accompanies the buses and planes on which aliens are returned to Mexico. Usually, buses are chartered to carry Mexicans back to their homeland, but in isolated areas—Utah, for example—commercial airline tickets are sometimes purchased.

The usual procedure of "voluntary return" is altered

somewhat to accommodate those undocumented aliens who are accompanied by their families in interior regions of the United States. Rather than jail a family group, Border Patrolmen usually issue an order of "delayed departure." In such instances, the family is given a grace period, ordinarily 15 to 60 days, in which it must return to Mexico. The purpose of delayed departure orders is to give families time to dispose of property, bank accounts and installment loans which they have undertaken while in the U.S. Family groups are usually allowed to return to Mexico without guard, and many go back in their own autos. When they reach the border, they are required to report their departure to Border Patrol officials at the international checkpoint or bridge where they cross into Mexico.

The preference shown family groups affects the customs of both married and single undocumented aliens. Because they know that the Border Patrol does not often provide them an opportunity to straighten out financial affairs before deporting them, unmarried *sin papeles* rarely save money in banks. Instead, they hide it in their apartments or send it to Mexico in the form of U.S. postal money orders. Likewise, they are reluctant to purchase automobiles in their own names. Many register them to legal residents or citizens who are either their relatives, or have befriended them. Most *sin papeles* acquire very little in the way of personal belongings while they are in the U.S. for fear that such items will be lost if they are deported. Since many *sin papeles* live with other undocumented workers, most of those who are arrested outside their homes do not give correct addresses, nor do they ask for permission to retrieve objects of personal property before deportation. At least 50 per cent of *sin papeles* go back to Mexico without so much as a piece of luggage in their hands.

"Voluntary return" is the preferred method of going home because it is speedy and does not prejudice the future. By confessing to illegal entry, *sin papeles* avoid long stays in jail and court proceedings which could complicate any future attempt to gain legal status. Though a handful of *sin papeles* have demanded formal deportation for political reasons, i.e., to challenge immigration law or focus attention on deportations, most of those who are subject to formal deportation proceedings did not elect to be tried:

rather, the government exercises its option to enforce federal immigration statutes.

Federal law makes illegal entry a felony offense, punishable by a maximum fine of $5,000 and a maximum sentence of five years imprisonment. In deportation proceedings, the accused is presumed innocent. Deportation trials are rare events, because they are trials in which the identity of the accused must be established by the prosecution. If a *sin papeles* maintains that he is a U.S. citizen, the prosecution must come up with documentary evidence—usually, a Mexican passport—that he is not who he claims to be, and that in fact, he is someone else, the person whose identity the prosecution has documented. For practical reasons, it is impossible to match the fingerprints or photo of an apprehended alien with all the birth, military or passport records which might exist in Mexico. Therefore, unless an alien's true name and birthplace can be discovered, either through informants, by confession, or by papers found in his possession, deportation proceedings are rarely started. One of the principal reasons why undocumented aliens as a rule carry *no* identification is that if they are apprehended, by giving false names they can make themselves practically immune to formal deportation.

Formal deportation proceedings are rare for another reason as well. Even if the identity of an alien is established by his confession or by informants, the prosecution must prove its claims by documents issued in Mexico. Ordering the passport of a suspect from the Mexican issuing office is a process encircled with red tape on both sides of the border. The suspect may be held for six months while such documents are on order, but no longer. If documentation is not available at the end of six months, the suspect must be "paroled" into the United States, i.e., released on his own recognizance. Release provides the opportunity for escape, and further, if documents are never found to identify the suspect, he can apply for residency status after completing a period on parole. Deportation charges, if not swiftly processed, can backfire into a legal situation beneficial to the undocumented immigrant.

In practice, deportation proceedings are reserved for aliens whom the Immigration Service seeks to punish for aggravated offenses. Undocumented immigrants who try to escape custody, or who attempt to pass off false immigration documents, or who are suspected of other criminal offenses are often arraigned for deportation—but ordinary *sin papeles* are not. In 1975, for example, the INS apprehended 680,392 deportable Mexican aliens, but only 14,-512, about two per cent of the total, underwent formal deportation.

Border Patrolmen and prosecutors are stern, however, with persons suspected of aiding undocumented aliens, especially profiteers. Besides smugglers and *coyotes*, there are persons who marry undocumented immigrants in order to provide them with the basis for claiming residency rights, and there are people, professional and amateur, who provide *sin papeles* with false documents. No estimates of the dollar volume of such traffic have been made, but available evidence indicates that INS activity has only recently begun to interfere with illegal activities associated with immigration.

Since 1977, the INS has concentrated on arresting and prosecuting smugglers. During the last six months of 1977, some 15,000 alleged smugglers were trapped at highway checkpoints, or arrested on tips from informers. Nearly 87,000 *sin papeles* or *pollos* were apprehended in their company.

The anti-smuggling campaign is being continued in 1978, and INS has asked Congress for an additional $18.7 million to fund it. No report of its effectiveness has been issued, but early results indicate that most of the smugglers netted are small-time operators and relatives of the families involved, not well-financed *coyotes* or profiteers. Serious efforts to prosecute are apparently being limited to cases involving U.S. citizens and resident aliens who are involved in alien smuggling for gain.

During January and February of 1978 federal courts in two Texas locations, El Paso and Laredo, convicted a total of 40 persons for alien smuggling. Most of the convictions grew out of arrests made at a checkpoint about 30 miles west of Laredo, in Hebbronville. A handful came from the El Paso district, where informants were apparently used to trapping professional smugglers.

Defendants in the 40 cases were fairly evenly distributed by immigration status. Twelve of the smugglers were U.S. citizens, 10 were aliens with residency rights, and 18 were undocumented Mexican immigrants themselves. Both the citizens and resident aliens averaged 30 years in age; the *sin papeles* convicted of smuggling were younger, averaging 23 years. All the defendants but two were persons of Spanish surname. About half of those arrested were in the company of six *sin papeles* or less. One defendant, however, was apprehended while directing the movement of three vehicles carrying a total of 46 undocumented immigrants.

Twelve of the 40 defendants received jail terms. One U.S. citizen of Anglo extraction suspected of heading a West Texas smuggling ring was sentenced to a 5-year prison term, and a *sin papeles* convicted for second-offense alien smuggling drew a 6-month sentence. Others sentenced to incarceration drew 90 days or less. Most of those not sentenced to jail terms were fined from $150 to $500, and in addition, received suspended sentences or probated terms. However, nine defendants got suspended terms and probation orders only.

Former INS Commission Chapman frequently decried the "fradulent marriage racket", citing the case of a Florida woman who married six aliens—without divorcing any of them—and received welfare in the name of all six, without living with any of them. Like most other examples Chapman cited, the Florida marriage racket is a fluke. Undocumented aliens from time to time encounter persons who will marry them, for immigration purposes only, at fees of from $100 to $1,000. But offers are rare; there is probably no city in the U.S. where aliens can easily arrange false marriages. Most marriages made to establish grounds for residency are made between members of friendship groups, and in these, money payments are never involved. The INS is practically powerless to halt such arrangements because of the nature of marriage itself. If an undocumented alien falls in love today, marries tomorrow, and two years later has a change of heart, there is no particular reason to suspect fraud, because divorce is common in the society as a whole. INS investigators sometimes visit newlyweds who have filed a residency claim to verify that they, indeed, live together. But INS cannot break down bedroom doors at midnight, and if it did, would probably be able to prove little in court. Instead, it customarily advises the couple under investigation that an agent will visit them at an appointed hour on an appointed day. The findings of such investigations, therefore, are largely formal. In 1975, less than 100 fraudulent marriages were uncovered, and most of these came not as the result of investigation, but as a result of windfall confessions.

The traffic in false documents is far more widespread and lucrative. On the Mexican side of most border cities, it is possible to buy papers of several different types from clandestine operators. Stolen residency cards, drivers licenses, and birth certificates are common, as are purloined Social Security cards. Some *coyotes* rent such papers from their owners to use in crossing *pollos*; if bridge authorities question the documents, the *pollo* reports that he bought them from a thief. Less common are altered residency cards and forgeries, though an increasing number of both have been discovered in INS raids. Ordinarily, such documents are confiscated. Frequently, those caught with them are set for formal deportation, and sometimes, for trial on federal false documents charges. However, in 1975 the INS convicted only 125 persons on documents charges. Its chief approach to enforcement has been the creation of a new residency card, designed to discourage forgery.

CHAPTER 11

———◆—◆◆◆—◆———

Why Mexicans Flee Home

The immigration law restrictions of 1965-68 closed the door on legal entry for most Mexicans. However, it is not law but economic imbalance which ultimately determines the course of great migrations. Despite laws to the contrary, there are Argentines in Brazil, illegal Turks in Germany, and even undocumented Salvadoreans in Honduras: the immigrant will go wherever he can in order to survive. During the late 19th century, when southern European poverty squeezed peasants out of their native lands, they came to America, often without any authorization whatever. Newcomers were processed on Ellis Island, near where the Statue of Liberty stands. The rudimentary immigration service of the era classified new arrivals as "without papers" or "with papers". "Without papers" was often abbreviated as "wop"—a particle of slang still around today as an term for Italian-Americans. There are ostensibly no reasons why "wetbacks" cannot attain respectability as have the descendents of undocumented Italian immigrants.

Mexicans, like the Italians, Poles, Irish and Germans before them, come to the U.S. for one fundamental reason: they cannot survive in their homeland, and they can survive here. Today Mexico is beset with crises her economic and political system can no longer manage or absorb. Inside the country, the crises are reflected in new levels of social turmoil, in strikes, terrorist incidents, and actual armed rebellion in the countryside. The prosperous classes in Mexico are apprehensive; they fear that a revolution may be smoldering. The working classes are listening to socialist agitators as never before, but the voices they hear most clearly are those of the television, movies and the neighbors, all of whom say—there's money to be made in *el norte*. The opportunity to work in the U.S. serves as an escape valve for the increasing misery of Mexico's millions.

United Nations statistics draw a picture of Mexico's poverty. There are an average of 5.7 persons per household in Mexico, compared to 3.2 in the U.S. Yet the average American home or apartment has five rooms, compared to two in Mexico. Nearly all American homes have running water, yet only a third of Mexican homes do, and only a fraction over half have electric connections. These statistics reflect the status of Mexico as a nation, with both rich and poor, rural and urban inhabitants. The average they provide does not show that most of the urban poor lack these facilities, and nearly all peasants are without them. *Sin papeles* do not walk out of statistical tables. By and large, they come from the poorest, most deprived segment of Mexican society. If, in Mexico, half of the homes are electrified, we may safely assume that much less than half of the homes from which *sin papeles* come are equipped with electricity.

The crises of modern Mexico are rooted in rapid population growth, and the inability of the economy to provide new jobs. Mexico today has 64 million inhabitants and the fastest growth rate in the world. Today, more children are born in Mexico than in the United States; the Mexican population is doubling every 17 years. By the year 2000, there will be nearly 200 million Mexicans.

The job market has already fallen far behind. Even during the relative prosperity of the 50's, Mexico was unable to solve the problem of "marginalization." In Mexico and other Latin American countries, where systems of social welfare are practically nonexistent, the unemployed seek a living by performing minor tasks. Thousands sell food, or soft drinks, or lottery tickets on the streets. Others become bootblacks or wandering musicians. Still others pass wet rags over the cars of the prosperous, begging a handout in return. Twenty years ago, the combined rate of underemployment and marginalization reached 25 per cent. During the 1960's, it inched up an additional 15 per cent. Today, based on 1970 surveys, government economists estimate that 4 out of 10 Mexican workers are jobless or marginalized. Private economists in more recent surveys have found that the current rate of joblessness and marginalization is closer to 60 per cent.

In Mexican cities, the consequences of industrialization now have created problems which nearly rival rural poverty in their severity. Mexico City, which 20 years ago had a population of 3 million, has 13 million inhabitants today. By 1980, it will have 16 million residents, surpassing Tokyo as the largest city in the world. Already, millions live in squatter camps, without sanitary facilities, mail service or electricity. Everyone in the city—where one-fifth of Mexico now lives—breathes the poisoned air, whose carbon monoxide level exceeds that of Los Angeles; yet no serious anti-pollution controls have been established. As a reflex of population growth and urbanization, Mexico, which once was self-sufficient in food production, now imports beans, vegetable oils and cereals. Yet her industrial output is not sufficient to establish a positive balance of trade. The Mexican government, which once saw urbanization as a solution to the nation's misery, now finds itself confronted with a new urban and national poverty for which it has no solutions.

The government's inability to manage the Mexican economy is measured by the nation's external debt, and its willingness is measured by widespread corruption. Mexico's foreign debt is already the highest of any nation its size; Mexico is on the "red alarm" list in portfolios of international lending institutions, and it has been denied new loans for such projects as agricultural development. The spectre of bankruptcy has brought about a reduction in public spending at a time when demand for it is peaking. Half of Mexico's population is under 15 years old, and when the new generation reaches adulthood, it will bring unprecedented strains upon health, education, housing and job markets which already are inadequate. In 1937 the

Mexican government nationalized the oil industry. Then its leaders sold off petroleum production at below-market rates, as a move to encourage the development of oil-consuming industries. The government nationalized the rail, telephone and electric industries, creating with each an enlarged bureaucracy which drew off revenue from cut-rate services; the government-owned industries, instead of turning profits, required subsidies to survive. Nationalizations, rather than contributing to the public treasury, contributed most to private industry and the bureaucracy. Today, the Mexican government promises its people that newly-discovered petroleum fields will bring relief to the troubled economy. But development capital is not available to the government from Mexican sources; already, 40 per cent of the nation's export income is needed to pay off the interest on foreign loans. Foreign capital has been offered for oil industry expansion, but the government fears external debt in excess of the present level, and therefore, has decided to finance the petroleum expansion from funds taken in on current oil and gas sales, and by public bond issue. Observers in Mexico doubt that funds can be raised quickly enough to head off worsening economic crises, and some now openly doubt that the new oil finds are significant; investigation may show that the new oil fields are more a promise than a reality.

Few Mexicans believe that the government could solve the nation's problems even if financing were available. A single political party, the Partido Revolucionario Institutional, or PRI, has been in office since 1929. By shrewd manipulation of patronage, by buying-off or terrorizing opponents, the PRI has manuevered itself into victory in literally every major election in 50 years. Each President—and all have been PRI nominees—hand-picks his successor, a practice which builds party loyalty, but takes the flexibility out of electoral politics. The jobs of public servants depend on the PRI, as do the jobs of many others, who must be licensed to their professions. Mexico's government over the five decades of PRI rule has been transformed into a vast conspiracy against the public coffers. Corruption is so thoroughly pervasive that in the summer of 1977 the president of the Association of Blind

Mexicans protested that even beggars in Mexico City must pay daily bribes to the police.

Until recently, the PRI stayed in power by turning out the voters, and by keeping other parties with populist programs off the ballot. To enroll children in a public school, adults must show voter registration credentials validated during the most recent election. Industrial workers are given a day off on election dates, but they are granted holiday pay only if they turn out at the polls. Peasants are often paid to attend rallies and cast ballots, as are the urban unemployed. At the polls, voters select between parties of token opposition, most of which run local candidates only. In the 1976 elections, for example, all recognized political parties endorsed the PRI's candidate for the presidency. The rare victories scored by the token opposition parties in local contests are usually stolen when election officials appointed by *PRIista* officeholders tally the results. In 1977, for example, members of the PARM party claimed fraud had prevented them from assuming office in Ciudad Mante, near Tampico. The *PARMistas* seized the municipal building in Mante, and the federal government sent in troops to take it back for the PRI. In Tuxtepec, Oaxaca, state police were sent to insure that power would be peacefully transferred to a regional administrator named as election winner by the PRI despite evidence that an opposition party polled more votes.

In late 1977 requirements for chartering new parties were eased, and bona fide opposition groups are now being organized. But they still must operate under rules which in most democratic countries would be unconstitutional. For example, the new parties must furnish the government—and that means the government of the PRI—with lists of their members. Activists in the nation's new parties fear that these lists will some day be used to crackdown on dissidents. The fear is a realistic one. Amnesty International in 1977 reported that there are more than 200 political prisoners in Mexico, and that critics of the PRI regime have been disappearing from public view following abductions by law officers.

The recent electoral reform in the cities has not touched Mexico's countryside. Pre-revolutionary conditions prevail over much of the rural south, and in many areas, federal police authority has never made itself felt. The result is that as many as a third of Mexico's peasants live under the *de facto* rule of *pistoleros,* armed thugs hired by large landowners. *Pistoleros* often encroach on peasant lands, taking them over for the cattlemen or planters they serve. They also from time to time exact tributes from the peasantry, whose only resort, now as in 1910, is in armed revolt. During the Mexican revolution of 1910, hundreds of thousands of peasants fled from violence to the U.S. Today, they are fleeing again, as violence rises to pre-revolutionary proportions. In 1977, for example, more than 200 peasants were killed in the state of Oaxaca alone, and many more fled the region when their villages became battlegrounds in the conflict between armed revolutionaries and *pistoleros.*

The conditions of peasant life make emigration attractive even when the threat of violence is distant. In rural Mexico, especially in the remote southern mountains, as much as half the population lives in circumstances which long ago disappeared in modern nations. Electricity, potable water, postal service and plumbing are beyond the reach of most southern farm communities. Cultivation in these areas is done, not with the help of mules, oxen or tractors, but by hand with long-bladed machetes. The southern peasant in Mexico, 60 years after the agrarian revolution Zapata led, still survives on a meatless diet of corn tortillas, beans and peppers. Most southern peasants have never seen a movie, and few among them can allow themselves the luxury of a soft drink as often as once a month. In the southern states, most women have never set foot out of the immediate region, and most men know nothing of the area beyond, unless they have made journeys to *el norte.*

Whether he comes from the arid north or the tropical regions of southern Mexico, the ordinary peasant spends most of his life working to survive, or looking for work. Rural schools do not offer education beyond third grade, and most peasant children are needed in the fields as soon as they are able to labor. Small landowners and residents of *ejidos,* the semi-collectivized farms agrarian reform created, eke a bare subsistence out of the plots they till. They do not provide themselves or the nation with a considerable surplus product because the land allotted them is often poor, and because funds are not available for fertilizers, machinery or irrigation improvements. Though as many as 4 million peasants have land of their own, an increasing number—estimated at over 4 million—do not. Even land-holding peasants usually work a part of the year on large estates or corporate farms as a means of acquiring cash income. Nevertheless, the average annual cash income of peasant families in Mexico is less than $100.

In the north, most peasants live in adobe huts with dirt floors; in the south, in palm huts with dirt floors. Peasant homes have windows, but no screens; a factor of importance in the south, where malaria threatens. Nearly the entire Mexican population, urban and rural, is afflicted with intestinal parasites which cause intermittent diarrhea. In the southern countryside, where sanitary facilities are least developed, parasites are a problem of grave proportions. The bellies of small children are often swollen with parasites. Nearly 20 per cent of these peasant youngsters die before reaching the age of five. Many die at birth, since obstetrical care is unknown. When peasants flee the countryside, it is not because they yearn for automobiles and televisions, which are only curiosities to them, but because they see no other way to survive. Compared to the hardships that make up peasant life in Mexico, the difficulties of living in America, even as *sin papeles*, are trivial. In federal courts along the border where multiple offender *sin papeles* are tried, defendants often hold up their hands in glee when sentence is pronounced. A prison term of five months, for example, represents five months of guaranteed survival and relatively humane care. In Mexico, peasants sleep in hammocks or on cots made by stretching towsacks across a wooden frame. In American jails, they sleep on bunks or beds with mattresses. In Mexico, peasants rarely eat meat. In jail, they get it once a day, sometimes twice. In their home villages, peasants bathe in rivers and creeks; American jails have showers. If in the U.S. *sin papeles* are unable to vote, in Mexico their ballots mean nothing. If here they cannot protest for fear of deportation, there they cannot protest for fear of imprisonment or abduction. When all the factors are weighed into the balance, working in *el norte* is a reasonable gamble for those who can endure a hostile and alien environment, and absence from their families. The gamble would not be half so attractive were Mexico half as prosperous, democratic and modernized as her leaders claim.

CHAPTER 12

Law and Reality

Over the past decade the attitude of the United States towards Mexican immigration has been changed by tolerance of contradictory realities in law and fact. Before the *bracero* program was ended, and before the immigration law restrictions of 1965-68, America welcomed Mexicans both as temporary laborers and as permanent immigrants. Today, U.S. agriculture and industry welcome Mexicans as cheap, mostly short-term laborers; the availability of jobs is testimony to this informal welcome. But while Mexicans are encouraged as workers, their immigration is discouraged, and is, in fact, practically impossible by legal means. The dual realities of the labor market and the law make Mexicans a prime target for labor exploiters. America today welcomes Mexicans, so long as Mexicans are willing to be exploited.

The current situation is a gift to exploiters. They violate no laws by hiring *sin papeles* and yet doing so provides them with a labor force that need not be hired permanently, and has no legal right to demand equal wages, job safety, or grievance procedures, much less unemployment, sick leave or other company-subsidized benefits owed to most American workers. On ranches where wages include room and board, undocumented workers will accept living and eating conditions that would cause U.S.

85

workers to go to court. In effect, employers can subject *sin papeles* to 19th century work conditions and management.

Furthermore, employers who hire mostly *sin papeles* can skip the considerable paperwork that other employees require, thus saving time and money. *Sin papeles* do not ask about health coverage, or make accident insurance claims; nor do they insist that Social Security reports be posted, or that W-2 tax forms be delivered on time. Although the boss runs the risk of losing his employee to *La Migra* at any time, his undocumented worker proves not only cheaper but more convenient in the long run. By hiring *sin papeles*, employers get the benefits of a youthful labor force, without having to pay money into the costs of employee retirement later on.

The presence of uncounted thousands of Mexican *sin papeles* offers advantages to government as well. Political leaders who can't resolve the problem of domestic unemployment can point to *sin papeles* as a cause. *Sin papeles* can and have been used as scapegoats for rising costs in health, education and welfare services. They even carry a share of the blame for balance-of-exchange difficulties, since they send American currency aboard. Population growth, rising crime and disease rates have also been laid at the feet of undocumented Mexican immigration. In contemporary American politics, the *sin papeles* functions as the factor x, the gremlin, the unknown which may be used to explain nearly any social disorder.

Unlike employers and politicians, Border Patrolmen have been trapped in the squeeze between de facto demand for Mexican labor and its de jure illegality. In most Border Patrol districts, there are worksites which cannot be raided because the employers are tied to influential politicians; to disrupt such workplaces might imperil the INS budget. For example, *sin papeles* work on the ranch of Texas Governor Dolph Briscoe, just yards away from a Border Patrol checkpoint.

Such incidental limitations, however, are only part of the Patrol's problem. For years, their spokesmen have told Congress that their service is understaffed, that they cannot possibly seal the border. Consequently, Border Patrol morale is a significant administrative problem. In 1975 Michael G. Harpold, representing unionized Border Patrol officers, told the Congress: ". . . We are frustrated . . . and angry. We feel that we are being deprived of a basic human right—the right to go home after duty, warm in the knowledge that we have served our country well. The ache that we carry instead . . . is the greatest single factor adversely affecting our working conditions today . . . We are here today to ask you most humbly: Give us a law we can enforce; allow us the pride of a job well done."

But most of all, the tussle between law and actuality has created a state of fear in Spanish-speaking *barrios*. The presence of *sin papeles* in virtually every Mexican-American community has provided grounds for Border Patrol raids on hundreds of businesses and thousands of homes. It has given both Border Patrolmen and policemen a pretext for questioning any brown-skin citizen about immigration status. Since some *sin papeles* do speak English, and do have such items as drivers licenses, no native-born Chicano has been safe from interrogation, and several have been deported. Hysteria over an "illegal invasion" has also intensified discrimination against the Spanish-speaking. Some employers refuse to hire *latinos* altogether, on the pretext that any Spanish-speaker might be a *sin papeles*, while others pay all employees substandard wages, on the grounds that the availability of *sin papeles* makes higher salaries unnecessary. Perhaps most serious of all, the issue of extra-legal immigration has divided the Hispanic community. Some Southwestern Chicanos see the *sin papeles* as the community's link to its ethnic culture; others see him as a threat to American living standards. Some Chicanos picture *sin papeles* as allies in the battle against discrimination; others say *sin papeles* invite discrimination and justify it. Often a Chicano creditor, romantic rival or in-law will denounce a *sin papeles* to immigration authorities. *Sin papeles* therefore live in fear of fellow *latinos* as well as *La Migra* and Anglo racist groups, like the Ku Klux Klan. Most try to lead exemplary lives, because if a *sin papeles* quarrels with a neighbor, is late with the rent, or merely offends someone without intent, *La Migra* may be waiting at the door. In this sense America and its Chicano community have become settings in which we are divided into a two-tiered status system, a higher one for citizens and *inmigrantes*, and a lower rung, without rights, for *sin papeles*.

Despite the hardships of border-crossing and finding jobs, and despite the scorn with which they are often treated even in Spanish-speaking neighborhoods, most *sin papeles* find life in America tolerable. The Linton report found that 59 per cent of the *sin papeles* interviewed who were in Border Patrol custody planned to come back to the U.S., usually for economic reasons. Most of those who had decided to stay home gave fear of apprehension as the chief factor in their decision. The Linton study merely confirmed what most observers already knew: if there is a breaking point in undocumented immigration, a point at which the risks of coming here outweigh the prospects of finding employment, current immigration policy has not reached it. Though the restrictive legislation of the 1960's has made immigration less alluring, the revised laws and their enforcement have not been sufficient to stop the Mexican influx.

CHAPTER 13

The Current Debate

The circumstance in which reality frustrates the law is not unique by any means. America faces an even more common discrepancy: the illegality of marijuana versus its popular and open use. In comparison to the furor over pot, immigration policy was not noteworthy until the middle Nixon years. On the one hand, important sectors of those directly affected by policy, i.e., agribusiness and the Hispanic community, were either content with the status quo or mildly in favor of more lenient alternatives. Labor and exclusionist organizations either demurred or advocated more restrictive policies—but did little or nothing to bring them about. Labor and liberals focused directly on unemployment and the problem of declining union membership, while conservatives were preoccupied with challenges from the women's movement and the fate of Vietnam war prisoners. Conservatives were also supporting candidates, whose chances of winning office appeared greater in the wake of a decade of liberal Democratic hegemony. But perhaps more important than anything else, immigration was seen as an essentially regional problem concerning only Southwesterners. The potential usefulness of *sin papeles* as scapegoats for aggravated social ills was unknown at the time. In order to make immigration into a popular public and national issue, politicians had to wage a public campaign. Two men, Leonard F. Chapman and Peter Rodino, came forward to assume the role of negative public relations men for *sin papeles*. Rodino was chairman of the House Committee on the Judiciary, which supervises immigration proposals. Chapman was Commissioner of the Immigration Service during the Nixon-Ford era. Rodino was a long-time labor politician; Chapman, a retired Marine Corps general. Both men put to work the skills they had learned in public service careers to provoke hysteria against "an alien invasion."

Peter Wallace Rodino, Jr., was born in a predominately Italian neighborhood in Newark in 1909, but not to immigrant parents. He attended public schools in Newark and in 1937 graduated from the New Jersey Law School. In 1940 he lost a race for a state assembly post, and some six months later, in March, 1941 enlisted in the Army. During World War II he was decorated in European theatre combat, and received a field promotion to lieutenant. Discharged with the rank of captain in 1946, he promptly entered politics again, this time as a candidate for the House of Representatives from New Jersey's 10th district, composed of parts of Essex and Hudson counties. Again, he lost.

In early 1948 attorney Rodino made headlines at home and in Europe as the organizer of a delegation of former U.S. servicemen, mostly of Italian extraction, who went to Italy to discourage that nation's voters from supporting Communist candidates in elections held that year. Following that highly-publicized tour, Rodino won election to the House seat he had sought two years earlier.

In Congress, Rodino showed himself as a Cold War liberal, a supporter of labor, civil rights and the anti-Communist crusade. He opposed the use of the Taft-Hartley Act to cool down the steel strike, again, a clearly pro-labor voting position. During the early 50's, he supported the expansion of public housing programs and opposed repeal of wartime rent controls.

Likewise, he followed labor's lead in the Cold War, voting for a bill to authorize wire taps on people suspected of treason and espionage, and for the McCarran Act, which made membership in the Communist Party a felony punishable by 20 years imprisonment. Along with labor, Rodino supported the social and civil rights legislation of the

60's, while at the same time endorsing the Vietnam war and its escalation. Like most politicians, Rodino belongs to the exclusionist American Legion and to half-a-dozen lodges one of whom, the Protective Order of Elks, excluded blacks from membership throughout the civil rights era. Rodino in every way has been the typical labor politician—liberal, but not radical; an integrationist, but not militant; a servant of the people, but also a lawyer with a profitable private practice.

Rodino, however, showed early in his career that he has one ability not common to all politicians, though common to the best of them: a nose for the dramatic. In 1951, to publicize his opposition to repealing price controls on meat, he worked behind a butchershop counter for several hours, then wrote an article in which he described the stunt as "a heart-rending experience . . . I only wish 400 other Congressmen would go behind meat counters to learn how people feel. There's be no question of a real price control bill being voted."

In 1951 he described Harry Truman's appointment of a Republican to a federal judgeship as a Democratic "Pearl Harbor." His knack for melodrama, which served him well as a rising politician, was one of the greater assets he was to use to stir fear in the nation's Chicano *barrios*.

On Jan. 26, 1971, Republican William McCulloch introduced an immigration bill for the Nixon Administration. The bill, H.R. 2328, was a reworking of a defeated 1952 measure to make knowing employment of undocumented aliens a federal offense. The bill never reached the House floor for debate. But the Judiciary Committee studied the proposal, and Peter Rodino saw in it the gleam of success. The measure had little chance of passing in a Democratic Congress, Rodino knew. But he could give it Democratic sponsorship by revising it and adding his name as author.

Prior to introduction of the McCulloch bill, Peter Rodino's interest in undocumented immigration was less than enthusiastic. Richard Brannick, a Border Patrol union representative, told Congress that:

In 1971, the employee unions went to Chairman Rodino, then chairman of the Judiciary Subcommittee on Immigration. He told us that he had been assured by INS officials that the situation was under control. . . . We assured Chairman Rodino that the situation had been out of control for at least six years. . . . Subsequent investigations by Congress proved our statements to be true. Not too long after that both the INS and Congress were aware of the problem.

The "subsequent investigations" Brannick referred to were called in 1971 and 1972 by Chairman Rodino.

The Immigration Subcommittee heard witnesses in Washington, D.C., Los Angeles, Denver, El Paso, Chicago, Detroit and New York. Labor spokesmen, church officials, INS employees and immigration lawyers were among the 186 who came before the Committee to call for changes in the current law. Following the hearings, Democrat Rodino authored a bill of his own to outlaw employment of *sin papeles*. That bill, H.R. 16188, introduced in August, 1972 passed the House of Representatives within 45 days.

The proposal then went to the Senate Judiciary Committee, headed by Mississippi's James O. Eastland, a long-time spokesman for agricultural interests, which were generally content with the status quo of immigration. He sought to delay Senate action on the Rodino bill. His tactics drew fire from the AFL-CIO which by now was backing the Rodino bill. The AFL-CIO Executive Board blasted Eastland in a public statement:

> Efforts to pass legislation that would make it a crime for an employer to have illegal aliens on his payroll . . . have been blocked by Senator James O. Eastland. . . . He refuses to consider any illegal alien bill that does not provide authority for importation of foreign farm workers."

Pressure from fellow Democrats forced Eastland to call hearings of his Judiciary Committee on the Rodino bill. But the result was not what sponsors of the Rodino bill had lobbied for: instead, Eastland drew up a bill of his own. The Eastland bill called for making employment of *sin papeles* a misdemeanor offense, as the Rodino bill did, but it also called for revival of the *bracero* plan created under Public Law 78. Eastland's judiciary committee deadlocked. Friends of labor could not broach the *bracero* provisions, and friends of agriculture, who predominate in the Senate, could not live with the bill's Rodino-like sections. Indeed, the deadlock served Eastland's interest well. So long as the Rodino proposal was bottled up, agribusinessmen could continue hiring *sin papeles*. The call for a new *bracero* program was largely a threat to cancel out the intent of the Rodino bill.

Rodino and other House members knew that the Eastland deadlock would not give way for years. Nevertheless, they got added mileage out of the alien issue by introducing new and improved versions of the Rodino bill at each session of Congress. Most of the new wave of anti-alien bills were written merely to placate labor backers in home districts. All of them contain the same thrust, modified only in minor ways for reasons of home district or intra-Congressional politics. The 1973 bill by Congressman Rodino in time became a model for a host of offspring. Its language provided that:

(b) (1) It shall be unlawful for any employer or any person acting as an agent for such an employer, or any person who for a fee, refers an alien for employment by such an employer, knowingly to employ or refer for employment any alien in the United States who has not been lawfully admitted to the United States for permanent residence, unless the employment of such alien is authorized by the Attorney General: *Provided,* That an employer, referrer, or agent shall not be deemed to have violated this subsection if he has made a bona fide inquiry whether a person hereafter employed or referred by him is a citizen or an alien, and if an alien, whether he is lawfully admitted to the United States for permanent residence or is authorized by the Attorney General to accept employment: *Provided further,* That evidence establishing that the employer, referrer, or agent has obtained from the person employed or referred by him a signed statement in writing that such person is a citizen of the United States or that such person is an alien lawfully admitted for permanent residence or is an alien authorized by the Attorney General to accept employment, shall be deemed prima facie proof that such employer, agent, or referrer has made a bona fide inquiry as provided in this paragraph. The Attorney General of the United States shall prepare forms for the use of employers, agents, and referrers in obtaining such written statements if they so desire, and shall furnish such forms to employers, agents, and referrers upon request.

(2) If, on evidence or information he deems persuasive, the Attorney General concludes that an employer, agent, or referrer has violated the provisions of paragraph (1), the Attorney General shall serve a citation on the employer, agent, or referrer informing him of such apparent violation.

(3) If, in a proceeding initiated within two years after the service of such citation, the Attorney General finds that any employer, agent, or referrer upon whom such citation has been served has thereafter violated the provisions of paragraph (1), the Attorney General shall assess a penalty of not more than $500 for each such alien employed in violation of paragraph (1).

(4) A civil penalty shall be assessed by the Attorney General only after the person charged with a violation under paragraph (3) has been given an opportunity for a hearing and the Attorney General has determined that a violation did occur, and the amount of the penalty which is warranted. The hearing shall be of record and conducted before an immigration officer designated by the Attorney General, individually or by regulation. The proceedings shall be conducted in accordance with such regulations, within the constraints and requirements of title 5, section 554 of the United States Code which shall be applicable to the hearing provided for herein, as the Attorney General shall prescribe and the procedure so prescribed shall be the sole and exclusive procedure for determining the assessment of a civil penalty under this subsection.

(5) If the person against whom a civil penalty is assessed fails to pay the penalty within the time prescribed in such order, the Attorney General shall file a suit to collect the amount assessed in any appropriate district court of the United States. In any such suit or in any other suit seeking to review the Attorney General's determination, the suit shall be determined solely upon the administrative record upon which the civil penalty was assessed and the Attorney General's findings of fact, if supported by substantial evidence on the record considered as a whole, shall be conclusive.

"(c) Any employer or person who has been assessed a civil penalty under subsection (b) (3) which has become final and thereafter violates subsection (b) (1) shall be guilty of a misdemeanor and upon conviction thereof shall be punished by a fine not exceeding $1,000, or by imprisonment not exceeding one year, or both, for each alien in respect to whom any violation of this sub-section occurs.

In other words, if this or any similar measure passes the Congress, businessmen will be required to have all employees, both current and future, sign statements alleging that they are either citizens or legal residents of the U.S. If an employer willfully neglects this duty, he will be cited by the Justice Department, i.e., he will be warned to take the *sin papeles* off the payroll. If within two years of citation he is again reported in violation of the law, he will be assessed a penalty of not more than $500 per undocumented employee. If he is afterwards again found outside the law, he will be subject to trial and conviction of a misdemeanor federal offense, punishable by a maximum fine of $1,000 and a maximum jail term of one year, or both.

On the other hand the Eastland measure would provide a means for employing *braceros* both in industry and agriculture. According to its provisions, an employer who wanted to hire foreign workers would be required to seek permission from the Department of Labor. Upon receiving his request, the Labor Department would have a period of 60 days in which to find American workers for industrial jobs, 20 days for agricultural jobs. If the Labor Department could not refer sufficient numbers of qualified citizens and legal residents for the jobs, it would have to issue the employer a permit to import foreign labor, for a period not to exceed one year.

The Rodino-Eastland impasse has essentially been a debate between AFL-CIO spokesmen and agricultural interests. A typical statement endorsing the *bracero* program from the National Council of Agricultural Employers reads:

1. NCAE firmly agrees with those who hold that employers should employ United States citizens and those aliens who are legally authorized to seek employment, *provided* such workers can be found who are willing, able and qualified to do the work. Historically, however, such worker have not been available in sufficient number at the times and places needed.
2. Agricultural employers need workers who will report

at the appointed time and remain to finish seasonal jobs. Employers' records are replete with employees who do not. As a single case in point, an agricultural employer organization in Virginia reported the following statistics at the end of its 1975 harvest season:

"This past season the Employment Service referred to us 172 people. Of this number 110 showed up and 14 finished the season."

Of the workers from within Virginia:

Fifteen percent completed the season.

Forty-two percent worked less than 1 week.

Twenty-five percent worked less than 2 weeks.

Six percent worked less than 3 weeks.

12 percent worked more than 4 weeks, but failed to complete the season.

Of the workers referred from other States, mostly Florida:

Nine percent completed the season.

Twenty-seven percent worked less than 1 week.

Thirty-five percent worked less than 2 weeks.

Seven percent worked less than 3 weeks.

Twenty-two percent worked more than 3 weeks, but failed to complete the season.

3. It has been alleged that the removal of all illegal aliens and a prohibition against the use of temporary foreign labor will eliminate the unemployment problem in this country. We have serious doubts that unemployed persons in, say Detroit, will travel to Virginia to harvest fruit, or even spend a full season picking peaches, cherries or apples in Michigan. The unemployment figures have been high for at least two years, but growers still cannot find workers, even through the State-Federal Employment Service, and in spite of aggressive local recruiting efforts.

4. The fallacious thinking exists that just anyone can do agricultural labor. Such is not the case. Physical fitness and manual dexterity are most essential. Many persons are afraid to climb ladders to harvest tree fruits. Others do not like stoop labor.

5. It has been alleged that bringing in foreign agricultural labor adversely affects the wages and working conditions of workers similarly employed. Quite the opposite is true. Any agricultural employer who employs one or more foreign workers must pay those workers, plus all his domestic workers doing the same work, "adverse effect rates" which are higher than would be paid if no foreign workers were employed.

6. When foreign agricultural workers are certified by the Secretary of Labor and the Attorney General, they

are brought into this country for a specified period of time to perform specified labor. When that job is completed, all such workers must be returned to the country whence they came. They can not remain to seek work elsewhere.

Labor counters with statements like the following, by Kenneth J. Meiklejohn, an AFL-CIO lobbyist:

We have maintained, and the subcommittee hearings have made clear, that their status as illegal aliens who are liable to be deported at any time upon discovery subjects them to serious discrimination and exploitation on the job. Because their presence in the United States is in violation of the law, and they are in constant danger of discovery and deportation or, if they came in illegally, of fines and imprisonment, they are in no position to complain if their employer pays them poorly or cheats them unfairly. As a result, their employment is characterized by substandard wages and denial of rights and benefits normally associated with employment in America. The net effort of their employment, the subcommittee hearings made clear, has been to depress and maintain low wage levels and substandard living conditions for American citizens, permanent residents and illegal aliens alike in areas where they are employed in large numbers.

In addition, of course, the availability of a substantial supply of illegal aliens able and willing to work for substandard wages and working conditions also results in loss of jobs and employment opportunities for American workers. Obviously, too, the effectiveness of the rights of union organization and collective bargaining is seriously undermined.

In initial debate about *sin papeles* Rodino and the Judiciary Committee could offer only weak evidence in support of the bill. For example, a 1973 statement by the Committee reports that "the number of illegal aliens appears to be between one and two million." It further reported that "illegal aliens are not generally involved in criminal or drug-related problems." Modest statements like these did not build the hysteria exclusionists and labor needed for a full-scale drive against *sin papeles*. What was needed was a set of new and enlarged accusations against undocumented immigrants. The Nixon administration, which supported the Rodino bill because exclusionist groups like the American Legion endorsed it, lent its own support by finding a man capable of creating demand for its passage. That man was Leonard F. Chapman, a former Marine general named INS Commissioner in 1972. During five years at the post, Chapman contributed to anti-alien hysteria as no one had since General Joseph Swing retired from the INS at the end of the Eisenhower presidency.

CHAPTER 14

━━━━━━━━━━━━━

Gen. Chapman's Smear Campaign

Leonard Chapman was not the sort of individual whom one expects to find at the center of any controversy. He had a record of patriotism, administrative service, and avoidance of politics. A Protestant, native of Florida and an honor student in college, in 1935 he began a seemingly lackluster career as an officer of the U.S. Marine Corps. When World War II came, Chapman directed Marine forces in the Pacific. During the 50's he served in Japan, and later worked as an administrator at Marine bases in the U.S., and behind desks in the Pentagon. His accolades do not point to a bent for controversy. For example, in 1967 he was awared a Distinguished Service Medal for leadership in "pioneering the development and utilization of the computer and other modern information machines" for the Marine Corps. The following year he was promoted to four-star general and named Commandant of the Marine Corps. In 1969, Korean dictator Chung Hee Park awarded Chapman the Order of National Security Merit for "distinguished services in strengthening the defense capabilities of the Korean Armed Forces"—an event which, in the light of Koreagate, hints of scandal. Shortly afterwards, he earned a Gold Star in lieu of a second Distinguished Service Medal for leadership of the Corps during the Vietnam war period. Chapman retired from the Marine Corps in January, 1972, after nearly 37 years of service.

Nothing in Chapman's record suggests that before Oct. 2, 1972, when President Richard Nixon named him to head the Immigration Service, he had any interest in Spanish, Mexico or the Mexican people. Chapman's nomination to head the INS cleared the Senate without debate, apparently because the post was not considered delicate and Chapman's record as an administrator spoke for his competence.

But the perspective Chapman brought to his new job was, quite simply, racist. His public speeches betrayed insensitivity to immigrant and minority problems, and often, an ignorance of facts. In an address to the Pennsylvania Fraternal Congress, an organization of European immigrants and their friends, Chapman declared that:

> There is a major difference in the patterns of immigration today compared with the early part of this century. The United States was then a melting pot, where persons came from other nations, were anxious to learn the language and become absorbed in the society of their new land. Though they may have settled with others from their own homeland, formed societies and kept the old ties, they became in every sense of the word . . . Americans. And good Americans.

> Today, America is becoming less and less of a melting pot of many nationalities, and is becoming more and more of a mosaic . . . a quilted pattern of races and nationalities, each clinging firmly to their own backgrounds, thinking less of the interests of the United States and more of the interests of the nation they left behind . . . forming power groups to influence American foreign and internal policy. I believe this must be a concern for all Americans, and perhaps especially for those of you who are the sons and daughters and grandchildren of earlier immigrants who did become a part of this great land and who helped build it.

Several points make his remarks noteworthy. Chapman said that the United States was once a "melting pot," but failed to observe that Africans, Orientals, and Mexicans were hardly allowed into the common mix. The implication he apparently intended to convey was that European immigrants, who were "melted" together, became "good Americans" while those with non-white skins did not.

Chapman offers proof that non-European immigrants did not become "good Americans" by pointing to the "quilted pattern of races and nationalities," i.e., ethnic neighborhoods. In doing so, he blamed ethnic and racial discrimination not on restricted housing, "last hired, first fired" employment policies, or any other aspect of prejudice, but on the supposed unwillingness of 20th century immigrants to give up their ethnic heritages. Further, his claim that this ethnic mosaic is composed of new, 20th century immigrants is historically false. Blacks were first brought here in 1619, and Mexicans lived in the Southwest long before it was a part of the United States. In fact, black immigration—if slavery can be called immigration—antedates at least Italian and Polish immigration. And whereas Italians and Poles maintain certain Old World traditions and customs, blacks were completely uprooted from their African pasts. They, more than any other ethnic group in America, have been "Americanized."

Chapman repeated the chronological error in the same speech and elsewhere by proclaiming that

> We are all the children, grandchildren or great-grandchildren of immigrants. It was the Poles, the Italians, the Lithuanians, the Czechs and literally hundreds of others who came to this continent, moved across the land, homesteaded and populated the prairies and the cities and provided the tremendous drive and power which have made this the greatest nation in the world.

The General apparently did not know or ignored the fact that many Mexicans and nearly all Native Americans did not immigrate here—ever. His list of productive nationalities failed to mention blacks, Mexicans or Orientals, on whose backs much of America's development was carried, though perhaps Chapman did include them in that generous phase "hundreds of others." In fact, Chinese, Japanese, and African immigration by far exceeds Lithuanian immigration, and Mexican immigration may exceed that of any European group in history. Certainly it does if Chapman's estimates of undocumented Mexican immigration are true, as the General would have had his listeners believe.

The General's claim that non-European immigrants "form power groups to influence American foreign and internal policy" rang of the loose rhetoric of the 1920 Palmer raids, of Nisei internment during World War II, and of McCarthyism. In no speech did he signal what group carried out the sinister purpose he attributed to associations of non-European immigrants, nor did he distinguish their functioning from that of the Fraternal Congress, which lobbies for relaxation of quota restrictions. It would seem that if non-European immigrants became citizens, they could vote on "internal policy" and form organizations as any other citizens might; the Constitution guarantees citizens a right to influence government policy. When reading the speeches of General Chapman, one gets the idea that citizens who live in ethnic ghettoes should be disenfranchised.

In addition, the research which went into Chapman's speeches lent to his racist image though his researchers probably never intended this effect. Time and again Chapman told Rotary clubs, business associations, and Congressional gatherings that "since 1820, nearly 50 million people have immigrated to America . . ." The figure 50 million, however, is based on a count of legal immigration only. Between 1820 and 1900, for example, head-counts of legal immigrants show only 81 Africans. Scholars have established from slave ship manifests that some 250,000 slaves were smuggled into the U. S. after importation was prohibited in 1820. Chapman's figure ignores these forced immigrants, as well as the Mexicans and Chinese who came here without documents during the first half of the 20th century. Ignorance of unofficial immigration leads to a skewed picture of the actual racial/national composition of history.

Chapman's contributions to exclusionist slander were not limited to public speeches. In articles for *Readers' Digest*, for example, Chapman termed undocumented Mexican immigration "a growing, silent invasion of illegal aliens," and sounded an alarm: "Action must be swift, for there is no time to lose." General Chapman pulled the military rhetoric of Operation Wetback from the grave and gave it new life.

CHAPTER 15

―――――――― ――◄―― ◄►― ―◄ ――――――――

Inflating the Estimates

One of Chapman's first moves in office was upward revision of the estimate of illegal aliens. In hearings conducted shortly after his appointment, he declared that there were not 100,000 illegal aliens as his predecessor, Raymond F. Farrell had said, but two million. The new estimate helped the Rodino Committee make its case for anti-alien legislation.

But it fell short of best evidence. The Chapman estimate was a tally of guesses by regional Immigration Service directors, not the product of any methodology. When quizzed closely about the alien figure by newsmen, Chapman responded that "If we could count them, we could catch them."

Under growing pressure from labor groups to pass the Rodino bill, Congress in 1975 authorized the expenditure of some $2 million for studying the subject of undocumented immigration. The initial fruit of that budget item was the $33,000 report by Lesko Associates, a private firm based in Washington, D. C. The Lesko study, commissioned for the INS and completed in 1975, gives the number of undocumented immigrants at 8 million, 5 million of them Mexicans.

The Lesko Report is the first effort in a longer study aimed at developing an unassailable estimate of the illegal alien population. The report admits itself to be a "quick-reaction study" some of whose figures, like those used in earlier estimates, "are not analytically defensible."

Appraised that the alien underground is, and generally has been, largely Mexican in composition, Lesko researchers began their efforts by drawing a lower limit on the number of Mexican illegals.

A document by a Georgetown University graduate student Howard Goldberg, produced for the Center on Population Research, gave the Lesko team its baseline information.

Goldberg applied life survival rates of the Mexican population to that nation's 1960 census, in order to estimate the population level Mexico would reach in 1970. He then subtracted his estimate from the figure on population reported by the 1970 Mexican census. Then Goldberg cast out the number of Mexicans who immigrated to the United States legally during the decade, and consulted American census figures on Spanish-speaking minorities.

His result was an estimate that 1.6 million illegal aliens were living in the United States as of 1970.

Although the Lesko Associates team passed on the Goldberg estimate as "analytically sound," it did not account for Mexican illegals present in the United States before 1960 who have maintained a continuous residence here.

With a figure of 1.6 million Mexican illegals as a lower bounds, the Lesko team developed an estimate of the 1975 population of the undocumented. The basic device used for post-1970 estimates was the "getaway" ratio.

The getaway ratio is an old device for measuring Border Patrol effectiveness, made complex and given a pretentious formula by the Lesko team. General Chapman in public speeches explained the ratio in more straightforward terms: "For every illegal alien our agents catch at entry, two or three more get away."

The getaway ratio is ordinarily a hipshot estimate made by Border Patrol agents on the basis of almost daily interviews with *sin papeles*. But it may also be dredged from INS statistics, the route taken by technically-minded Lesko researchers.

In 1975, for example, of 756,800 illegal aliens of all nationalities apprehended, 88 per cent, or 667,700, had entered the country clandestinely, without visas of any kind. Of that number some 662,000, or 99 per cent, were Mexican nationals who slipped over the Southwestern border. Among apprehended Mexicans, 98 per cent lacked documents at the time of apprehension. The Lesko Report terms these *sin papeles* "Entries Without Inspection," or EWI's.

The Lesko Report distinguishes between those undocumented Mexicans apprehended within 72 hours of entry, and all those netted later on, regardless of their status at entry. To arrive at its prime getaway ratio, it divides the number in the later-caught group by the number in the earlier-trapped group. The result is what is called the "minimum getaway at entry ration" or MGAER.

Lesko methodology sets up an MGAER for 1970, assumes that the MGAER for other years varies by a constant factor from that of 1970, and then limits the 1970 MGAER with other considerations.

Calculations for 1970 show that for every EWI caught within 72 hours of the border, another 2.9 Mexican *sin papeles* got away and were later caught.

The raw 2.9:1 MGAER falls short of an actual getaway rate for several reasons, but primarily because an unknown proportion of *sin papeles* are never caught, and are therefore, never counted.

Limiting factors which do get consideration in the Lesko formula are death rates of *sin papeles* once they are safely in the United States, and the rate at which they emigrate back to Mexico. The function of these considerations is to distinguish between the *flow* of illegal aliens and illegal alien *stock*.

Its chief gambit is adaptation of a United States Census Bureau report that between 1960 and 1970, one of every seven *legal* aliens returned home permanently.

For its own calculation, the Lesko study uses a higher figure of one in five over a 10-year period, or 20 out of 1,-000 annually. The report explains the change by saying that "the study team assumed that the migration rate of illegals is somewhat higher than that of legal aliens."

The admittedly arbitrary annual emigration ratio did not sit well with the research team, which noted that it "intuitively" felt an even higher rate should be used, but could find no factual basis for the inkling.

Another restraint on MGAER computations is the death rate of *sin papeles* once they are safely inside the United States. The Lesko Report lifted life survival tables for Mexicans age 25-40 from a reference source, and calculated that 6.2 *sin papeles* per every 1,000 die off annually. Adding both its return and death rates together, the report comes up with a 26.2 attrition rate for the stock population of illegal aliens.

Details of the Lesko study are given mathematical pretensions in a formula which, even modestly considered, merits uninhibited incredulity:

$$T_y = \sum_{i=1}^{Y} A_i (MGAER)_i XR^{y-i} - \sum_{i=1}^{Y} BiR^{y-i} + T_0$$

Plugging Goldberg's 1.6 million estimate into the left side of the formula, at T_y, or total number of illegals in 1970, it adds getaway data into the system, survival and apprehension information, and arrives at what the study terms an "analytically defensible" and "actual" ratio of getaway, 1.58:1. This figure is proffered as the key to estimating the population of the alien underground.

Armed with this ratio, the Lesko team then calculated the illegal populaton in years since 1970, and produced an estimate of 5,204,000 for 1975:

Year	Getaway-at-Entry Ratio	Successful Illegal Entries (000's)	Illegals Remaining from Previous Years (000's)	Mexican Illegals in U.S. (000's)
1970				1,597.0*
1971	8.61	544.6	1,555.2	2,099.8
1972	7.64	648.9	2,044.7	2,693.6
1973	6.89	845.0	2,623.0	3,468.1
1974	5.67	972.3	3,377.2	4,349.5
1975	6.26	968.4	4,235.6	5,204.0

The methodology and findings of the Lesko study may be challenged on a variety of grounds, but the most critical is that the study does not make any allowance for uncounted thousands of EWI's who are apprehended and deported more than once in a given year.

Many *sin papeles*, especially those who commute to work along the border, are apprehended and returned to Mexico several times a year. Yet for a *sin papeles* who is deported three times, for example, INS statistical tallies will show three EWI's. The Lesko report errs in presuming that for each EWI, there is a separate alien. INS records are not computerized to allow for dropping-out of multiple EWI's, and therefore, only an estimate could repair the Lesko formula. No such estimate is made. By necessity, any such estimate would lower the figure for total *sin papeles* in the U.S. Failure to compensate for multiple EWI's inflates the actual number of *sin papeles*.

Criticism of Lesko estimates has come from a range of agencies, but most responsibly from a Labor Department study team which in early 1975 interviewed 481 Mexican *sin papeles* as part of a study on the economic impact of undocumented immigration. The study, performed by a private research firm, Linton and Company, differs with the Lesko Report in several important ways.

In its own report, which did not seek to estimate the underground's size, the Labor Department research team pointed out several problems for Lesko defenders, and plainly said:

". . . in the context of other available information, we believe that the estimate is on the generous side—by millions."

It cited Mexican census data showing population of 23,-229,000 between the ages of 15 and 29, or roughly, the workforce age from which most EWI's are drawn. Lesko's estimate of 5 million illegals, mostly from that age group, would indicate that between one-fifth and one-quarter of all Mexicans of that age are illegally in the United States, a contention the Linton study calls "most improbable."

Another body of evidence in apparent contradiction is the Current Population Survey estimate of the Bureau of Census. This document, the Linton team noted, estimates that 10,795,000 Spanish-origin persons are residing in the United States, both native and foreign-born. Lesko's 5 million estimate, then, would indicate that fully half of them are illegal aliens, a conclusion unacceptable to anyone familiar with Mexican-American populations, even along border areas.

A second part of the Lesko study estimates the total population of illegal aliens of all nationalities, including the Mexicans. Conclusions of the second-part study were based on subjective information, and are not analytically defensible, the report warns.

To make the aggregate estimate, the Lesko team asked a blue-ribbon committee of church, civic and education leaders to guess the number of illegals in their destricts. Attention was given, for example, to Poles in Chicago, West Indians in Miami, and to Oriental illegals on the West Coast, all groups not considered in the team's painstaking Mexican report.

Initial estimates from the second-part study indicated an undocumented population of from two to 25 million, a range beyond the tastes of the Lesko team, which sent tallies to its sources and asked them to guess again.

The second round of responses narrowed the numbers spread to between five and 11 million. A third series of questionaires then went out, and brought back an estimate the Lesko team could live with: that there are between 4.2 and 11 million undocumented immigrants in the United States.

For practical use, the Lesko team recommended, and INS leaders accepted, an average of the high and low estimates of 8.1 million undocumented immigrants, with 5.1 million attributed to Mexico, according to data in the getaway ratio study.

The sheer guesswork of the second part of the Lesko study has been pointed out by government officials and scholars alike. Vincent Barabba, former Census Bureau Director, told researchers that "the estimates of the current illegal alien population shown in the study are based on weak and untenable assumptions, and add very little to our knowledge of the size of the illegal alien population."

Demographer Charles Keeley reviewed the estimates and concluded that "budget needs and organizational dynamics" guided the makers rather than a concern for reliability.

The Lesko estimates, like earlier ones, fall short of the requirements of best evidence. Unlike earlier reports, the Lesko estimates were high, and so was their cost to the public.

CHAPTER 16

───── ▶◀ ◀▶ ▶◀ ─────

They're Stealing Our Jobs

Chapman decided that the Rodino bill stood its best chance of passage if presented to the public as a remedy for domestic unemployment, not merely as an extension of immigration law. In his *Reader's Digest* article he urged that "if we could locate and deport the three to four million illegals who currently hold jobs in the United States, replacing them with citizens and legal residents, we could reduce our own unemployment dramatically—*as much as 50 per cent*." To develop and sharpen his claim, Chapman downplayed the traditional assumption that *sin papeles* work mainly at low-paid jobs in the Southwest. Instead, he declared that Mexican undocumented workers had spread across the nation, taking well-paid jobs from Americans as they advanced. "The problem is not restricted to any geographic area. It is nationwide in scope and impact, and affects everyone," he told a national VFW gathering. In an article for the *U. S. News & World Report*, he proclaimed that:

"... These jobs. ... are not low-paying jobs that are unwanted by legal residents. ... One of the difficult tasks the Immigration Service has before it is to dispel the myth that the illegals take only jobs picking tomatoes or planting cotton, which pay a few dollars a week and couldn't be filled if the aliens were sent

home. That may have been true at one time, but is no
longer so."

In order to provide evidence for his thesis, Chapman instructed the INS to "concentrate our limited capacity on
those that are working at good jobs, that we think an
unemployed American would be very happy to have. . . ."

The results of the campaign to arrest undocumented im-
migrants who held attractive jobs were proclaimed in
speeches to civic and exclusionist group across the nation.
In these addresses, Chapman relied heavily on the unusual.
His strongest examples did not involve Mexicans at all.
For example, in March 1975 Chapman told the National
Security Committee of the Veterans of Foreign Wars that:

"Many [undocumented immigrants] are students or well-
educated and skilled persons who obtain good paying jobs.
One example of this type of illegal alien is an East Indian
national whom we apprehended in Houston on January
22. He held a masters degree in electrical engineering
from Stanford University. . . . When he was apprehended he was employed at an electronics firm as a product development engineer earning over $17,000 a year."

Needless to say, there are very few East Indian engineers, or Pakistani restaurant managers—another favorite Chapman example—in Houston or anywhere else. Only
the smallest fraction of *sin papeles* are college-educated, as
the Linton study—which found an average education level
of 4.9 years among the Mexicans—proved beyond any
doubt. There are not enough M.A.'s in the whole Western
World to account for a tiny fraction of the more than
700,000 *sin papeles* apprehended each year.

Chapman, like Rodino, had an eye for the dramatic. In
the VFW and other speeches he reported that:

"Another good example [of highly-paid undocumented
workers] is provided by two brothers of Greek nationality
whom we appehended here in New York in mid-January.
One had entered as a tourist for 10 days, and had been
here for five years. The other had jumped ship when the
freighter on which he worked had put into New York
harbor. He had been here about four years. When we
caught up with them, they were both employed as

painters, earning $9.71 per hour. And where do you suppose they were working? On the Statue of Liberty. They were part of a contractor's crew, refurbishing the statue, and were being paid out of federal funds."

Another dramatic example, but one Chapman did not take to the public in his speeches, was the 1974 arrest of four undocumented aliens who were working as janitors at INS headquarters in Washington D. C.

For nearly two years Chapman attempted to develop statistics to convince readers and listeners that *sin papeles* indeed occupied attractive jobs across the nation. For example, in early 1976 Chapman told the Phoenix Metropolitan Chamber of Commerce that:

"In the first seven months of 1975 we located in the major cities more than 50,000 illegal aliens who were employed. More than half were earning in excess of $2.50 an hour. In Chicago, 75 per cent of those we find are earning from $2.50 to $4.50 an hour."

Comparison of the earnings Chapman cited with data kept by the Labor Department in Chicago indicates that the wages paid *sin papeles* there were substandard for 1975. The Labor Department reported an average wage of $5.75 cents an hour for Chicago in 1975. The city's lowest-paid workers that year were guards in service industry settings, who earned an average of $2.70 an hour. Janitors on the whole earned $3.90 per hour. The conclusion to be drawn is that *sin papeles* in Chicago were mainly employed in menial jobs.

In May, 1975 Chapman told the Dallas Rotary Club that:

"Last week in Dallas, a special detail of Border Patrol agents, operating here temporarily, checked an aluminum storm door factory. They apprehended 52 illegal aliens, which was one-sixth of the total work force of 300. They were earning from $2.50 to $3.10 an hour."

Labor Department figures for Dallas during that time period show that janitors averaged $2.93 per hour, and that materials handlers in light industry—employees with jobs comparable to the storm door workers—average

$3.75 an hour. Again, Chapman's citations of prestige wages actually point to labor exploitation.

Reporters for the *Washington Post* who looked behind Chapman's charges in 1975 found little to support them. In Los Angeles, for example, they found that:

"Of 842 illegal aliens who were reported holding jobs in the Los Angeles area in the first three weeks of January, 60 per cent were making $2.50 an hour or less. A total of 96 per cent were making $3 an hour or less."

Labor Department studies indicate that janitors in Los Angeles averaged $3.42 to $3.52 an hour during late 1974 and early 1975, and the lowest wage reported for food services workers during the same period was $2.66 an hour. Clearly, *sin papeles* in Los Angeles by and large did not hold prestige jobs.

The INS effort to depict *sin papeles* as prosperous job competitors was largely silenced when early reports of the exhaustive Linton & Company study became public in mid-1975. The Linton study, commissioned by the Labor Department, drew on interviews with some 793 undocumented aliens in Border Patrol custody, all of whom had worked two weeks or more in the U. S. Interviews were conducted in 19 cities, including Los Angeles, New York, San Antonio, Chicago, Miami, Newark, San Francisco, Detroit, Seattle and Washington, D. C. When the study's full findings were released in March, 1976, it proved that undocumented workers earn substandard wages that Mexican *sin papeles* are especially exploited, and that the locus of *sin papeles* is the Southwest.

The majority of Mexican respondents in the Linton study were employed either in manufacturing (27 per cent), agriculture (26.2 per cent), or construction (20.8 per cent.) Altogether, more than 90 per cent were employed at unskilled, menial, or blue-collar jobs. The study found that the average wage earned by the Mexican *sin papeles* in manufacturing was $2.92 an hour, compared to an average of $4.73 for American industrial workers as a whole. Those in construction average $2.98 an hour, compared to $7.15 for construction workers nationally. In agriculture, the average wage of Mexican *sin papeles* came to $2.07 an hour, three cents below the national minimum wage at the time.

The study found that Mexican *sin papeles* on the average earn less than other undocumented workers, and that undocumented workers earn less on the average than legal residents and citizens. The Linton report summarizes that:

> "The average hourly wages of the illegals interviewed for this study fell markedly below the norm in each of the . . . industrial divisions for which there are comparable data on U.S. workers, and well below the average hourly wage of most of the U.S. workforce. As a group. . . . the respondents employed in those . . . industrial groups earned an average of $2.66 an hour—about 60% of $4.47, the average hourly wage in 1975 of the some 50 million similarly employed production and nonsupervisory U.S. workers."

A similar study completed by the INS in 1975 showed even lower average earnings for Mexican *sin papeles* than those unearthed by the Linton team. Summarizing results of the two studies, the Linton report points out that:

> ". . . Both studies of the hourly wages of apprehended illegal aliens are in agreement that (1) at least three-quarters of all respondents in farmwork earned less than $2.50 an hour; (2.) at least two-thirds of all respondents employed in the Southwest Region earned less than $2.50 an hour; (3) at least three-quarters of all respondents earned less than $4.50 an hour, regardless of their type of employment, location in the U.S., or. . . . region of origin; and (4.) at least 98% of all respondents earned less than $6.50 an hour."

The Linton study also found evidence that Mexican *sin papeles* are more subject to unemployment than other undocumented workers and the workforce as a whole. Of those who responded to the study, only 20.6 per cent had held a job in the U. S. for two years or more, though they averaged 2.4 years inside the country. Of those employed in agriculture, only 11.8 per cent had been continuously employed as long as a year, a finding which points to the persistent importance of *sin papeles* as seasonal workers. In the Linton sample as a whole, including non-Mexican workers, average job tenure was between one and two years. Comparable figures for American workers in the same age bracket are 3.1 years for whites, 2.8 years for blacks. Unemployment for the sample as a whole averaged 10.2 per cent, compared to 9.4 per cent during the same period for black Americans, and 3.8 per cent for the workforce as a whole.

Another significant finding of the Linton study was that about 23 per cent of the illegals interviewed had received less than the minimum wage. A third of the farmworkers, a quarter of those in construction, and about 10 per cent of those employed in manufacturing reported black market salaries. Mexican *sin papeles* were especially likely to report wages below the federal minimum. Nearly 40 per cent of those hired below the minimum wage reported that they had been hired *because* they were undocumented, and many claimed that they were paid salaries lower than those of legal workers on the same job. Nearly one quarter of the Mexican *sin papeles* reported that they were paid in cash, and along the border area, the figure rose to 63 per cent.

In addition, the Linton study found that undocumented immigrants worked longer hours than American workers—and earned less, even when overtime pay was counted into earnings. On the average, the 793 *sin papeles* in the study worked 44.5 hours a week, 8.6 hours longer than the national average. Yet take-home pay averaged $117 weekly, compared to $160 for the workforce as a whole.

Wage exploitation was sharpest in the rural Southwest, and especially in the 23 counties bordering Mexico. The Linton study interviewed 68 *sin papeles* from that region, who averaged earnings of $1.74 per hour, the lowest of any regional group in the sample. Wages across the Southwest averaged only $1.98 per hour, again a figure below the federal minimum wage.

The interviews indicated that as Mexican *sin papeles* become established in the U. S., they seek to leave the border country, usually for urban industrial jobs in the northwest and midwest. "Mexican EWIs are deliberately leaving the notoriously back-breaking, low-paying, and unstable jobs offered in southwest agriculture for jobs in urban areas, where they are also less likely to be apprehended . . . ," the study concluded. Study data

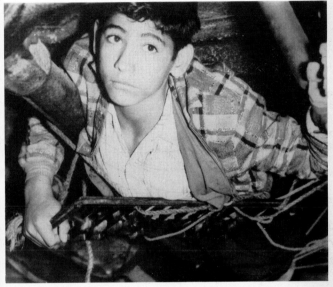

Attempt to smuggle 13-year-old alien into the United States under a car. *Official U.S. Immigration and Naturalization Service Photograph.*

Undocumented aliens travel across the border any way they can: these pictures show some of the ways they are packed into automobiles, and trucks. Many die in the attempt to escape the grinding poverty south of the border.

Official U.S. Immigration and Naturalization Service Photograph.

Smuggling 28 illegal aliens in a U-Haul truck.

Official U.S. Immigration and Naturalization Service Photograph.

Girl getting out from under the hood of a car after attempt to enter the United States.

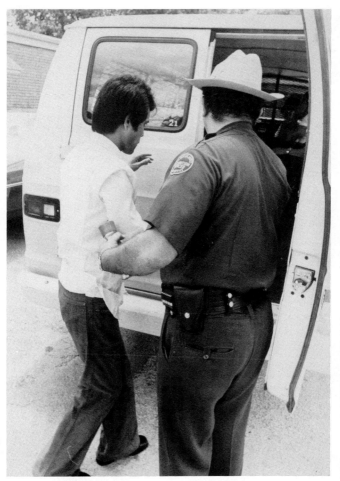

San Antonio pick-up.

Photo courtesy of Mario Cantu

INS investigators question a suspected *sin papeles*.

Photo courtesy of Mario Cantu

Apprehension on the border.

Photo courtesy of Dick J. Reavis

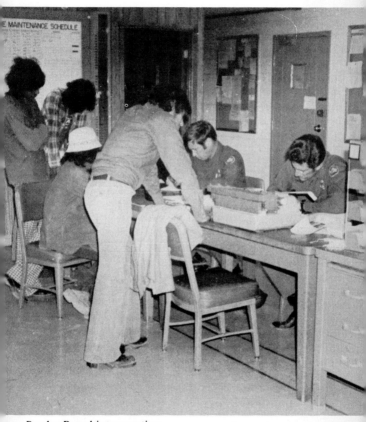

Border Patrol interrogation.

Photo courtesy of Dick J. Reavis

A recent protest march.

Photo courtesy of Dick J. Reavis

pointed out that *sin papeles* who have been in the U. S. two years or more are only half as likely to be working in agriculture, another indication of the northwestern and midwestern immigration drift. However, the Linton researchers were unable to show that great numbers of *sin papeles* actually escape the Southwest, even when they do find industrial jobs. Nor could it be shown that the percentage of *sin papeles* employed outside agriculture had increased over the previous decade.

INS tables show that 95.3 per cent of the Mexican *sin papeles* apprehended in 1964 were found within the agency's Southwestern District, which includes California. Ten years later, 94.6 per cent were located in the same region, a scarcely noticeable change. In 1964, 66.6 per cent of those apprehended worked in agriculture; in 1974, 61.2 per cent did. INS tables clearly show that the total proportion of Mexican apprehensions is growing, as is the absolute number. In 1964, 50.6 per cent of all undocumented workers apprehended were Mexican. By 1974, the figure had risen to 90.1 per cent. In absolute terms, the increase was greater than tenfold: 41,799 undocumented Mexican immigrants were apprehended in 1964, compared to 671,-901 ten years later.

Apprehension tables, however, are not sound indicators of the distribution of *sin papeles* across regions or sectors of the job market. As the Linton study noted, "apprehending illegals at the southwestern border is far more cost effective than in the interior of the nation." Apprehension statistics provide only a pointer: they say where undocumented immigrants may most easily be caught, along the Mexican border and on farm jobs. They do not disprove the contention that successful *sin papeles* move both away from the border and from agricultural work.

However, evidence on hand and the current theories of immigration all indicate that the concentration of *sin papeles* remains the Southwest. Recently arrived legal immigrants tend to cluster in cities where members of their nationality already live: the immigrant populations of both the East and West Coast are testimony to this, as is the distribution of legal Mexican immigrants. Scholars of immigration and the Linton researchers therefore hypothesize that undocumented immigrants also cluster where their countrymen already live. Several field studies, and one apprehension project of the INS—which used addresses of recent legal immigrants to locate unapprehended *sin papeles*—have borne out this theory, for Europeans and Mexicans as well. If the facts correspond to the hypothesis, then most *sin papeles* still reside in Texas and California, since more than half of all Mexican permanent resident immigrants live in California, and another quarter are to be found in Texas, the two states which lead in INS apprehensions.

CHAPTER 17

――――――― ✖ ―――⬥――― ✖ ―――――――

Tax Evaders! Welfare Cheats!

A second part of the campaign to impugn *sin papeles* was circulation of the claim that they burden welfare rolls and evade social security taxes. Labor again took the lead. A 1974 statement in the AFL-CIO *Federationist,* for example, said:

> It is estimated that illegal aliens cause an annual wage loss to U.S. workers of $10 billion. These are tax-free wages that escape the community levies attached to the salaries and wages of all legally employed persons in this nation. Our social security and welfare systems are heavily penalized by illegals, too. . . . In thousands of cases, illegals have worked in the United States for years and then gone home to collect social security benefits from a nation of which they never become legal residents and in which they never paid income or social security taxes. . . . Welfare and other relief agencies must modify their screening procedures so that illegal aliens cannot receive benefits from tax monies paid by legal residents and citizens.

General Chapman echoed the charge in his 1976 *Readers' Digest* article:

> Illegal aliens and their offspring also benefit from public services such as wlfare, medical care and free education.

117

Few, if any, pay their share of the cost. . . . In addition, illegal aliens routinely avoid hundreds of millions of dollars in both state and federal taxes. . . .

Detractors of the *sin papeles* did not attempt to present objective findings to buttress their claim. The "estimates" the AFL-CIO talked about were those of General Chapman, whose only evidence was anecdotal. Typically, Chapman's speeches included an assertion that *sin papeles* were freeloaders on the public economy, followed by a listing of incidents—which created the impression that hard statistics were available—but which in no way accounted for the possibility of contrary evidence.

From the first, the charge was doubted in quarters where *sin papeles* were well known. Like other workers, undocumented Mexicans are subjected to withholding of Social Security and other taxes; like other consumers, they pay sales taxes on purchases. Most know little or nothing of welfare programs, which are non-existent in Mexico. Further, *sin papeles* generally avoid contact with government agencies and personnel—even census-takers—for fear that their illegal status will be discovered. Since most are young men capable of physical labor, serious ailments and instances of hospitalization are rare among them. Because few have families in the U. S., they do not send their children to American schools. In a word, their status as workers obligates them to contribute to public programs financed by taxation. But their characteristics as a group are not those of a population likely to be eligible for public assistance programs, which are designed for the aging, the infirm, and the improverished family head. If in exceptional instances *sin papeles* do receive aid, the critical question is: do they take out as much as they contribute to the public till?

The Linton researchers attempted to gather credible figures on the participation of *sin papeles* in tax, welfare and social insurance programs. What they discovered speaks sharply against tax evasion and welfare fraud charges. Of the 793 undocumented immigrants the Linton team interviewed, 73.2 per cent reported paying witholding taxes. But only 31.5 per cent of the group as a whole, and 22 per cent of the Mexicans, filed returns to claim refunds on witholding taxes paid, though doubtless many were eligible, as many Americans are at the end of each tax year. Their reluctance is a reflex of their fear of discovery, though in fact, the Internal Revenue Service cannot report the names or addresses of its clients to the Immigration Service or anyone else. It also reflects their ignorance of English and their relative transciency. The effect is that *sin papeles*, instead of evading taxes, overpay them. The public treasury millions of American draw on is enriched by the unclaimed refunds of undocumented workers.

The Linton survey also showed that 77 per cent of undocumented immigrants, and 74.5 per cent of the Mexicans interviewed, had Social Security deductions taken from their paychecks. The finding is all the more significant in light of the way in which the Social Security system is financed—and in light of moves to cut *sin papeles* off from particpation in it.

Deductions are made from the checks of salaried and hourly workers for deposit in the Social Security trust, which the Department of Health, Education and Welfare administers. Though all workers must pay into the system, not all ultimately qualify for its benefits. In order to establish eligibility, a worker must have paid deductions on regular earnings over a specified period of time; wage and time requirements vary with the age of the prospective worker when he enters the Social Security system by paying his first deduction. The Social Security trust is designed essentially to pay today's retirees from current deductions, so that each generation subsidizes benefits to the generation before it. Had U. S. population growth continued on an upward keel, the Social Security system probably could have looked foward with confidence to its future.

But since 1950, the birth rate has declined so that today, population growth is negligible. When the generation now in the workforce comes to retirement age, the ratio of workers to retirees will be the narrowest in Social Security history, and the system could face bankruptcy. In 1970, about 56 per cent of the total population was of working age, and about 9 per cent was age 65 or older. The Census Bureau estimates that by 2025, the retirement age population will double in proportion to the working age base.

The total amount of Social Security retirement benefits will be forced upwards, with no increase in income sources. The demographic problems Social Security faces are compounded by inflation and the international monetary market: dollars paid in today may be worth only fractions of their value when the "baby boom" generation leaves the labor market.

Sin papeles have essentially been donors to the Social Security system, and therefore, a factor mitigating in favor of its future solvency. Under the law, *sin papeles* who meet payment-over-time requirements can become eligible for benefits. But as the Linton Study shows, few *sin papeles* are likely to have been regularly employed in the U. S. over a time span long enough to satisfy SSA standards. Furthermore, while beneficiaries may receive SSA checks in foreign countries, they must be present in the U. S. at the time eligibility is established. A 1974 survey by the Social Security Administration showed that some 37,113 accounts were being paid to claimants in Mexico, compared to 41,236 in Italy. Reviewing its files on foreign claimants, SSA administrators found that about half were U. S. citizens who had moved back to their homelands in order to take advantage of lower living costs and family ties there. Information in SSA files did not indicate what proportion of the remaining 50 per cent were former legal residents of the U. S.; however, given the transient situation of *sin papeles*, SSA Retirement Bureau Chief Pasquale F. Caliguiri concluded that relatively few alien workers who worked long enough to be insured would have been here illegally.

There are parallels in European studies of temporary immigrant workers, or "guestworkers." A German study in 1974, for example, pointed out that guestworkers received in benefits only about 10 per cent as much as they paid into social insurance programs. A similar finding was reported in 1968 by the *Economic Review*, the newsletter of the National Bank of Paris: "The foreign wage-earner, if he is healthy and has no children, leaves a not inconsiderable part of his wage with the social security system of the receiving country and thus contributes to a better distribution of the expenses which a higher proportion of inactive people places on the community."

The conclusion to be drawn is that the millions of *sin papeles* who have contributed to the Social Security system since its initiation in 1937 have taken very little away in benefits. They have, in fact, subsidized the system, and therefore, the retirement of other workers. For from weakening it, their continued participation as donors, and de facto exclusion as beneficiaries, might conceivably save the SSA from bankruptcy by providing unencumbered revenue.

Passage of a 1972 proposal to prohibit the issuance of SSA cards to undocumented immigrants has not imperiled their future ability to pay into the system. Prior to passage of the 1972 act, SSA made no inquiry into the immigration status of those who applied for Social Security numbers.

Millions of *sin papeles* were routinely issued Social Security cards, and most of them who stayed here more than a few weeks got them. Today, however, applicants who are not native-born American citizens must provide proof of legal residency before a card may be issued. The 1972 law has excluded *sin papeles* from collecting SSA benefits, but it has not stopped them from contributing to the system, because Social Security procedures make paying in simpler than drawing out.

Two considerations ostensibly motivated passage of the prohibition bill. Many Congressmen claimed that they voted for it out of a desire to limit SSA benefits to citizens and legal residents. However, this end could have more logically been accomplished by requiring that *benefit* applicants prove legal residency. The measure to prohibit issuance of cards probably passed for a different reason: backers of the Rodino bill believed that it gave them a shortcut way to keep *sin papeles* out of the labor market.

Citizens, employers and their agents commonly believe that it is illegal to employ persons who do not have Social Security *cards*. This belief proceeds from federal requirements regarding the collection and remittance of withholding and Social Security tax deductions. According to the law, employers must deduct withholding and Social Security taxes from each paycheck they issue. Every three months, they must remit deductions to the SSA and IRS. On their quarterly reports, they must list the name and

SSA number each employee has given them, along with the amount deducted. Because they confuse the requirement that a Social Security *number* be reported with the notion that the Social Security *card* be inspected, many employers do demand that prospective employees show Social Security cards.

In fact, however, the demand for a showing of Social Security cards is illegal. The Social Security Act stipulates that Social Security cards are not to be required for employment or any other purpose of identification—only Social Security *numbers* are required. Congress imposed this limitation out of the fear that SSA cards might become de facto internal passports. National identity cards are used in many nations, but traditionally have been viewed in the U. S. as totalitarian trappings. Because it sought to protect the system's users from federal spying, the Social Security Act also gave card holders the right to change the names—but not numbers—in which their accounts are held, simply by requesting it. Also as a safeguard to privacy, the Social Security Act did not require employers to determine if the numbers given them were valid. Fraud detection in Social Security and tax matters is the prerogative of the federal agencies involved, not of private parties.

Rodino bill proponents sought to take advantage of widespread confusion over the law. If *sin papeles* could not show SSA cards, they reasoned, many employers would deny jobs to them. While it is reasonable to assume that many employers did behave as expected, those who traditionally have exploited *sin papeles* were by and large not fooled.

Therefore, the result is that *sin papeles* have begun to dream up Social Security numbers, and to borrow them. Social Security numbers are composed of a series of nine digits. Each digit informs SSA of data about the client, such as the region and office through which his card was issued. However, any combination of nine digits will fit onto reporting forms. When the names and numbers reported for an employee do not correspond to SSA files, computers in agency headquarters in Baltimore spit out an error notice. The error notice, a pre-addressed computer card, informs the employer of the discrepancy, and asks that he report a corrected number. Error notices are not usually received by employers until about six months after the report on which the error was made has been submitted. If error notices are disregarded, no one comes to investigate; instead, additional error notices are sent out at intervals. If an employee who has supplied an erroneous number supplies another series of nine imaginary digits, as a replacement, the process is only repeated. SSA does not follow-up with investigations because the presumption built into the system is: if you don't report your number correctly, you're only cheating yourself.

The 1972 prohibition has given profiteers and unscrupulous employers a new means of exploiting illegals. Prisoners, students, housewives, habitual drunks and others who are not economically active give their SSA numbers to employers of *sin papeles*, who record deductions from the checks of *sin papeles* in the names and numbers of the card donors. In this way, the donors can establish eligibility for benefits, without working. The practice is also sometimes linked to an income tax racket, wherein the name/number donor files for a refund on withholding taxes actually taken from the wages of the *sin papeles*. Previously, the SSA racket could not be worked so easily, because *sin papeles* had SAA numbers of their own and therefore, had the right to ask SSA for an accounting of their contributions. Since taxpayers identify themselves to the IRS by the Social Security numbers under which withholding taxes are also paid, those who were eligible could collect tax refunds, though few did. Today, the *sin papeles* without an SSA account of his own cannot provide proof of refund eligibility.

The net effect of the 1972 SSA prohibition was not what many of its backers had hoped. It was not a shortcut to limiting the employment of *sin papeles* as the Rodino proponents thought. The Linton study indicates that it did not keep *sin papeles* off the job market which is traditionally theirs. Instead, it merely shortened job tenure. The *sin papeles* who might otherwise have stayed on a permanent job may now move on when error notices advise his employer that he is probably not a legal resident. Moreover, the measure did not end the presumed exploitation of the Social Security system by *sin papeles*, for that was mythical. Instead, it intensified the exploitation of both *sin pa-*

peles and the Social Security system by conscienceless Americans. It took future benefit dollars out of the hands of workingmen, both citizens who might have been subsidized and *sin papeles* who might have been eligible, and put them in the hands of profiteers. It took tax payments out of the treasury and refunded them to claimants who did not work to earn them. In sum, it penalized workers, both immigrant and native-born, and created new opportunities for profiteers to feed off them.

Critics say that when *sin papeles* do pay income taxes, they use dishonest means to avoid paying their fair share. General Chapman told a Dallas audience, for example, that interviews with 87 undocumented workers arrested in Dallas during January, 1974 pointed up that they were "fraudulently claiming a total of 429 dependents for tax withholding purposes." Fraud in ordinary usage indicates an intent to deceive. Due to the technicalities of tax law, it is possible that many *sin papeles* claimed dependents whose support is not an allowable deduction. The assertion that they defraud the tax system, however, is far from the truth.

Mexican *sin papeles* generally send money home to support wives and children, if they are married or for their parents and younger brothers and sisters, if they are single. The Linton team found that "Though . . . apprehended illegals were less likely to be married than U. S. males of the same age, and although only about half of them had children, their family obligations were substantial. . . . Mexicans reported a dependency ratio of 5.4 persons per illegal." If the average *sin papeles* supports 5.4 persons in his homeland, then a group of 87 could be expected to claim 469 dependents, 40 or more than the number actually claimed by the Dallas deportees. Chapman undoubtably knew that most *sin papeles* do not read English and are not tax authorities. Like other workers, when asked how many dependents they have, they generally tell the truth. As a group, they cannot be reasonably expected to know that federal tax law makes allowance only for dependents living inside the boundaries of the U. S. Chapman's claim that *sin papeles* defraud the government is therefore dubious.

His report that "we often find that they are receiving

welfare or food stamps" is even less credible. Applicants for food stamps and all welfare programs even partially funded with federal monies are required to show proof of legal residency as a condition for eligibility. The Linton team found that "only 10 of the 793 respondents, or 1.3%, reported that they had received food stamps. . . . we found four illegals . . . who said that they had received welfare assistance. This is a rate of .5%." The 1.3 per cent rate for food stamp eligibility compares to a rate of about 9.4 per cent for the population as a whole. The comparison is all the more striking when one considers that *sin papeles*, as a group, are nearly all poverty-striken; were they legalized residents, most would be eligible for food stamp assistance.

CHAPTER 18

Unemployment

In addition *sin papeles* are characteristically blue-collar workers; as a group, they are frequently laid off and unemployed—prime candidates for unemployment compensation. And since mandatory payroll deductions finance most state systems of jobless insurance, *sin papeles* are also contributors to unemployment insurance systems.

The Linton study found that unemployment among its Mexican respondents was high—10.2 per cent—more than twice the rate for the workforce as a whole. But only 3.6 per cent of its Mexican respondents reported ever having received an unemployment check.

Undocumented workers in the sample, including non-Mexicans, reported a total of 10,309 weeks of unemployment over the past 2.5 years, but between them, had received only 207 unemployment checks. The observation leads to the conclusion that although 3.6 per cent may have received an unemployment check at one time or another, their real rate of coverage was much lower than simple one-time receipt suggests: for every 100 weeks of joblessness they experienced, *sin papeles* received about two weeks of compensation.

The fundamental cause of the exceedingly low rate of unemployment insurance is fear of authorities. But another factor has recently developed as well. Today, many *sin pa-*

peles who pay into unemployment systems are denied eligibility for benefits. Courts in California, for example, have ruled that *sin papeles* are ineligible for benefits because they are not legally "available for work." In fact, there is no law against *sin papeles* working, and if *sin papeles* were not available for work, they would not be here. Once again the law (or its interpretation by courts) conflicts with the realities of the workplace, and fosters added injustice. Once again, *sin papeles* are forced to finance social programs but denied access to their benefits.

CHAPTER 19

Health, Education and Welfare

The public institutions *sin papeles* deal with most frequently are hospitals. A *sin papeles* who is injured or seriously ill may have no alternative other than reporting to an emergency room, and most hospitals with emergency receiving centers are public-supported. However, *sin papeles* know that if they cannot pay bills, their undocumented status may be discovered in the process of investigating their eligibility for medical benefits. Therefore, they pay hospitals when they can. The Linton team found that some 22 per cent of the Mexican *sin papeles* in its study had visited either hospitals or clinics. But 83 per cent had paid for services, either in cash or through job-related hospitalization insurance. If there is an "illegal invasion" of our hospitals, the invaders, by American standards, are reasonably well-paying patients.

Newspapers in recent years have often carried tales from the border in which pregnant Mexican women cross into the U. S. when their labor pangs begin, so that they may rush into an American hospital for free medical care. If it is known that these women are *sin papeles*, and if they do not pay, they are presumably deported. Yet INS figures report that less than 10 per cent of the apprehended *sin papeles* are women. It is common, however, for Mexican women who have border-crossing cards, or who have "green cards," to come to the U. S. side of the border to deliver babies. Their chief object is to secure American citizenship, not for themselves, but for their children who, at the age of 21, U. S.-born children may elect to be American citizens regardless of the immigration status of their mothers. This practice cannot be limited, for the basis of citizenship is birth, not legacy.

The issue of alien impact on schools is patently artificial. All native-born citizens and legal residents contribute to school finance, either indirectly, by paying rent, or directly, by paying the property taxes from which schools are supported. Likewise, the few *sin papeles* who do own homes must pay property taxes, and the majority, who are renters, nevertheless pay school levies indirectly. The conclusion to be drawn is that *sin papeles* finance the school system as much as citizens do; yet most of them are denied its benefits because they are unaccompanied by their families. The Linton study found that only 2.7 per cent of its Mexican respondents had enrolled children in public schools, though nearly half of them had children in Mexico.

However, some school districts in Texas and California have sought to determine which students might be undocumented immigrants, and have asked for authority to deny them enrollment. A 1977 Texas legislative act enables schools to demand proof of legal residency from students, and further, to charge the parents of *sin papeles* an annual tuition of $1,000 for each child enrolled in a public school. As a result some parents withdrew their children from schools, exposing themselves to prosecution under the state's mandatory education laws. The campaign to deny undocumented children an education is still being waged by some educators, but now with little hope of success. In February, 1975 the Justice Department filed a brief in Tyler, Texas, on behalf of 16 children turned away from the schools there. The Justice statement argued that the Texas tuition statute for *sin papeles* violates the equal protection clause of the 14th Amendment. In response, the Federal District judge who heard the case ruled in favor of the students.

The results of the Linton study show that for the most part, Mexican *sin papeles* work in low-wage, low-skill, low-status jobs in the Southwest; that they contribute more than they take away from government-funded education and assistance programs, and that they are prey to special and extreme forms of exploitation, such as the Social Security card racket. There is little evidence that *sin papeles* are particularly aware of social benefits available in the U. S., or that they frequently seek such benefits. However measures like the 1972 Social Security prohibition, the California unemployment and Texas schools rulings, are evidence that they are progressively being denied access to even those programs where their role as donors cannot be doubted.

CHAPTER 20

———— ⊷◄►⊷ ————

Balance of Exchange

In his campaign to defame Mexican immigrants, General Chapman also popularized the charge that *sin papeles* aggravate the nation's balance of payments deficit. The accusation is not without a basis in fact: most undocumented immigrants send money home. However, Chapman exaggerated the charge by claiming that they send *most* of their earnings abroad.

The Linton team found that Mexican *sin papeles*, when compared to other undocumented immigrants, send home both a greater sum per month and a greater proportion of their earnings. Mexican *sin papeles* in the sample averaged monthly salaries of $455, and monthly remittances home of $129, compared to $838 in earnings and $37 in contributions to foreign relatives for the European sample. Of the Mexicans who regularly sent money home, 89 per cent of the sample, the average monthly remittance figure was found to be $169.

The impact Mexican remittances have upon the U. S. economy is difficult to assess, given the lack of reliable estimate of the number of *sin papeles* in the country. Arbitrarily taking an estimate of 1 million as the number of Mexican undocumented workers, the Linton team calculated an annual loss of $1.5 billion to the American economy.

Even were the estimate doubled, it would not pose serious problems for the American economy. Commercial relations between the U.S. and Mexico are extensive, and work to the advantage of *el norte*. The U.S. exports some $4.9 billion in goods to Mexico annually, and imports some $3.5 billion; the result is a favorable balance of trade of about $1.4 billion. Further, Mexico currently owes an external debt of about $30 billion, most of it in dollars. Interest on the debt alone is estimated at $3 billion, again, most of it payable in dollars. Beyond this, the U.S. takes in uncounted millions of dollars each year in sales to Mexican shoppers, who account for as much as 90 per cent of retail commerce in many American border cities.

Even in terms of the Mexican economy, *sin papeles* are a minor factor in the flow of U.S. dollars southward. Tourism provides Mexico's second largest source of foreign income, after exports. Each year some 3.2 million visit Mexico and 2.7 million of them, about 85 per cent of the total, are Americans. Tourists from the U.S. spend an estimated $2 billion annually in Mexico, foreign aid by the U.S. to Mexico averages about $80 million a year, and American investments there are estimated at just under $4 billion.

Still it is entirely possible that remittances by *sin papeles* do account for Mexico's third largest source of foreign exchange though a distant third, if so. This thesis would explain in part the Mexican government's reluctance to enforce its laws against undocumented emigration. In Mexico, it is a criminal offense, punishable by 10 years imprisonment and a fine of 10,000 pesos, to leave the country without a passport, as most *sin papeles* do. But arrests are rare, apparently because the Mexican people and economy have nothing to gain by halting undocumented emigration. In 1976, Mexican President Jose Lopez Portillo told a correspondent for *U. S. News & World Report* that "illegal immigration will end when we solve Mexico's economic problems, when we create enough jobs here at home . . ."

CHAPTER 21

The Breeder Myth

In recent years undocumented immigrants, especially Mexicans, have been accused of aggravating several social ills—unemployment, welfare crises, and school overcrowding among them. The most exaggerated charge yet laid at their door, is that they inflate the rate of population growth. Surprisingly, the charge has come from a usually liberal organization, Zero Population Growth.

ZPG is a national organization founded in 1968 to encourage population control and ecological caution. It claims as sponsors such notables as science-fictionist Isaac Asimov, Norman Borlaug, Kingsley Davis, ecologist Paul Ehrlich, millionaire and patron Stewart Mott, Nobel prizewinner Linus Pauling—and even a former television host, Arthur Godfrey.

Zero Population Growth is dedicated to the proposition that the world's population cannot long survive if it keeps growing. To stabilize population growth in America, ZPG has proposed voluntary birth control, plus restrictions of *legal* immigration. Spokesmen for the organization advocate that the present ceiling on legal immigration, 240,000 per year, be reduced to 54,000. In addition, ZPG has urged passage of the Rodino bill and the issuance of national identity cards to all citizens. These demands place ZPG in the camp of hard-line exclusionists, beyond even the demands made by labor. In 1975 and again in 1976, ZPG representatives argued their position to the House subcommittee on immigration.

ZPG's professed concern is that of stabilizing population growth within the U.S., and across the world. Calculations by its study committees indicate that over the next 25 years, the present U.S. population will increase from about 220 million to about 258 million. In addition, continued legal immigration will add another 16 million inhabitants, if new restrictions are not voted by the Congress. This much is generally uncontested by both the friends and foes of continued immigration.

However, Dr. John Tanton, an opthalmologist and chairman of the ZPG study committee on immigration, and Melanie J. Wirken, the organization's political director, have told Congress that undocumented immigration will add more than 40 million more to the U.S. population. Ms. Wirken told the Congress in 1976 that:

An indirect effect of immigration on population growth is the fertility of immigrant women. Insofar as they come from under-developed countries, their fertility is higher than that of American women. In the U.S. in 1970, the number of children born to women aged 40 to 44 was 4.4 per woman for those of Mexican origin and 2.9 for all women. Taking into account the higher birth rate of persons from the less developed countries, we conservatively estimate that illegal immigration at the rate of 800,000 persons yearly would contribute some 40 million additional persons to the U.S. by the year 2000.

Her statement closely parallels one given a year earlier by Dr. Tanton:

Now, if you take 800,000 as a figure for illegal immigrants per year, and take into account the fact that illegal persons from the lesser developed countries have higher birth rates than the persons from developed countries; and if you project 800,000 persons per year to the turn of the century, it comes out to at least an additional 40 million persons.

The AFL-CIO has an even larger estimate than that. They project that by 1985 we could have 35 million illegal persons in this country if present trends continue.

Both statements ignore the simple fact, cited even in INS literature, that at least 90 per cent of *sin papeles* are males. This factor entirely alters the calculations that can legitimately be made regarding the effect of undocumented immigrants on population growth. Ordinarily, population growth is determined by dividing the number of births in a given nation by its population for the year in question. In 1975, for example, there were 3,150,555 births in the U.S. from a base population estimated at 220 million. Carrying out the division produces a birth rate of .0143 per capita, which when doubled—on the basis that women and men are about equally numbered—produces a fertility rate of .0286 for each woman in the population, the figure which ZPG for convenience reports as a rate of 2.9.

According to ZPG, Mexican-American women have a fertility rate of 4.4 per woman, compared to 2.9 for U.S. women as a whole. Therefore, the rate of birth per capita in the Mexican–American community is 2.2, or .022 annually, because the birth rate for any community in which the male-female ratio is about equal is half the rate of female ferility alone.

However, that birth rate cannot be attributed to *sin papeles* because the sex ratio is not 50-50 among them. If undocumented immigrant women may be assumed to have a fertility rate of 4.4 in America, then the *sin papeles* community would have a rate of 2.2 were the sex ratio even, as it is with Mexican-Americans. However, since women account for only 10 per cent of the *sin papeles* population, the female fertality rate must be divided, not by two, but by 10, an operation which produces a group birth rate of .4—the lowest in the nation.

Alternately, if in the nation as a whole there are .0143 births annually per inhabitant, there are 14.3 births per thousand inhabitants each year. In the Mexican-American community, if ZPG claims are true, there are 22 births per thousand population. And the corresponding rate for *sin papeles* would be 4.4 births per thousand each year.

However, even these figures do not tell the whole story. Birth rates for the nation are calculated by dividing births by the whole population, including infants, and those who are past child-bearing age. Only 6.2 per cent of the Linton study's Mexican respondents were over 45, compared to

34.3 per cent of the U.S. population as a whole. Though the Linton study did not interview anyone under 16, INS statistics show that the percentage of children among Mexican undocumented immigrants is negligible. The result is that most *sin papeles*, perhaps as many as 80 per cent of them, are of parenthood age. The reproduction rate for Americans age 16 to 44 is certainly higher than that of Americans older than 44 or younger than 16. Yet the reproduction rate of *sin papeles* of parenthood age is lower than the reproduction rate for Americans as a whole. Therefore, it is probable that the reproduction rate of *sin papeles* is several times *lower* than that of Americans of reproduction age. The claim that *sin papeles* are "breeders" is wholly false.

In fact, *sin papeles* lower the birth rate by depressing the sex ratio without adding new population. They enrich the nation's resources, without enlarging the population pool which draws upon that enrichment. They provide, in effect, pure, disposable labor power. For each American worker, there is in gross terms a corresponding mate, and corresponding children, all of whom must be maintained after the worker's useful years have passed. With *sin papeles*, no familiar needs outlive his usefulness as a worker. Once exhausted, he may be deported, with no pardon begged his children, and with no pensions paid.

CHAPTER 22

The Chicano Movement

Since the turn of the century, agribusiness and labor have vied for influence over immigration policy, and Congress, at one time or another, has favored both interests. The current immigration debate, however, includes a third party, the Chicano movement.

The movement's roots can be traced back to mutual aid societies formed in Texas and California during the Mexican revolutionary era, and to simultaneous labor battles by Mexican-American copper miners in Arizona. But the Chicano movement in its contemporary form is molded more on the black civil rights struggle of the sixties, and dates from September 16, 1965, when Cesar Chavez led Chicano vineyard workers out on strike in Delano, California.

The date September 16 is symbolic in Chicano affairs for it is Mexican independence day. Mexico stood in the background of the largely Chicano strike in another way; the *bracero* program had been eliminated at the end of the 1964 harvest, removing the greatest obstacle organizers faced in prior efforts to unionize California fields. Chavez, aware of the new importance of ethnic politics, gave the strike the moral atmosphere of the black civil rights movement, by promoting non-violence as a philosophy and tactic, and by openly contrasting the ethnic and linguistic differences between grape workers and their employers. Strikers added to the image by practically adopting the Virgin of Guadalupe, Mexico's patron saint, as a symbol of the strike. Within six months, these moves had won the support of church leaders and prominent liberal Americans, like Mrs. Coretta Scott King.

In December 1965, Chavez buttressed strike action with a call for a national boycott of products made by firms which refused to negotiate with the farmworkers union. The boycott, again a tactic borrowed from the civil rights campaign, proved immensely popular in liberal circles, and gave added publicity to union effort. Nevertheless, grape producers did not cede to union demands. Over the next five years, they succeeded in staving off union recognition with a variety of tactics, one of which was pitting Mexicans against Chicanos, legal residents against *sin papeles*. Mexicans with "green cards" or legal permission to live in the U.S., who nevertheless lived in Mexico, were brought to the fields as strikebreakers, as were *sin papeles*. From time to time, INS investigators raided UFW picket lines, arresting *sin papeles*, and more than once, UFW organizers called the immigration agency to deport *sin papeles* who had not joined the strike.

The complexities of immigrant involvement in the grape strike attracted the eye of long-time maritime organizer Bert Corona and an associate, Chole la Torre, who in 1968 founded with others the Centro de Accion Social Autonomo, or CASA, in Los Angeles. Under the leadership of Corona and la Torre, CASA soon provided immigration counseling to some 15,000 area residents, and spread to Oakland, San Jose, and Los Angeles. Typically, CASA chapters charged a fee, as low as $15 per year, for aiding immigrants to obtain documents, like the Social Security card, to which they were legally entitled. CASA representatives also spoke for members at Immigration Service appeals, and helped prepare forms for obtaining citizenship and residency status. Leaders of CASA encouraged political radicalization and cultural awareness, through rallies, fiestas, and community meetings. When the Rodino bill was brought before Congress, CASA spearheaded a drive to protest it. When General Chapman became INS Commisioner and began slandering *sin papeles*,

CASA countered with demonstrations and warnings to the Chicano community that it, too, was endangered by rising anti-alien sentiment.

CASA's growth paralleled that of the campaign to impugn the Mexican-American community. By 1974, new chapters had been formed in Chicago, San Antonio, and more than two dozen small cities from Texas to California. That year CASA founded a newspaper, *Sin Fronteras*, published under the editorship of San Antonio leader Mario Cantu. The bilingual newspaper disseminated CASA's political perspective, summed up in the slogan, "Somos un pueblo sin fronteras" ("We are a people without borders.") What CASA advocated, essentially, was unconditional amnesty for *sin papeles*.

CASA's drive to bring the Chicano community into the campaign to defend *sin papeles* succeeded, and similiar activist organizations sprang up. Church and humanitarian agencies began providing immigration counseling in the Southwest. By 1976, when CASA ruptured, its counseling services had largely been taken over by better-financed organizations, which unlike CASA, could not plunge into protest activity. After editorship of *Sin Fronteras* transferred to Los Angeles in 1976, the large San Antonio chapter of CASA split in a dispute over moves to centralize political leadership of the national organization.

The San Antonio split reflected in part a trend inside CASA towards new ideology, and the rise of new leadership. Corona resigned from CASA, not over political matters, but to found an organization devoted exclusively to unionizing *sin papeles*, and la Torre also left the group. Their legacy fell to Antonio Rodriguez, who has been intent on two goals: continuing agitation against restrictive immigration laws, and infusing Leninist ideology into the movement. Under his leadership, CASA has been molded along political and organizational lines similar to those of disciplined Marxist parties. *Sin Fronteras*, though once devoted almost exclusively to immigrant issues, now carries wide coverage of world events, always from a radical leftist perspective.

In some ways, CASA's overt leftward shift contributed to a decline in its membership. So, too, did the fact that other organizations had absorbed much of its counseling functions. Though CASA was still the largest pro-immigrant group, by the fall of 1977, its prominence had faded enough to allow the Raza Unida Party of Texas to make a serious stab at providing leadership to the movement. In October, 1977, nearly 3,000 delegates from across the Southwest gathered in San Antonio for an immigration conference sponsored by La Raza.

The general growth of the pro-immigrant movement was evident at the meeting but so was the movement's internal disunity. Spokesmen for conservative Chicano groups, like the League of United Latin American Citizens, shared the platform with CASA and RUP leaders, and Peter Camejo, a frequent Presidential candidate of the Trotskyist Socialist Workers Party. Camejo's role in the conference was challenged by Rodriguez and other CASA supporters, who called for the SWP's expulsion from the meeting. They lost the vote, overwhelmingly, because La Raza's leadership allied with Camejo. But in the wake of the conference, various Chicano groups, especially in California, denounced the Trotskyist group for allegedly manipulating Chicano affairs. The conflict appears to have partially split La Raza as well. The conference therefore did not produce hoped-for unity, nor did it give rise to a new wave of protests. The introduction of the Carter plan, Senate Bill 2252, in February, 1978, found the pro-immigrant movement internally more divided than ever before, though with more allies outside the Chicano community. Most critical was the death of nationally-respected leadership. To a certain extent, a lack of clear issues to contend with has also confused the movement. By taking steps to reform the Border Patrol, INS Commissioner Leonel Castillo had in effect taken one complaint—the mistreatment of *sin papeles*—out of the realm of protest into that of administration. And since church and civic agencies have largely assumed the movement's counseling functions, and the Carter plan, by promising amnesty to some *sin papeles*, has undermined movement support from the families of immigrants who might be eligible under the plan's provisions.

To restore the movement's momentum, in early 1978, San Antonian Cantu began attempts to lead it in a new direction. Cantu, who founded CASA in Texas, led the split of the San Antonio faction away from the national organization. In the spring of 1977, he also resigned from TU-CASA, the organization founded after the San Antonio CASA split. His break with TU-CASA was predicated on a novel premise: that the immigration movement should link up with leftist groups in Mexico.

"The Chicano movement is based on a feeling of belonging. We begin by seeing that culturally, we are still Mexicans. Cultural awareness leads us to look into all of Mexican life, and when we see Mexico's political institutions, we realize that we are not one people without borders. Borders are very real, and very necessary."

Unlike other immigration spokesmen, Cantu no longer assails the idea that immigration can or should be restricted. Like most Chicano leaders, he argues that Mexicans leave their homes to escape poverty, and blames trans-national American corporations for Mexico's plight. But *sin papeles,* in his view are an important escape valve for the Mexican economy. "If the border could be sealed off, Mexico might face a revolution like Cuba had. Socialism would give Mexico control of her natural and industrial resources, and would put an end to widespread misery," he maintains.

Cantu believes that the task of the Chicano movement is protesting American economic and political intervention in Mexico, rather than "encouraging" undocumented immigration. "We want to speak up for our people, and that means the working people of Mexico. We have to support them, not just as immigrants, but before they become immigrants as well." The thrust of his argument is that the emphasis of the pro-immigrant movement should shift from the amnesty issue to questions like the role of American banks and corporations in Mexico, and to political solidarity. "When the Mexican police in 1968 murdered 500 demonstrators at Tlatelolco, 10,000 Parisians protested in the streets, but there was not one massive demonstration in the United States. We can't support the Mexican people if we are unconcerned about their fate at home, where they want to live," he declares.

Cantu is a well-known Chicano spokesman, a founder both of the Raza Unida Party and CASA. He was one of a dozen Hispanic spokesmen from across the U.S. who sued the Ku Klux Klan in an effort to enjoin its "border watch" campaign. His credentials as a friend of *sin papeles* are unquestioned: in a precedent-setting 1976 trial, he became the first American to be convicted of shielding undocumented aliens from arrest. But because Cantu is closely allied with revolutionary organizations in Mexico, he has been shunned by many former colleagues in the Chicano movement.

Most Chicano leaders, and prominently, Reieses Tijerina of New Mexico and Jose Angel Gutierrez of Texas, have cultivated friendly relations with the Mexican government, relations which preclude pacts with oppositionists south of the border.

Cantu, however, has made himself known in Mexico as a spokesman for Chicanos revolutionaries, and *sin papeles;* Mexican newspapermen parade through his San Antonio home with clockwork regularity. In March, 1977 he won support for his thesis from a conference of some 150 Midwestern Chicano activists, some of whom joined the effort to spread the Mexican solidarity movement. As an immediate goal, the Cantu faction proposes that Chicano students protest university involvement in economic and military support programs for Mexico, as black students have done in regard to the apartheid government in South Africa. If the Cantu faction prevails, immigration policy will become only part of the Chicano movement's protest against American dealings with Mexico, and the movement itself will take on an internationalized outlook. The question that the faction's proposal does not answer, however, is whether or not it is premature to lay aside immigration as a chief concern of Chicano activism.

CHAPTER 23

———◆—◀◆▶—◆———

The Carter Plan

The tumult over immigration has defined three interest groups, each of which demands a different solution to the problem. Exclusionism, headed by the AFL-CIO, demands passage of Rodino-type legislation; radicals in this camp, like ZPG, demand a reduction in legal immigration quotas and the issuance of national identity cards as well. A second alliance, headed by the American Association of Agricultural Employers, the American Farm Bureau, and the National Restaurant Association, speaks out of what might fairly be called the interest of exploitation. This group represents the traditional employers of *sin papeles,* and its chief Congressional spokesman is Senator James O. Eastland. Essentially, this food lobby wants no change in the status quo of immigration. As an alternative, it will accept passage of a new *bracero* bill, covering both agriculture and industry. Cheap labor is not the only benefit immigration, legal or illegal, provides the food industry. The agricultural lobby need not worry whether Americans are prosperous or poor, because its position in the economy is unique: people will buy food, even if they cannot afford televisions, tourism and cosmetics. An expanded population, whatever its source, means expanded food sales. The agricultural lobby therefore has no interest in limiting immigration.

The newest interest group in the immigration dispute is the Chicano movement. The movement's concern for *sin papeles* is relatively recent, dating back to 1968 and the foundation in California of the Centro de Accion Social Autonima, or CASA. In less than 10 years, CASA has become the focus of a wider movement based in two dozen cities. CASA and similar groups defend *sin papeles* from INS abuses, and help eligible *sin papeles* file for immigration papers. The influence of the current CASA initiative was seen in early 1978, when nine national Chicano leaders visited Mexican President Jose Lopez Portillo and afterwards issued a joint statement of opposition to Rodino-type legislation. In its immigration activity, the Chicano movement carries the support of liberals, civil libertarians, progressive labor and church spokesmen. Its minimum demand is for humanization of the deportation process; its maximum demands include the abolition of all restrictions on Mexican immigration. The movement has been united, and to a great extent held together, by the threat of Rodino action.

By mid-1975, along with energy and unemployment, Mexican immigration had become a question of top national importance. Congress, however, was deadlocked by the conflicting pressures brought by the labor, business and Chicano lobbies, each of whom began seeking support for its proposals from Presidential hopefuls. Spokesmen for all three lobbies went to Jimmy Carter to ask support for their demands, and to each of them, he promised something.

The result was an amorphous mix of contradictory measures called the Carter plan, a program whose limits are still unknown and whose features change from month to month. As originally conceived, the Carter plan included:

1. Passage of Rodino-type legislation.
2. Beefed-up enforcement of immigration laws.
3. An amnesty program for undocumented aliens already in the U.S.

The program as originally conceived would have halted *future* undocumented immigration. However, despite Labor Secretary Marshall's protestations that "No issue, with the possible exception of energy, has been studied as long and as intensely as immigration"—the features of the Carter plan have been fluid. Its details have contradicted its main points, and its main points have come and gone like phantoms.

Originally, the Carter administration promised to endorse Rodino-type bills which would prohibit the hiring of *sin papeles*. However, the question of enforcing any Rodino-type law has become critical for Congress and the Carter administration has not clarified itself on the key enforcement issues. The Rodino bill and its successors would require that employers procure signed statements of legal residency from all employees. Employers would be liable to prosecution only if they "knowingly" hired undocumented aliens, i. e., if they accepted statements which they knew to be false. Labor spokesmen do not believe these provisions are sufficient. They argue that many employers will encourage *sin papeles* to sign the forms, and that *sin papeles* themselves will quickly learn the necessity of lying. Once they do, employers will be absolved of any responsibility for hiring workers whom they might reasonably suspect are *sin papeles*. Therefore, labor lobbyists have argued that the requirement of "knowing" violation of the law be deleted; instead, they would have penalties applied to any employer who hires an undocumented worker, whether he knows the worker's immigration status or not. Radical exclusionists have gone beyond even the AFL-CIO in demanding the issuance of national identity cards. If such cards were issued to all legal residents, employers could easily determine a worker's immigration status, proponents urge. The Carter administration originally balked at the idea of a national identity card. However, in May 1977 Labor Secretary Marshall declared his support for the demand. His version of the Carter plan calls for the Social Security administration, to issue a tamper-proof identification card as a replacement for both current and future Social Security cards.

Administration endorsement of the ID card demand came as a surprise to many observers, especially to those in the Department of Health, Education and Welfare, which manages the Social Security system. SSA Deputy Commissioner Arthur Hess in 1973 told the House Immigration Committee that "The social security number is not a reliable mechanism to use as a work permit or identification card, nor was it ever so intended . . . ," and repeated his warnings in 1975. In 1976, HEW undersecretary Dr. William A. Morrill again laid out the Department's objections to use of the Social Security system as an identifier bank. He told the Eastland Committee that:

> There was a large study commissioned a few years ago when Secretary Richardson was serving at HEW. It relates around the problem of the "universal identifier," and the social security card is probably the closest one to it, if in fact it is not already.
>
> The use of that number could put one in the situation where the confidentiality, or the privacy of an individual could be invaded, not necessarily by the governmental use of that, but if this then became a common identifier for credit bureaus, and what have you; and that without protection of privacy, on how that was used, that were generally applicable, not only to the governmental side, but the nongovernmental one as well, that inappropriate invasion of privacy could occur.
>
> I think that has been the source of our concern. In the use within the Government they tend to be proscribed in such a way that we can make use of the information for the purposes for which it was collected, or specified by law. But there is not much out there to protect the individual from what totally nonpublic entites could do with that information.
>
> So, its general use as an identifier without those protections raises some serious civil liberties concerns, or privacy concerns.

Spokesmen for the SSA have consistently told Congress that using the Social Security system to issue national identity cards would also be a costly and drawn-out endeavor. Arthur Hess estimated that it would take more than two years merely to call on current card holders to prove that they are legal residents. Some 230 million Social Security cards have been issued since the program began in 1937, and perhaps half that number are still active. In the 1976 Senate hearings, SSA representatives estimated that tamper-proof cards would cost about $100 million—apart from processing and administrative expenses. Photo identification cards would be more expensive, and would require reissuance every few years. Once begun, the program would involve issuance to a minimum of 9 million new system participants each year, plus replacements for cards lost—about 3 million more each year. Issuance of Social Security cards as identifiers would also create another problem: SSA has no authority to revoke the cards of current enrolees in its system, nor can any such authority be granted under the Constitution's prohibition of *ex post facto* legislation. Therefore, those undocumented aliens who currently have cards would be entitled to the national identifiers, and once they got them, would be pratically immune to discovery and deportation.

The Carter administration has maintained one part of its stance towards agriculture, and waffled on another. As a candidate, Carter promised the agribusiness community that despite his opposition to a renewed *bracero* program, he would insure that no shortage of field labor developed, even if providing workers meant allowing the entry of temporary Mexican labor. He fulfilled that pledge in August, 1977 when he ordered the admission of temporary harvest hands from Mexico at Presidio, Tex., in response to complaints from growers that domestic labor was not available. At the same time, he renewed his pledge to oppose any future *bracero* plan. But in early 1978, a leading administration spokesman gave a different report.

Agriculture Secretary Robert Bergland visited Mexico in January for talks with President Jose Lopez Portillo. On Jan. 26, the leading daily in Mexico, *Excelsior*, reported that Bergland had told Portillo that the United States needed 3 million *braceros* for agriculture work each year—a figure far in excess of the number of *braceros* imported under the prior program. On Jan. 30, President Carter told a press conference that "We have no plans whatsoever to reinitiate a *bracero* program." The same day, Bergland, who had been in contact with the White House through the U. S. Embassy, told reporters in Mexico that his remark about the need for 3 million *braceros* had been misunderstood, but that he did not preclude the possibility of a new, more limited, *bracero* program.

Equally hazy is Carter's promised amnesty program, details of which have never been clearly spelled-out. In August, 1977 the administration unveiled an amnesty proposal which would grant permanent residence to *sin pa-*

peles who can show that they have been in the U. S. continuously since Dec. 31, 1969, or earlier. The "7-year rule" was immediately assailed on the grounds that few *sin papeles* could qualify. Most have either been deported or have returned home for visits since 1969, and therefore, cannot meet the continuous presence rule. Furthermore, *sin papeles* who remain in the U. S. more than a year or two in time acquire drivers' licenses, Social Security numbers, and other documents which indicate permanence. Many have learned English. Long-term *sin papeles* are therefore practically safe from deportation without amnesty; they are "documented" illegals. The "7-year rule," its critics say, offers amnesty to those who do not need it, and denies amnesty to those who need it—recent entrants. Since the original announcement, Carter cabinet members have been variously quoted as favoring a five-year rule, and a three-year rule. The President however, has not spoken in favor of liberalizing the proposal. Meanwhile, the "7-year-rule" has with time become an 8-year-rule.

A second part of the amnesty package was the proposal that a 5-year non-deportable status be given *sin papeles* who had resided in the U. S. continuously between the first of January, 1970 and the first of January, 1977. According to the plan, *sin papeles* who met the requirement would be given work permits valid for five years, but would be excluded from food stamp, welfare and other social programs. Nor would they be eligible to apply for permanent residency or citizenship. Their status at the end of the 5-year term would be determined by Congress in the interval. Three options would then be open under the Carter plan: extension of non-deportable status, legal residency, or deportation.

The second part of the amnesty plan is no more popular with Chicano leaders than the first, because it does nothing for recent immigrants, and because it creates a new tier of noncitizenship, below parole status and below residency status. Jose Angel Gutierrez, Raza Unida Party leader, has denounced the 5-year grace plan as "the beginning of an American apartheid for Chicanos." The proposal is also subject to criticism on the grounds that it is but a new version of postwar "storm and drag" immigration. It provides a humane alternative to deportation for those *sin papeles* already here, perhaps, but does nothing to confront the issue of undocumented immigration itself. The proposal's humane value may also be questioned, for as with the 7-year-rule, few *sin papeles* eligible for nondeportable status are likely to fall into Border Patrol nets.

Ironically, news of the amnesty proposal spurred undocumented immigration. Newspapers in Mexico reported that within days after the program was announced, thousands of former *sin papeles* headed back to *el norte,* hoping to slip in before measures for determining continuous residency were established. Undoubtably, many did get across, and today have witnesses who will testify that they have been here since—whatever date the Carter administration chooses. Other *sin papeles* were inspired to come north by Secretary Bergland's statement that the U. S. needed three million agricultural laborers, more than six times as many as had been imported during the *bracero* program.

A move towards finalizing the plan was taken in late 1977 when leading Democrats joined to endorse a new bill, S. 2252, introduced by Senators Eastland, Kennedy, Bentsen and DeConcini. The "Carter plan" bill, as it was called, provides for:

* civil fines of not more than $1,000 per offense for employers who hire *sin papeles*
* fines of up to $2,000 and a prison terms of up to 5 years for *coyotes*, or others who for financial gain seek work for *sin papeles*
* legal residency for *sin papeles* who entered the U. S. prior to Jan. 1, 1970 (amnesty)
* five-year non-deportable status for *sin papeles* who entered the U. S. before Jan. 1, 1977

However, the bill is as notable for an ommission as for what it provided. It does not say how employers are to determine the immigration status of employees. The bill neither provides for a national identity card, nor speaks against it. Since there are currently some 71 different kinds of proof which may be offered by defendants in deportation trials, presumably those documents would be acceptable—unless the law makes other provision. A requirement that 3.5 million American employers familiarize themselves with 71 more documents is clearly a requirement begging for alteration. Before the "Carter plan" can be passed, the issue of suitable identification must be resolved.

Labor lobbyists do not like the bill, as they have not liked other measures which have won Senator Eastland's signature. The penalty provision for employers is weaker than that set out in the previous Rodino-style bills, because it calls for civil, not criminal, penalties. To fine an employer for hiring *sin papeles*, the Justice Department will have to bring suit. Under S. 2252, employers may not be arrested nor may they be convicted in speedy administrative hearings. The Rodino bills included a step-ladder prosecution scale, providing stiffer penalties for repeat offenders. S. 2252 does not, again to labor's displeasure. But the sharpest labor objection is to the non-deportable status provision; they see in it a new form of *bracero* plan.

Agricultural interests, however, are not entirely placated by the bill, which offers no promise of cheap Mexican labor beyond the 5-year non-deportable status plan. Food lobbyists have not given up the demand for a *bracero* program and Secretary Bergland's announcement that the U.S. needed 3 million Mexican farmworkers may have been a test balloon to measure the strength of opposition.

Congress will come closer to passing the "Carter plan" measure than any before it, because it promises to break the Rodino-Eastland deadlock, despite grumblings from both agriculture and labor. But the Carter plan cannot satisfy Chicano leadership. Senators and Representatives will only vote for the bill if they believe that organized Chicano groups do not speak for the *barrios*. Whether or not they do will perhaps be seen as Chicano leaders muster forces for what may be the final test of the demand that employment of *sin papeles* be banned.

CHAPTER 24

The European Parallel

The "Carter plan's" proposal that *sin papeles* be given 5-year work permits and a non-deportable status is not a new one. Plans based on a similar principle have been in effect in Europe for some 30 years, and provide some insight into how the Carter scheme might affect American society. In Europe, what began as a temporary solution to a post-World War II labor shortage has now become a necessity. Over 11 million migrant imported workers live in Western Europe, excluding those in Great Britain. International migrants composed about 6.3% of the total labor force in France, 7% in West Germany, and nearly 30 per cent in Switzerland.

The massive post-war immigration in Western Europe resulted from two basic tendencies: economic growth in the industrialized host nations, and population growth in the underdeveloped emigrant nations. Reconstructing the war-devasted economies of France and Germany, aided by the Marshall Plan, resulted in a long period of virtually uninterruped economic growth which soon absorbed all available labor. Switzerland, a neutral country, whose economy was left intact during the war, used its strong position to capture a large part of the European market immediately after the war, so its economy also grew rapidly. European nations approached a position of virtual

153

full employment, which allowed native workers to demand and receive higher wages. Growing industry needed a large source of cheap labor.

Simultaneously, in the underdeveloped nations, modern medicine had improved the mortality rates and increased the average life span. Nations like Turkey, Greece and Algeria experienced population booms out of proportion to economic growth. These economically backwards nations, which had always suffered from unemployment, developed labor surplus. The natural result of labor shortages in one country and labor surplus in neighboring ones is immigration—legal or not.

To provide temporary immigrants for the labor-hungry economy, the French Government set up the Office National d'Immigration (ONI) and gave it a monopoly on recruitment. French employers seeking migrant labor had to apply to the ONI, which found workers, gave them medical examinations and arranged for transportation to France.

In the late forties and the fifties, the largest group of ONI migrants came to France from Italy, but that number declined later as higher wages in Germany and Switzerland began to draw Italians away. Spaniards became the predominant group in the early sixties, but in recent years the largest number have come from Portugal, the least industrialized nation in Western Europe. The French Government allowed Algerians free entry and exit from France as long as their homeland was a colony. Thousands of Algerians migrated freely without having to go through ONI from 1945 until 1955, the year of Algerian national independence. Afterwards, immigration continued almost as before under agreements signed by both governments. Today, Algerians form the largest non-European enclave in western Europe.

By 1968, the increase of undocumented immigration into France had broken the ONI's monopoly on migrant recruitment; an estimated 82 % of that year's immigrants bypassed ONI. Workers entered France clandestinely because the procedures of the offical system were complicated and time-consuming. Some feared medical exams would exclude them, and others came from countries like Portugal which prohibited emigration. As in the U.S., many

French employers preferred hiring undocumented workers because they accepted lower wages than others. To reassert some control over immigration, the government had to pass legislation allowing undocumented workers to "regularize," to register with the ONI after showing proof of employment and passing a medical exam.

The first organized recruitment of migrants in West Germany (Federal Republic of Germany) came in 1955, when the government concluded an agreement with Italy for seasonal agricultural and construction workers. Later, as labor needs grew, Germany contracted for year-round industrial workers as well and signed labor import agreements with Spain and Greece in 1960, Turkey in 1961, Portugal in 1964, and Yugoslavia in 1968.

The Federal Labor Office in Germany supervises the immigration process, operating recruitment centers in the labor-supplying nations. After paying a fee, German employers give the agency specific requests for migrants, listing the jobs available and the terms of employment. The FLO passes on the information to the labor officials in the recruitment nations, who in turn choose suitable native workers. The recruitment centers process the applicants, give them medical exams, test them for industrial skills and check to ensure that none have criminal records. Workers who pass the requirements sign one-year labor contracts; then the Federal Labor Office transports them to Germany and places them with employers.

Unlike France and Germany, the Swiss government does not handle the recruitment of foreign workers; they leave that up to the employers. But the state exercises strict control over admission and residence of immigrants. Immediately after World War II, Swiss immigration policy was comparatively tight; it kept the number of entrants to a minimum for fear of an impending economic crisis. In the fifties and sixties, however, after uninterrupted periods of economic growth, the restrictions loosened and large numbers of immigrants came in to fill labor shortages. Though in 1964 anti-foreign sentiment in Switzerland prompted the government to limit official immigration again, the number of immigrants has continued to grow because of undocumented entries. The Swiss government usually grants relatively short-term (one- to two-year) work visas to discourage permanent settlement. Most of the immigrants to Switzerland come from Italy, Spain, Germany, and Yugoslavia.

Like *sin papeles* in the United States, the majority of migrant workers in Europe come from peasant villages where they can no longer make a living at agricultural work, because there is not enough land to go around, or the land available is not productive enough to support the growing populaton. Nor do the cities offer any hope of work; street hawkers fill the cities to sell rugs, cigarettes or to shine shoes, because they cannot find steady work.

A typical first-time migrant to Germany is a peasant from a rocky, arid village in southern Turkey. Agriculture contributes 60% of the gross national product of his nation, yet 90% of agricultural labor is performed with hand tools, without modern technology. Many peasants find work only during harvest season. The typical Turkish farmworker has a large family he needs clothe and feed, but no prospects of employment. He hears from another villager. a returning migrant, about the high wages and ample opportunity in Germany. He knows nothing about places like Hamburg and Berlin, and has probably never visited the urban centers of his own country. He doesn't speak any German nor can he read the Roman alphabet, but he hears that in Germany he can work. So he doffs his workman's cap and his one suitcoat, and takes a bus for Istanbul, where the German recruitment center will process him.

Immigrants in Western Europe assume the lowest paid, the least comfortable and the most dangerous jobs host countries have to offer. They cluster in the building trades as unskilled labor, in seasonal agricultural work and also in unskilled manufacturing positions. These are the jobs that native workers dislike, and most have moved out of them into better paid white collar jobs created by the post World War II economic boom. According to the French National Office of Immigration;

Immigration has to a great extent contributed to the revival and expansion of our economy. Jobs which were no longer of interest to Frenchmen, for which there were not enough applicants, have been taken by foreigners, without any difficulty from national workers.

Immigrants take what jobs are offered; they have no choice because they lack the education and skills necessary to demand prestige work. Furthermore, laws and regulations of the host countries prevent guest workers from moving up into skilled labor or white collar work. Short-term visas make it difficult for migrants to achieve promotion. In France and Germany, the terms of work contracts prohibit immigrants from changing jobs, and they face immediate deportation if they break a contract.

The jobs assigned to immigrants tend to be menial and tedious, like assemblyline work, which demands the repetition of one bodily motion for hours at a time. Since the migrants attempt to make as much money as possible in a short time, they often volunteer for overtime. Many factory workers receive pay on the basis of the number of pieces produced, and once again, the migrants are in a hurry to earn, so they work faster. Overtime and speed-ups cause greater job stress and fatigue, which in turn can cause industrial accidents. Not surprisingly, the accident rate for industrial migrant workers in France is eight times as high as the rate for natives.

The other great employer of migrants, the construction industry, involves arduous and dangerous work, and conditions are generally more hazardous for foreign workers than natives in the same field. Migrants do not have full civil rights and since they tend to be unaware of the rights they do enjoy, they often accept the most miserable job conditions. Some employers segregate foreign workers to prevent them from comparing conditions with native veteran employees.

The construction of a drainage tunnel in Geneva in 1971 illustrated how employers abuse migrant labor. The job was particularly hazardous because it required workers to drill through sandstone, whose dust can cause silicosis, a lung disease common to coal miners. What was not sandstone was mud, which had to be dug out by hand, a task demanding considerable endurance. Swiss workers refused to work in the tunnel because the wages offered were not high enough to compensate for the danger and discomfort. Their places were taken by migrant tunnelers, from Italy, Spain and Yugoslavia. Two engineers and the foreman hired for the project came from Germany.

Safety conditions in the tunnel were poor, with faulty ventilation, insufficient lighting and a high noise level. A conveyor belt, running above head level, occasionally dropped clumps of mud and dirt from the diggings. During a year of activity with a work force of less than 100, two tunnel workers died in accidents, a third broke both legs, another injured his spine, and one more lost his hearing because of an explosion. In 1973, when a group of Spanish workers staged an impromptu strike over conditions in the tunnel, the company fired them. The Swiss construction union did nothing to help the Spaniards, who, without jobs, had to leave the country.

Although Western European unions attempt to organize immigrants in industries where they work side by side with natives, they tend to ignore workplaces that only employ foreign labor. Futhermore, in labor disputes between employers and immigrants, the tendency is for unions to remain neutral. In a strike organized by Spanish seasonal workers against a Swiss construction firm, the unions actively opposed the immigrants, calling them irresponsible and accusing them of violating industrial peace. This quote from the president of the Swiss Clothing and Leather Workers Union testifies to the second-class status of immigrants in Switzerland:

> Our foreign colleagues should know that we act in their interests without any reservation where their interests coincide with those of the Swiss. Where collisions are perhaps possible, we act in just consideration of the general interest.

The refusal of the Swiss trade unions to support the Spanish tunnel workers points to a general failure of organized labor in Western Europe to represent the interests of foreign workers. A joint statement from the two largest trade union confederations in France, the CGT and the CFDT, says:

> Immigrant workers are an integral part of the working class and are not competitors with French workers. We in-

tend to place action with and for immigrant workers within the general struggle of all workers.

Whether it is a question of jobs, purchasing power, living conditions or trade union rights, immigrant and French workers are both concerned.

But, despite lip service on behalf of migrants, the French trade unions actively opposed immigration of workers to France from the late forties until the late sixties. Opposition ended only after the unions realized the inevitability of immigration.

Besides taking the worst jobs offered by the host countries, immigrants also have to accept substandard housing. In Germany at the beginning of its immigration program, Italian, Spanish and Greek workers were actually quartered in the dilapidated huts of the Dachau concentration camp.

Today, over half the migrant workers live in company-owned housing. The typical company hostel consists of wooden barracks, sleeping from four to eight men to a room, with public shower facilities in the main building of the complex. Some of the hostels have been converted from old warehouses, cold storage halls, airplane hangers and unfinished buildings. Some housing lacks adequate plumbing and heating. Almost all of the barracks lack the amenities that native workers enjoy, such as chairs, lamps and curtains, yet migrants spend most of their leisure hours in the quarters.

Private housing for immigrants tends to be even less attractive. A shortage of living space plagues all of Western Europe, particularly urban industrial centers. Migrants, being newcomers, poor, and often the victims of discrimination, have even greater difficulty than natives in finding private living space. The housing crisis in Paris has led to the development of "bidonvilles," shanty-towns of huts made by migrants from rubbish—old signs, oil drums, scrap metal and pieces of wood left at construction sites. An estimated 360 bidonvilles skirt the city, housing over 50,000 migrants, most of them from Algeria, but also others from Morocco, Spain, Portugal and black African nations. These shanty-towns have no plumbing; inhabitants have to haul water from the nearest source—as many as a thousand migrants may have to use a single water tap.

Without toilets, the bidonville dwellers defecate behind their huts, in pots or the nearest empty lot. Their open sewage leaves a pervasive stench, and, along with exposure to cold and rain, augments the danger of disease. Fire presents a constant hazard; without water to douse them, flames spread quickly from shack to shack.

Although invited in to work, migrants receive a lukewarm welcome from the general population in the host countries. Opinion polls indicate that more than two thirds of the citizens of Germany believe that too many foreigners work in their industries. Dark-complected people often find themselves the victims of harrasment and verbal abuse. Racist slurs against migrants include "rag-pack," "camel-driver," "snake-eater" and "skunk." Natives often attribute negative characteristics to the immigrants—consider them to be lazy, or accuse them of "chasing women," even though most migrants are completely segregated from native women. The mythology of the Old South is resurrected on Continental soil.

Every large group of immigrants to seek work in a foreign land has come up against prejudice. Indigenous workers fear the competition for jobs and housing, and employers foster racism to divide the labor force. In some cases as in France, governments have encouraged prejudice. During the war against Algeria, war-time propaganda depicted Algerians as inferior, cunning and brutal. Today, French racism is most pointed against North Africans, particularly Algerians. Right-wing extremist organizations in France make anti-Arab sentiments their rallying point, and one of the most vocal groups, the fascist l'Ordre Nouveau, has staged terriorist attacks against North Africans in Paris, using gasoline bombs and guns.

In Switzerland, anti-immigrant feelings take the form of an hysterical xenophobia. In 1970, a group called the Action Committee Against Foreign Domination of People and Homeland, initiated a national referendum on whether to limit the number of immigrants to ten percent of the population. If passed into law, the move would have caused the expulsion of thousands of migrants. The Action Committee's propaganda argued that, if allowed to continue, foreign immigration would undermine the "national character" of the Swiss. It theorized that because of "hereditary physical and mental characteristics," the mostly Italian and Spanish immigrants could not be assimilated; rather the Swiss would have to assimilate to them. The referendum, which drew a higher voter turnout than any in decades, was narrowly defeated, 46% in favor and 54% against.

Despite the uncordial reception they receive, foreign workers have sparked the productivity and increased the growth rates of the economies of Western Europe. The "Economic Miracle" of post-war West Germany and the reconstruction of the French economy would have been difficult without the ready reserves of cheap immigrant labor. According to a writer in *Welt der Arbeit*, a publication of the German Trade Union Federation:

> Without immigrant workers there would be no motorways! What would we lack in addition? The approximate calculation is that every worker in our country would have to do about four hours overtime per week if our standard of living were to remain at the same level. . . . In North Rhine Westphalia alone, 500,000 jobs would be vacant if the guest workers were sent home and the annual social product would decline by 12 thousand million deutschmarks.

Foreign workers also benefit from the immigration programs. They make wages they never could in the underdeveloped nations. At home, their families use the earnings to improve their standard of living. But in the host countries, the immigrants are exploited; they compose a subclass of workers making less than native workers, and they have no civil rights. When they return home to the underdeveloped countries, they find that there are still no factories and no available land to employ them. Many times they become chronic migrants, constantly having to travel between two nations, not really belonging to either.

Migrant worker programs have not halted undocumented immigration. In France the level of undocumented residence stands at 60%, in Germany 10%, and in Switzerland, although how much is not known, the foreign population continues to grow despite cutbacks on official immigration. Probably, immigration from underdevelped areas to advanced industrial centers will occur whether it is organized by the state or expressly illegal. And probably, immigrant workers will be exploited by industry and discriminated against by society with or without papers.

CHAPTER 25

The States Get Into the Act

The campaign to create public fear of a "Mexican invasion" has lead agencies of local government beyond their range of competence, resulting in passage of state and municipal anti-alien measures. In 1971, before the Rodino bill was presented to Congress, California—historically the leader in exclusionist legislation—passed a measure to forbid hiring *sin papeles*. California's lead was followed by Kansas in 1972, and would probably have been taken up by other legislatures, had the California statute not run aground on legal questions. In 1972 the Los Angeles Superior Court enjoined its enforcement on grounds that no authority for state interference in immigration matters had been established. California appealed to the U.S. Supreme Court, which in a 1976 decision, *DeCanas vs. Bica*, ruled that state actions had not been pre-empted by federal legislation. The ruling opened the way for a patchwork of state laws, and the following year, Florida, Virginia, New Jersey, Vermont and Massachussetts passed anti-alien bills of their own.

Four states, Nevada, Colorado, Texas and Illinois, turned back 1977 attempts to pass Rodino-style bills. In early 1978, similiar proposals were delayed or defeated in Indiana, Nebraska and Washington, D. C. Nevertheless, in four other states, Michigan, Ohio, Rhode Island and Wisconsin, anti-alien bills were set for hearings before 1978 legislative committees.

The severity of state legislative acts in the immigration field varies widely. Some states define hiring undocumented workers as a civil offense, while others make it punishable as a misdemeanor or felony offense under criminal law. Penalties range from fines of as little as $100 to a jail term of two years.

The Massachusetts Act, for example, makes "knowingly" hiring an undocumented worker a misdemeanor offense, punishable by a fine of $200 to $400. Employers may defend themselves from prosecution by proving that they have made a "bona fide inquiry" into the immigration status of their workers, but no precise guidelines for determining alien status are provided by the law; nor was any affidavit of legal residency created by the Act. Employers are therefore left in the position of having to determine alien status without expertise in the field, and employees are forced to prove their legality without knowing with certainty what documents might clear them. By mid-1978, there had been no prosecutions under the act. "We were not given additional staff to enforce the law, and we're too tied up with other duties to bother with it," says a spokesman for the Department of Labor and Industries, which is charged with putting the law into effect.

Non-enforcement is not unique to Massachusetts. With the exception of the California cases, which did not produce valid convictions, no charges were filed until early 1976. The first successful case under a state statute was recorded in Kansas, where a farmer pled guilty to hiring a *sin papeles*—and paid a misdemeanor fine. Since then, prosecution of state Rodino laws has been universally abandoned.

Many observers doubt that state legislative acts proceed from serious intent to prevent undocumented immigration. The stipulation that violations be "knowing" and the vagueness of "bona fide inquiry" requirements serve as safeguards to prosecution. Accused employers are not required to maintain records on the documents employees have shown to prove legal residency; therefore, an employer can safely avoid prosecution by merely claiming that his employees did show documents of one kind or another. The state, in such cases, would be left the duty of finding *sin papeles* who would testify against the men who hired them. State legislative acts have been carefully studied by the immigration project director of the Georgetown University Law School, Jose Medina, who says that he believes that "all the state laws are merely demagogery. They were written to win votes, not to be enforced."

However, Medina reports the state acts have an effect of a different kind: they intensify discrimination against Spanish-speaking immigrants and foreigners in general. "What is happening is that employers who do not understand the laws, or who do not want to hire Spanish-speaking workers are using the laws as a pretext. We've had reports from Virginia, for example, where legal permanent residents have been denied jobs or even fired because employers refused to accept their residency cards as appropriate documentation of legal status. We can bring lawsuits in cases like these, but the process is slow and costly. It has also been complicated by a Supreme Court ruling that discrimination based on national origin is not racial in character." In a word, the state legislative acts have not halted the exploitation of undocumented workers. They have provided headlines for politicians who want to exploit anti-alien hysteria, and they have given discrimination a new, and patroitic, guise.

CHAPTER 26

Ku Klux Klan Diplomacy

Popular hysteria against Mexicans also provided an opportunity for the Ku Klux Klan to flaunt its brand of racism. A Klan crusade to terrorize *sin papeles,* though only two weeks long and waged mainly in the press, developed into an international incident which Mexico will not soon forget. The success of the campaign is owed to David Duke, 27, a resident of suburban New Orleans, Grand Dragon of the Klan, and a skillful press manipulator since his college days at Louisiana State University, where he identified himself with the American Nazi Party.

On Oct. 17, Duke showed up in San Diego, California to announce that the Ku Klux Klan would patrol the border "until the government does its job" in stopping undocumented immigration. The Klan, he said, saw itself as an auxiliary to the "understaffed" Border Patrol, in whose ranks Duke claimed to have members. Klansmen, he said, would drive up and down the border in unmarked cars, searching for illegal entrants. When they found them, they would notify the Border Patrol by radio. In order to "protect" themselves, they would carry handguns.

Duke's announcement was headlined by most newspapers in Mexico, including its most prestigious dailies. The press echoed the sentiment of most Mexicans, which was that it is not in the interests of good international relations that private parties be allowed to threaten Mexicans and go unpunished in the U. S. Most Mexicans expected that the FBI or another law enforcement agency would simply jail Duke; they were dismayed when no such action was taken. In Mexico, the story was one of the top 10 newsmakers for 1977—because it grated on the sensitive nerves of Mexican patriotism.

The day following Duke's announcement, a largely Chicano group demonstrated against the Klan in San Diego, and a clash with policemen resulted. One man was arrested on charges that he smashed the windshield of a car belonging to the Ku Kluxers. Meanwhile, Duke met with two INS officials, District Director James O'Keefe, and local office head Alan Clayton, who told the Grand Dragon that the agency did not need help from the KKK. Their meeting with Duke produced new protests, however. On October 21, some 50 religious, labor, and Chicano organizations and prominent individuals, including farmworkers, leader Cesar Chavez and California lieutenant governor Mervyn Dymally telegrammed President Carter, demanding that he fire O'Keefe and Clayton for having "honored" Duke by meeting with him. Further, the telegram's signers demanded that Carter take steps to halt the Klan's border patrol.

Though Duke maintained that the Klan's aims were nonviolent, on the nights of October 21 and October 22 the homes of two San Diego Chicano leaders were defaced with Klan grafitti, and a cross was burned near the home of Leon Williams, a black city councilman. Following the incidents, U.S. Ambassador to Mexico Patrick J. Lucey in an interview with the newspaper *Excelsior* promised the Mexican people that the American government would not tolerate the Klan's attempt to impose vigilante law on the border. Journalists across Mexico interpreted Lucey's statement as a promise that the Klan would be jailed. Front-page headlines said: "The U. S. Will Punish the Ku Klux Klan," "The U. S. Will Prevent KKK Vigilance on the Border, Lucey Promises," and "Ku Klux Klans Threaten."

Duke meanwhile announced a one-week postponement in the starting date for the "Klan Bodrer Watch." In the interval, five residents of the border town of San Ysidro with support from several Chicano organizations filed a federal suit asking for an injunction to stop the Klan from implementing its program. On Wednesday October 26, U. S. District Court Judge Howard Turrentine denied the request. "You're asking me to restrain them from crimes that haven't yet been committed," he told the plaintiffs. Later that afternoon, Duke and a fellow Klansman posed for press photographers in a radio-equipped car on the border at Dulzura, Calif. The following morning, Border Patrolmen in the area reported that they had seen no other Klan cars along the border. Hours later, Duke declared that the Klan's efforts had brought about the apprehension of some 44 *sin papeles* and had reduced undocumented immigration even more by putting fear in the hearts of Mexicans. Therefore, he claimed, the Klan would move its anti-alien drive to agricultural areas in northern California—which some six months later, had not reported sighting any Klan patrols. Duke did not go to northern California, but instead left San Diego for Arizona and Texas, to "extend" the Klan's phantom "Border Watch." His departure coincided with the arrival of several thousand Chicanos, unionists and libertarians for a massive protest on the border October 28-29.

Duke was reported in Tucson early October 28, and later, he held a press conference in San Antonio. "We feel the massive flow of illegal aliens is a real threat to the American way of life. They're taking jobs, creating a crime problem and disrupting the welfare program," Duke told the press—echoing the sentiments of General Chapman and Congressman Rodino. "We feel this rising tide washing over our border is going to affect our culture. All the politicians talk about the problem but do nothing."

Duke and a sidekick, Louis Beam, Jr., Grand Titan of the Texas Knights of the Ku Klux Klan, promised that the Kluxers would not simply do nothing. The Klan, Beam claimed, had three light aircraft at its disposal and had already dispatched some 150 vigilantes to the border. After making the announcement, Beam joined Duke on the airport runway. Minutes later, they boarded a small private plane and flew off, supposedly to patrol the border at Del Rio.

Duke's cameo appearance in the San Antonio airport coincided with the opening of a Chicano conference on immigration attended by some 3,000 delegates and sponsored by the Raza Unida Party. After his departure, two militant Chicano groups, the Barrio Club of Crystal City, and the state-wide Brown Berets, announced that they would patrol the border—to insure that the KKK did not brutalize Mexicans or Chicanos in the area. On the morning of Saturday, October 29 some 30 Brown Berets reached the border. A contingent of 15 was halted by sheriff's deputies at a roadblock outside Del Rio, and encamped there. Sheriff's department officials told the Berets that they planned to prevent both the Klan and the Chicano groups from patrolling along the border; but no Klan caravans were intercepted over the weekend. Other Brown Berets were able to work the border between Del Rio and Brownsville, but saw no signs of the KKK.

"We ran into a lot of deer hunters and immigration people, but no Klansmen. Nobody we talked to had seen the Klan," says Brown Beret Martin Delgado of Austin. Delgado also noted that he saw no Mexicans crossing the border; hard rains had hit the area, swelling the normally-shallow Rio Grande to dangerously torrential proportions. Fearing the river as much as the Klan, would-be *sin papeles* stayed home.

When the weekend was over, there was scant evidence that the KKK had actually been on the border. A reporter from the Dallas *Times-Herald* wrote a report of his experiences with one Ku Klux patroller, and residents of a Brownsville apartment complex found Klan leaflets scattered around their parking lot. The leaflets bore a crudely-drawn skull-and-crossbones design and said: WARNING TO ILLEGAL ALIENS AND OFFICIALS OF THE U.S. GOVERNMENT. THIS BORDER SUBJECT TO RANDOM PATROLS BY THE KU KLUX KLAN." Since the leaflets were printed in English, it is doubtful that they frightened any undocumented aliens. Like the rest of the campaign, they were designed for domestic consumption.

Nevertheless, the scandal did not die as quietly in Mexico as it did on the American side of the border. On November 2 at a press conference in Juarez, Ambassador Lucey reiterated that "Any suggestion of contact between the United States government and an extremist group like the Ku Klux Klan is totally ridiculous." He missed the point. Mexico wanted to see the U.S. government, in the name of neighborliness, stand up to the Klan.

Back in Louisiana by November 3, Duke got in the parting shots of his publicity stunt in an interview with Mexico City's *Excelsior*. His remarks summed up Chapman's speeches, with a little of candidate Carter's concern for "ethnic integrity" thrown in. "We don't have anything against Mexicans, even though you are invading us, occupying our territory, even though you want to dominate us, convert us into a political force inside our own country, and destroy our cultural integrity," Duke told *Excelsior's* reporter, Fausto Fernandez Ponte. Then he threw in the Klan's own trademark: "We are not directed against the Mexicans, but against our own government, which is dominated by the Jews. . . . The Jews want to use the undocumented Mexicans as a force for politics here, to destroy us." If any sane note came from the interview, it was only Duke's claim that he had never received any telegram from U.S. Attorney General Bell warning the Ku Kluxers that racist violence would not be welcomed on the border. Duke's comment and the success of the campaign made Mexicans wonder if Bell had sent a warning to Duke—and if, indeed, American officials had not secretly been pleased by the KKK terror.

CHAPTER 27

Is Leonel Castillo the Answer?

The President Carter's choice to replace General Leonard Chapman as INS chief was Leonel Castillo. Castillo is a wily Texas politican with a record for championing two causes, himself and minorities in general. As a city official in Houston, he succeeded in his administrative duties, in building minority strength within the Democratic party, and in making himself a man to be reckoned with. In the INS job, he is pitting his considerable political finesse and his command of ethnic clout against the legacy Chapman left and the still-formidable hysteria he created. This time, however, Castillo's gamble may not pay off. If it does, Castillo can set his eyes on a governorship or a Senate chair.

Castillo comes to the job with several advantages, not the least of which is his ethnic background, an inroad to the community most affected by immigration policy.

Leonel Castillo's grandfather walked across the international bridge at Brownsville in 1880, and paid a nickel to become a U. S. citizen. His father was a unionized dock worker in Galveston, and Leonel in his youth was studious, apart from and somewhat afraid of the rowdy working class culture of the Chicano *barrio* around him. Though he played football on the high school team, Leonel was

173

given the nickname "Lone," a designation of his aloofness from the school spirit.

Texas in 1961 was largely a part of the Old South, and Dixie itself had not changed much since Reconstruction. The 1963 march on Washington was still in the future, there had been no Birmingham crusade, no Selma walk, no Nobel Prize for Dr. Martin Luther King, Jr. Chicanos were not subject to legal segregation, as blacks were. Like most whites in Texas, they generally felt above the nascent civil rights movement. Castillo, however, was different. Then a student at St. Mary's University in San Antonio, he joined a sit-in movement to integrate downtown facilities which were closed to blacks. It was a bold step for anyone, especially for anyone with political ambitions in Texas.

His civil rights internship, though a brief one, earned him the careful eye of school gossips and administrators, but did not deter him from graduating *cum laude* with a major in English. After college, the path he took shows in how many ways he differed from General Chapman. When Chapman graduated from college in 1935, he joined the Marine Corps. When Castillo graduated in 1961, he joined the Peace Corps. Chapman saw the Philippines as a soldier and an officer; Castillo, as a Peace Corps volunteer, and later, staff member. In 1965, while Chapman was preparing the Marines to step-up their campaign in Vietnam, Castillo was on his way home from the Pacific to begin graduate study in Philadelphia. Castillo studied community organization while Chapman ordered community "pacification." In 1967, the year of the Tet invasion, as Chapman watched American gains turn sour in Vietnam, Castillo moved to Houston, where he watched toddlers in the day care centers he supervised.

Houston in the late sixties was a growth ring for the ethnic movements which had already risen to prominence elsewhere. Castillo heard the call of opportunity, and heeded. In 1968, he won the top post in a government jobs training program. It was the sort of appointment which might have lulled others into thinking that they, at last, had arrived—Castillo, however, wanted more. Among other things, he wanted to see the Catholic church on the Gulf Coast overcome its reluctance to side with minorities on social equality issues. He lambasted church leaders, then accepted when they offered him the directorship of the area Catholic Council on Community Relations.

The new post, like others before, was a pinnacle for seeing opportunities beyond.

Just 10 years after he graduated from college, Castillo decided that he wanted to be mayor of Houston. The city charter blocked him, however, by requiring mayoral hopefuls to have a record of five years residence in Houston. Unphased, Castillo researched the requirements for other offices and discovered that there was no minimum residency requirement for the post of city comptroller. He entered his name on the ballot, and ran as a Democrat. Luck was with him, the incumbant, a conservative Anglo, was in failing health and had a right-wing rival in the Democratic primary. They split the vote, putting Castillo into a runoff. He came out a winner.

The city comptroller's post is neither glamorous nor usually a political stepping stone. Castillo set about changing that. He exposed the undertaxing of a Houston country club, went after attorneys and physicians who evaded city income taxes, and made headlines when he drove an electric auto to conserve on city fuel bills. Meanwhile, he became something of a power broker in Democratic Party politics. In 1973, he won re-election to the comptroller's job, and a year later, tried to unseat conservative leadership inside the Democratic party. At a 1974 state Democratic convention in Austin, he polled 42 per cent of the delegate votes. The near-win whetted his appetite for what friends say is his long-run ambition: to become the first Chicano governor of Texas.

Castillo backed off from confrontation after the 1974 close showing. Though he had earlier promised to improve the status of Houston's city laborers, who were hired on a day-to-day basis, without either union or civil service protection, he let the issue pass. He had previously complained about the pollution created by industries in the Houston ship canal, and had exposed their favorable tax status; now he hesitated to press for the kill. He played backroom cards skillfully, trading ethnic posture for the power of real politics. His far sightedness was evident in the spring of 1976, when he signed into the state Democratic con-

vention as a Carter delegate, though he personally favored
Sargent Shriver. "He's forever asking questions like, 'What
asking questions like, 'What do you think the odds are?'," a
Castillo aide told reporters.

When Carter won, the payoff came. Though he would
have preferred to be Ambassador to the Philippines—a
post for which he is no doubt qualified—that spot was not
offered. Still in office as Houston comptroller, but bored,
Castillo turned down several offers to take federal fiscal
control jobs, because he wanted to get involved in "real issues."

The chance to take over the INS was as dangerous as it
was tempting. Here, without any doubt, was a real issue. It
offered national limelight, always good for boosting home-
state political standing. But it also threatened to spoil his
reputation with the Spanish-speaking community in Texas
and across the nation, for though *sin papeles* are often
scorned, nobody in the *barrios* has kind words to say
about *La Migra*. Taking the job was a calculated risk:
Castillo wanted national prominence but could not have
wanted the name of Judas among his own people. A less
self-confident and less ambitious man would have said no.
Instead, in April, 1977 Leonel Castillo went to Washington.

He spoke with savvy about the risk involved, and perhaps with too much optimism about the opportunity before him. "If I do a good job, it'll be good for me
politically. If I do a bad job, it could prove fatal to any
future political plans I may have. . . . If I can come up
with a good immigration policy with positive effects on
employment and the economy, I'll have the backing of
both business and labor," he told the *Texas Observer*
shortly before he assumed office.

More prudent and less strident men would have assumed a new post quietly and waited on the bidding of the
President. But Castillo, like Andrew Young, quickly
showed that he was not entirely bought or bossed. Even as
early as his appearance before the Senate during confirma-
tion hearings, he spoke against that part of the Carter plan
which would make it illegal to employ *sin papeles*. "There
would be problems in safeguarding the rights of U.S. citizens who appear foreign," he said. He also expressed op-

position to any plans for a national identity card. As soon as he took office, he ordered INS officers to quit testifying in favor of Rodino-type bills.

Castillo has dropped the term "illegal alien" from his vocabulary in favor of "undocumented immigrant," the neutral terminology of demographers and sociologists. From time to time he speaks of "our undocumented brothers," publicly employing the nominative of the Chicano movement. Rather than referring to *sin papeles* as welfare cheats and job competitors, Castillo says they are "young, ambitious but not educated people, who have been hardy and agressive enough to reach out for something better." The change in tone at INS pleased liberals and Chicano activists, and rankled old-line hands in the Border Patrol.

Castillo has also set out to reform the INS. Some of the changes he has made are cosmetic: "I have been in too many offices which are drab, foreboding, unfriendly and depressing. We have ordered some Peter Max paintings to help brighten them up to give our employees a better outlook and a more friendly manner, and make INS a more pleasant place to visit for business." Others were substantive. The INS is charged with two functions, service and enforcement. Its service function includes processing applications for permanent residency and citizenship. During the long years of INS neglect, and especially when the agency was headed by generals, the police function, that of the Border Patrol, was given priority. When Castillo took over, he found that some INS offices had backlogged nearly four years' work. He ordered new staffers into impacted offices, and in a period of six months, set the agency on its way catching up with paperwork. In June, 1977 there were 97,000 naturalization applications pending; in December, the number had been reduced to 21,000. Application for residency status, some 239,000 in June, were reduced to 190,000 by December, despite a 30 per cent increase in filings.

During the Chapman years, immigrants were often unable to contact the agency became its phone lines were perennially busy. Castillo admitted the problem in public speeches:

A survey earlier this year revealed that 12,800 callers to one large office were unable to get through in a two week period. We handled about 8,500 calls in that period, but 60 per cent of the calls were unsuccessful in reaching anyone.

To remedy the situation, he ordered the use of automated phone answering equipment, an impersonal solution, by his own admission—but a start.

In the past, letters to INS were rarely answered, and when they were, the delay stretched over months. Castillo found that the agency sent foreign-language letters to the State Department in Washington for translation, which routed them back to INS offices through bureaucratic channels. To cut down delay, Castillo ordered the creation of an in-house translation service.

In the fall of 1977, Castillo visited Los Angeles. While there, he learned that Border Patrolmen and local policemen were stopping churchgoers in Mexican-American neighborhoods to demand that they show immigration documents. He ordered Border Patrolmen to halt the Sunday morning harrassments, and publicly condemned the practice. Castillo also denounced an attempt by federal prosecutors, with collusion from Border Patrolmen, to frame activists from a Tucson community service agency on immigration charges.

He courted the wrath of seasoned Border Patrolmen and the administration itself when in December 1977, he called for implementation of a concept of his own making, called "positive repatriation." Under the plan, a "trust fund" would be set up for apprehended *sin papeles*, with funds coming mainly out of a tax on bridge crossings. The funds would be used to give medical tests to deportees, so that they might be advised of any serious ailments; to provide them with a minimum of training in such arts as home improvement, and "by putting a few dollars in their pockets [it would put them] in a position where they need not recross the border immediately in search of work, or face the prospect of no food, no bed, no friends and no money."

At the same time he was preparing reform, however, Castillo beefed-up the Border Patrol. He focused initial efforts on the Chula Vista, California area, which his agents said had been long out of control. In June 1977 Castillo dispatched 100 additional Border Patrolmen to the sector, a measure which six months later produced 192,000 apprehensions, 55,000 more than in the same period of 1976. To attract attention to the move, Castillo himself flew out to Chula Vista to direct apprehensions from a patrol helicopter—a dramatic act which cost dearly in Chicano support. Undeterred, in early 1977 he asked the House for a total of $298 million to last the INS through the next fiscal year, an increase of nearly $19 million. With the increase, he promised to hire 1,000 new employees, bringing the total INS staff to nearly 12,000. Nearly 300 of the new workers were slated to go into Border Patrol uniforms.

Leonel Castillo has not pleased either conservatives or liberals with his behavior. Exclusionists grumble when he talks about agency reform, and they regard "positive repatriation" as a subversive move: if allowed, it will encourage undocumented immigration, they say. The Chicano movement and its liberal supporters cannot wholeheartedly praise a man who leads a para-military helicopter action against defenseless *sin papeles*—and tells the press he enjoyed the stunt—even if he has generally acted to counter anti-alien hysteria. Nor can they applaud the called-for expansion in Border Patrol numbers. The right dislikes his opposition to Rodino-type legislation, and the left is uncomfortable with Leonel Castillo in the role of "lesser evil." Castillo is imperiled, isolated from both liberal and conservative bases of support. He has lived up to his high school nickname—Lone.

His isolation comes as no surprise. Friends and journalists who knew him in Houston believe that Leonel is acting in accord with his own character—and perhaps with the times. In 1976, before he was tapped for the INS post, Houston writer Tom Curtis pointed out the paradox which awaited Castillo

> . . . In these times of apparent slide to the political right and a return to consensus politics, ambitious minority leaders are facing a basic dilema: to succeed they must move away from their political base in order to appeal to a larger constituency. The moment they do, they are inevitably barraged by accusations that they have "sold out".

Leonel Castillo cannot solve the problems of undocumented immigration, because their roots are in international economic imbalance. He cannot write State Department policy, nor can he abandon the use of deportations as an instruments of immigration strategy. What he can do is counter the atmosphere of "Mexicanophobia" which Chapman and Rodino encouraged. His public speeches indicate that he is attempting to do this. He can also "humanize" the INS, both in its dealings with *inmigrantes* and *sin papeles*. He can restore the service functions of INS which Chapman neglected. Castillo may lose political popularity as Commissioner of the INS, but the nation has gained a sensitive and intelligent administrator.

CHAPTER 28

UFW Dualism

A conspicuously quiet voice in the immigration controversy has been that of Cesar Chavez, who is unchallenged
as leading spokesman for the Chicano minority. Chavez
has not joined with other prominent Chicanos in crusading
against restricted immigration, because he is also chief of
the United Farm Workers union, an AFL-CIO affiliate
with a unique relationship to immigration issues.

Practical problems of organizing as well as the UFW
membership have prevented him from either endorsing a
policy of open immigration or supporting the AFL-CIO's
push for exclusion. The UFW is the product of more than
a half century of organizing attempts, many of which were
defeated when growers used *braceros* and *sin papeles* as
strikebreakers.

In 1947, workers on the DiGiorgio farms, now covered
by UFW contract, went out on strike—and were replaced
by *sin papeles*. In 1961, the now-defunct Agricultural
Workers Organizing Committee of the AFL-CIO called a
strike of Imperial Valley lettuce workers—who were replaced by *braceros*. The United Farm Workers Association, parent to the UFW, organized several thousand farm
laborers in California during the early 60's, but was unable to go successfully out on strike until 1965, after the
bracero program had been halted.

Today, INS agents often show up just days before a collective bargaining election to deport *sin papeles* whom

growers have denounced. Usually, those on the pick-up list are union members; because it is not in their interest, growers rarely turn in non-union *sin papeles*. In 1977, Cesar Chavez told *Excelsior* of Mexico that the Border Patrol is "the worst police force in the United States, similar to the Gestapo," but despite this, in recent years, the UFW has also called the Border Patrol to deport *sin papeles* who have not joined the union. It has also turned in the names of individual strikebreakers whom it knows or suspects are undocumented. Deportation has become a tactic for both union and management, especially on the eve of collective bargaining elections and during strikes.

Since growers want a reliable source of cheap and temporary labor, they generally favor reinstatement of the *bracero* plan. The UFW, on the other hand, needs for its existence a stable labor force of well-paid workers. Therefore, it is opposed to any new *bracero* program. In 1976 it showed it's opposition and strength by winning the passage of a California legislative resolution against re-enactment of any *bracero* program by Congress.

Cesar Chavez in 1974 told the *New York Times* that "the illegal workers from Mexico are a severe problem. It is a problem that is out of control. These illegals will accept 30 per cent to 50 per cent less than the Chicanos." That same year, at the urging of the UFW and AFL-CIO, Congress passed a federal law requiring farm labor contractors to refuse their services to undocumented workers. The 1974 measure was, in effect, a mini-Rodino bill for agriculture, a measure to restrict the employment of *sin papeles*. Chavez and his union do not complain that it sparked ethnic discrimination so much as that it has not been enforced. "As with most protective legislation for farmworkers, the law has not been thoroughly enforced," says Marc Grossman, an assistant to Chavez.

Nevertheless, the UFW has not joined the AFL-CIO push for restrictive immigration laws. Chavez and the union have refused to support both the Rodino bill and the Carter plan, which they say would result in "wholesale discrimination against Latinos." In 1976, the UFW convention instead urged Congress to grant amnesty to all undocumented workers, a measure which would protect union members *sin papeles* from deportation.

CHAPTER 29

———◆◆—◀◀—◆◆———

Inside the Border Patrol

There are 2,200 Border Patrolmen, all but 200 of whom work along the U. S.-Mexico border at tasks which are unique in American law enforcement. Typically, Border Patrol staffs are divided into "city", "border", and "brush" crews. "City" crews patrol downtown streets, inspect boxcars and train yards for aliens, and question passengers of busses bound for points away from the border. The jobs of city crews are largely done in the daylight hours, and produce few apprehensions; their purpose is chiefly as a deterrent. "Border" crews work evenings and nights, and do not patrol at all, for headlights give away their positions, and the border, 1,945 miles long, is too vast to cover on foot or by horseback. Instead, they park their vans at watchpoints along the Rio Grande or western desert, and wait for *sin papele*s to come up trails which are commonly used. When they draw near, the Patrolmen hide themselves, springing out to make apprehensions when their unaware suspects pass by. Usually, the officers need only shout "alto" or "parrase" (stop), and their catches submit. Other border crews spot their prey with the aid of electronic sensors given to the Border Patrol from surplus Vietnam-era army supplies. Sensors are of two types, magnetic and seismic. Magnetic sensors send out a radio signal to Border Patrol stations whenever a metal object passes by them. Seismic

sensors register impact on the ground above and around
them; when four thuds are recorded, the sensors emit a
signal. Their radio beams trip a switch in surveillance centers, lighting up a bulb on an area map and initiating a
print-out of the sensor number, date and time. Radio
dispatchers in the surveillance centers report to units in the
field whenever a sensor is tripped. The "border" crews, in
turn, move to the area where the sensor is located, hoping
to run upon *sin papeles* in the vicinity. The sensor system
provides the Border Patrol with relatively accurate information, but Border Patrolmen like it more because on
cold nights, it allows them to wait inside warm vans until
they know with certainty that *sin papeles* are crossing in a
particular area.

The sensor system is not infallible. Dogs with metal tags
can set off magnetic sensors, and any wandering animal
can trip a seismic device. Sensors cannot be used in areas
where public traffic is heavy, nor in areas which are often
flooded by runoff or the rising Rio Grande. They are useless in areas where vehicles or trains pass, and, like any
electronic equipment, are subject to breakdowns. For these
and other reasons, only 97 sensors are in use. Not even
that many are needed. Because its staff is not large
enough, the Border Patrol can respond to only one of every three sensor alarms.

Most sensors are located within a mile of the border.
When sensor information or informers tell the Border Patrol that *sin papeles* have gone past that limit unapprehended, "brush" or tracking crews are sent to work. The
Border Patrol academy is the only law enforcement school
in the United States which routinely trains enrollees in
tracking, or "sign cutting," as it is called in the agency.
"Sign cutters" or "brush men" set up "dragstrips," smooth
sandy areas, which they read for information on the number of *sin papeles* in a group, the direction of travel, and
other details. When sign cutters determine how many persons crossed a "drag strip" and when the crossing took
place, they radio Border Patrol pilots. The air crews, if
they locate the *sin papeles*, radio instructions to the track-
ers, who close in for apprehension.

Once a Border Patrolman has apprehended a group of
sin papeles, he searches them and locks them in the rear

of his van or auto. Then he proceeds to find new suspects. Only when his van is full or quitting time is near does he take his captives into the station for booking and lock-up. Usually, the apprehending officer is also responsible for interrogating subjects and completing forms required for booking. In many instances, he is also given the task of driving a group of prisoners to the bridge or border crossing point which goes into Mexico, where they are released.

Apart from their jobs, Border Patrolmen have little in common. Like other federal uniformed personnel, they come from different regional and ethnic backgrounds; it is not unusual, for example, to find an Italian-American from New York working with a partner from rural Georgia or Oklahoma. Nor are Border Patrolmen recruited from similar occupations. Among 30 agents at the Del Rio, Tex., office, for example, there is a former film technician, a former elementary school teacher, a geologist, and a bus driver. The staff there and elsewhere includes college graduates as well as men who completed high school by taking an equivalency exam. Only a few Border Patrolmen are recruited from the ranks of other law enforcement agencies. What attracts men, and now, women, to the Border Patrol is its pay level and the promise of civil service security.

Ordinary non-supervisory Border Patrol jobs are within the federal civil service G-7 classification; this means that, with about 10 hours overtime counted in each week, most Border Patrolmen earn $15,000 to $20,000 a year. Supervisory officers earn up to $25,000. Morale in the Border Patrol is essentially good because pay levels are high.

Most Border Patrolmen are also content with the service for a reason beyond income: they like their jobs. Many relish the comraderie that comes from working with a partner, and others find satisfaction in the suspense and surprise of tracking. Because Border Patrol work is rarely hazardous, and because weather conditions are mild, it attracts outdoorsmen. In fact, most Border Patrolmen liken their jobs to fishing, hunting, or picnicking.

Military and police agencies often attract personnel whose life-long fantasies involve wearing uniforms and exercising power over other men. The typical Border Patrolman, however, had no contact with the agency until reading about it in a civil service bulletin encountered at a federal employment center. Many recruits never heard of the Border Patrol before taking federal civil service exams. Less than 20 per cent speak Spanish before arriving at the Border Patrol Academy in El Paso. At the academy, nearly 10 per cent are discharged over the 4-month internship, usually because they are unable to make sufficient progress in language training. Because federal exams and academy training are demanding, Border Patrolmen, as a group, are conversant and literate, perhaps more so than any other group of uniformed officers in the nation. Privately, many of them say they are over-qualified for the jobs they do. However, this evaluation is subject to a condition: the belief that other lawmen are sufficiently qualified. The general courtesy and intelligence with which most Patrolmen do their jobs may be testimony that they are, indeed, suited to the human tasks at hand.

Every profession has its unethical practicioners, however. Despite the relative lack of men with prior power fantasies in its ranks, and despite the superior pay and training provided them, many Border Patrolmen are sadistic. Certain details indicate that their penchant for rough treatment developed after they got into their jobs: during the administration of General Chapman and prior to it, racist and brutal attitudes were actually encouraged in the force by such things as the official use of words like "wetback"; suspensions of officers for mistreating their captives were rare; and the Border Patrol had no effective means of policing itself internally.

Incidents of brutality and racism are still common in the Border Patrol. Suspected *sin papeles* are frequently threatened, sometimes beaten, and now and then, actually murdered.

The very nature of Border Patrol work contributes to such practices, because apprehensions are not made in public view. Most *sin papeles* are arrested in remote brushy or desert areas, and usually, at night. There are no witnesses to their apprehensions except Border Patrolmen and themselves. The time span between apprehension and booking is ordinarily two hours or more, a relatively long gap, one which abusive officers may use to their own advantage. Since *sin papeles* are not arrested on the basis of warrants, accountability suffers; a Border Patrolman who has abused a prisoner may avoid discovery by merely letting his subject go.

Furthermore, conditions themselves are abusive. Border Patrol jails are inadequate; it is not unusual to find as many as 100 *sin papeles* packed into a 20' x 20' holding tank, lying side by side exactly like sardines in a can. Border Patrol vans, in which *sin papeles* sometimes wait for hours, are not equipped with water tanks or toilets. Neither the vans nor the holding tanks provide for segregation of female and child prisoners, nor are they equipped with emergency medical supplies. Pay phones are available at some Border Patrol stations, but lock-up and handling personnel are not. Therefore, few *sin papeles* are given the opportunity to call attorneys or family members to report that they have been arrested. Once a prisoner has been shut behind the door of his holding tank, he cannot ordinarily obtain cigarettes, food, coffee—or medical care—because in most cases, there is no officer he may call for help. Few *sin papeles* complain about these conditions, however. They are docile while in custody because in Mexico, uncooperative or demanding suspects are very frequently beaten, and sometimes disappear entirely. *Sin papeles* are not usually informed that in the United States, suspects have rights to fair and humane treatment. Based on what they know of police practice in Mexico, few are courageous enough to complain about anything.

Other circumstances also contribute to the complex cause of brutality. Few criminal suspects in the U. S. are actually arrested or detained by civilian citizens, because criminals are not easily recognizable. We cannot ordinarily know, for example, whether the passerby on the street outside is a man or woman going shopping, or a thief calmly walking away from a mugging. Even when suspects are sighted in a criminal act, such as armed robbery, they normally move swiftly away from the scene. Further, if an ordinary citizen attempts to halt a hold-up man or even a shoplifter, he is likely to be pushed, struck, or stabbed, and so losing the suspect, because criminals, generally speaking, do not fear ordinary men and women. But *sin papeles* are somewhat recognizable. Any border area rancher who spots a group of four or five men in peasant's clothing walking north across his property, carrying bottles of water or bags of food, may reasonably suspect that he has spotted *sin papeles*. If he wishes, he may question them, and in most cases, they will answer his questions truthfully, out of fear. Because this situation prevails, and because the Border Patrol will take custody of *sin papeles* whom private parties have detained, there are sadistic civilians along the the border who keep an eye out for *sin papeles*—or actually track them—as a hobby. Many of them carry arms or patrol with hunting dogs merely to increase the terror they visit upon their prey. In border areas, anyone who has fantasies of power may discharge them in "wetback catching," and for his efforts, will receive the friendship and praise of Border Patrolmen, whose jobs are made easier by gratuitous private captures.

Internally, Border Patrol abuse takes the form of harrassing fellow officers. Border Patrolmen who openly criticize other officers find themselves reprimanded for infractions of little consequence. Every government agency and large corporation has regulations which serve little purpose, but particularly in police and military organizations, such rules are used to punish "out-of-line" personnel. For example, Border Patrolmen are required to buy cowboy hats and to wear them on the job. But such headgear does not suit their jobs. Border Patrolmen must crawl through brush, jump over draws, climb into railroad cars, and run against the wind while chasing down *sin papeles*. To keep a broad-brimmed hat in place, the wearer must hold it with both hands while jumping or crawling, clearly a disadvantage. In practice, Border Patrolmen do not wear cowboy hats. They go hatless or wear golf caps instead. They also almost universally roll up their shirtsleeves when working, because regulation clothing is a mixture of wool and cotton, too warm for most daylight work along the border. Rolling up one's shirtsleeves is also an infraction of the rules. As in all military and police services, some officers in the Border Patrol get pleasure out of petty harrassment of fellow men in uniform. Border Patrolmen who do not conform to the generally racist standards of co-workers or superiors, or those merely unlucky enough to be assigned to a sadistic supervisor, often find themselves under reprimand for violation of the useless hat and shirtsleeve rules.

They may also find themselves under pressures to meet unrealistic standards. Though Anglo Border Patrolmen are taught to speak Spanish, few of them are fluent. Yet they are required to meet vague standards of "fluency and proficiency." "Fluency" is essentially a subjective standard; it is measured by the ear of the listener. Since most Anglo Patrolmen speak Spanish with heavy English accents, few are "fluent" in the most technical sense of the word: and that means, most of them can be reprimanded for lack of language ability. The serious question to be considered is whether or not the Border Patrol, in the past or present, has ever taken the fluency standard seriously and with sincerity. Most fluent among Americans in the Spanish language are Chicanos, who until a few years ago, were rarely hired on Border Patrol jobs. Even today, not more than 20 per cent of the agency's personnel are of Mexican-American parentage.

Border Patrolmen in some districts are also subject to off-the-job pressures. The Border Patrol in every district sponsors pistol marksmanship teams, and participation is sometimes an unspoken requirement of good relations on the job. Enthusiasm for marksmanship has led Border Patrol teams to more than 25 state championships, to 12 wins in National Police Bullseye competitions, six wins in National Police Combat contests, and six others in National Police Individual Championship meets. Border Patrolmen, unlike members of many local police teams, receive shooting ammunition at government expense. Yet, very, very few Border Patrolmen are called upon to fire a pistol while on their jobs. *Sin papeles* do not carry guns for a simple reasons: arms ownership is tightly restricted in Mexico, and a gun is an expensive item on the black market. A pistol worth $50 in the U. S. will see for four times as much almost anywhere in Mexico. If a *sin papeles* owned a pistol or a rifle, he would be inclined to see it in order to survive, for *sin papeles* are universally poor. Further, few of them know how to use firearms, since military training in Mexico is skimpy and conscription laws go unenforced in the countryside, from which most *sin papeles* come. Today, even smugglers who cross the border go unarmed, for they know that weapons will set off the Border Patrol's magnetic sensors. Despite all this, a Border Patrolman who is not disposed to marksmanship may find that he is under scrutiny ostensibly for other reasons. Former patrolmen often claim that, in fact, they were fired because their superiors wanted to replace them with agents who had reputations as sharpshooters. Even if all such charges are exaggerated, there seems to be little reason why the Border Patrol should encourage and subsidize a fascination with pistols. In actual practice, Border Patrol work is more akin to social welfare or probation work than to hard-line criminal catching, and the pistol is more a relic of the past than a response to present needs.

The underlying racism and brutality of some Border Patrolmen has recently come into conflict with the realities of survival in the agency. Leonel Castillo, the Commissioner of the INS since 1977, has ordered a series of measures destined to reform the agency. Most notably, he has announced the hiring of agents who will pose as *sin papeles,* purposefully falling into Border Patrol traps in order to observe the treatment *sin papeles* are given. These internal policemen, called "aides" in Border Patrol parlance, are being hired from outside the agency. Their activities will be kept secret from the Border Patrol agents in districts being investigated. Already, "aides" have visited Immigration Service offices across the nation, and a popular rumor among Border Patrolmen has it that Leonel Castillo himself, dressed in poor man's grab, visited several offices on his own. Though reports from "aides" are not yet available to the public, there is every reason to believe that their work will lead to a weeding out of some sadistic agents.

Already, a crackdown on beating cases is underway. Border Patrolmen have been encouraged to report incidents of brutality by fellow officers, and several agents have received 45-day suspensions following investigation of internal complaints. Castillo has also encouraged attempts to rid the service of overt verbal racism. Border Patrolmen are now under instructions to refer to their subjects as "undocumented guestworkers" or "undocumented immigrants," not as "wetbacks."

Border Patrol supervisory and administrative ranks are almost entirely Anglo in composition, and the same is true of the INS as a whole. Castillo has proposed that some 1,-200 jobs in the INS & Patrol be removed from civil service listings and reclassified as appointive posts. His object is to overcome the time lag which would be necessary, under seniority rules, to promote Chicanos and personnel from outside the agency into supervisory positions. If his proposal wins approval, Castillo will appoint Chicanos and others who are presumably uninfluenced by agency racism to these positions. However, the proposal has met opposition in powerful quarters. The American Federation of Government Employees, which represents Border Patrolmen and INS employees, has challenged it as "a return to the spoils system." The AFGE, however, has not developed any alternative proposal for overcoming INS racism nor has it admitted that racism is a problem. Its interest is in protecting those who are already union members, and therefore, it is not likely to acquiesce to reform.

This and other proposals have made Leonel Castillo an almost demonic figure inside the Border Patrol. Many agents believe that Castillo has entered into a conspiracy with radical Chicano leaders to "give everything up to the Mexicans." Aware that Castillo has political ambitions in Texas, many charge that his INS activities are simply a ploy for building a political base. Castillo, it is charged, wants amnesty for aliens and is weakening the Border Patrol so that Mexicans who come to Texas become citizens in short order, and vote for Castillo when he runs for governor. Castillo, they think, is trying to import a political base. Most Anglo Border Patrolmen are entirely unaware that their Commissioner, though Mexican-American, has come under fire in his own community for measures taken to build up the Border Patrol's numerical strength.

Chicanos in the Border Patrol do not say so in the company of their Anglo co-workers, but most of them are pleased by Castillo's reforms, for they see in them a chance for rapid job advancement. To a lesser extent, they also see an opportunity to humanize the agency. Several Chicano agents have been suspended for brutality, and like Anglos, they harbor no love for *sin papeles*. Most favor stronger enforcement measures, for example, a law allowing the Border Patrol to confiscate vehicles used by alien smugglers. By and large, Chicano agents do not believe that Castillo has weakened the Border Patrol, although they do believe he has countered its racism.

While Chicanos and Anglos in the agency are divided in their opinions about Castillo, they share a common view about immigration restrictions. Virtually all believe it is impossible to seal off the border, for two reasons. First, the Border Patrol cannot cope with what is called "massing." Along the border west of El Paso, *sin papeles* often gather into groups of 40 to 60 and cross the desert *en masse*, sometimes in broad view of Border Patrol agents. In these cases, the agents order the group to halt, but it usually does not. Therefore, Border Patrolmen each chase down and grab one or two *sin papeles;* one out of perhaps every five is caught, and the others run away. The Border Patrol cannot mass as many agents on the American side as *sin papeles* on the Mexican side, and therefore, no method short of total military occupation of the border will seal it shut. Further, as any Border Patrolman is quick to point out, the legalities of interrogation have opened a loophole through which any *sin papeles* can pass. Court rulings since 1970 have made it clear that Border Patrolmen have no right to require that citizens produce documentary evidence of their citizenship. This means that a Border Patrolman who detains a suspect until he proves his claim to citizenship may be sued in civil court under the doctrine of false imprisonment. In theory, any suspect who claims that he is a U. S. citizen may not be required to prove his statement true, and therefore, may not be held for interrogation, unless compelling reasons make his claim seem doubtful. In theory, the burden of proof has shifted from the suspect to the Border Patrol, and the Border Patrol cannot easily disprove citizenship claims, because to do so, it must produce documents—necessarily from a foreign country—showing that the suspect is a citizen of that country. It matters little that it is illegal to make false statements to Border Patrolmen because it is almost impossible to prove the falsity of citizenship claims without a simple confession. Most *sin papeles* are ignorant of the technicalities of American law, however, and therefore, do not hide their alien status. But Border Patrolmen believe that the naivete of *sin papeles* will disappear, and when it does, undocumented immigrants will make deportations difficult to effect.

Richard Brannick, president of the Border Patrol council of the AFGE, has repeatedly warned Congress that Border Patrol morale has soured. His statement is accurate, but more accurate in regard to supervisory personnel than ordinary officers. Higher-level Border Patrolmen and INS administrators tend to identify alien exclusion with patriotism, anti-subversive activity, and public service. Younger, newer, more practical Border Patrolmen view their jobs as games. Undocumented immigration is not slowing, nor can they ever entirely halt it, they know. Most believe that *sin papeles* have no choice but to emigrate, and most say, almost apologetically, "but it's our job to stop them." Most do not pay attention to the political dispute over immigration, for that would disturb the day-to-day nature of their approach. As one younger officer reported: "Nothing is really being done to stop immigration, and I don't really care. I'll still have my job no matter what, and I think it's too good a deal to ruin by worrying." Like most Americans, Border Patrolmen derive satisfaction from paychecks and social contacts on the job, not from analyzing their roles in the world or society at large.

CHAPTER 30

Life, Limb and Legality:
The Civil Liberties Issue

Mistreatment of immigrants predates the Old Testament. In Leviticus, Jehova tells Moses:

> And if a stranger sojourn with thee in your land, ye shall not vex him.
> But that stranger that dwelleth with you shall be unto you as one born among you, and thou shalt love him as thyself; for ye were once strangers in the land of Egypt.

Whether for economic or political reasons, most countries have treated immigrants as invaders. The Spanish crown expelled the Moors in the 15th century, Edward I ejected Jews from England in the 1200's and Louis XIV drove the Protestants from France in the 17th century. In many cases American policy has also fallen short of the principle of hospitality put forth in Leviticus. *Sin Papeles* have been chased, detained, and expelled in cursory style. Courts have traditionally refused to guarantee undocumented immigrants the same share of civil liberties and constitutional protections enjoyed by Americans facing detention or prosecution. Curtailment of legal rights for *sin papeles* has another consequence as well: sadists, swindlers and other anti-social elements know that *sin papeles* are safe prey. Newspapers on both sides of the border are replete with tales of abuse of these immigrants whom legal institutions rarely protect.

A particularly brutal case involving three peasants from the state of Chihuahua attracted wide attention recently in Mexico. Manuel Loya, Bernabe Mata and Eleazar Zavala crossed the border into Arizona on August 18, 1976 on their way to Elfrida, near Bisbee, to seek work. According to the story they told prosecutors, they had walked only a few miles across the desert when an armed Anglo jumped out of his pickup truck and ordered them into its camper.

Because the *sin papeles* believed their captor was an immigration agent, they did not resist. The Anglo drove them to a ranch house, picked up two younger men, and then headed for a secluded spot where he stopped the truck again. While the older Anglo held a shotgun on the trio, his two younger assistant ordered them to strip naked and bound them with ropes. The three *sin papeles* later told the Cochise county superior court that the Anglos carved slashes along their bodies with knives, and cut their hair down to the scalp. They allegedly also strung a noose around one peasant's head, threw a rope over a tree branch, and pretended to hang him. Then they reportedly burned the feet of the three captives with a poker from an open fire, and dragged them across the desert floor. After several hours of torture, the two assistants released the Mexicans one by one, firing on them with birdshot as they attempted to run. The wounded men limped some 10 miles back to the Mexican side of the border, where they checked into the hospital at Agua Prieta. Doctors there removed 125 shotgun pellets from one victim's back and 60 from another.

Following a bitter protest by the Mexican consulate, the Cochise county prosecutor's office investigated the case, and a county grand jury indicted a wealthy rancher and restaurateur, George W. Hanigan, along with his sons, Tom and Pat. The indictment against them contained fourteen counts of kidnapping, conspiracy, assault, and armed robbery; however, none of the three accused men was arrested.

The elder Hanigan died before the case was brought to trial, in September, 1977. During court proceedings, the three *sin papeles* stripped to the waist to show their scars. Medical records and photos of their wounds were also introduced as evidence. The two Hanigan sons did not take the stand, but defense attorneys called up testimony that both were elsewhere at the time the alleged assault took place. A doctor testified that at the hour of the reported beating Hanigan was in a hospital emergency room receiving stitches to a hand wound received earlier that day when a bull gorded him. After three weeks of testimony, an all-Anglo jury found the Hanigans innocent on all counts. With aid from the Mexican consul, however, the three *sin papeles* continued efforts to prosecute a civil suit against their alleged abusers.

Undocumented immigrants have more to fear than the occasional brutal sadist or theiving employer. The Immigration and Naturalization Service fields an entire network of inspectors, investigators, and Border Patrol officers, all charged with the task of apprehending, interrogating and expelling as many *sin papeles* as possible. In expediting their duties, the federal agents are rarely sensitive to civil liberties of individuals they catch. Sometimes they criminally overstep the bounds of duty in the process of apprehension.

Typical is an August, 1976 deportation involving Cornelio Balderas Loredo, an immigrant from central Mexico. When Balderas returned to Ciudad Valles in the state of San Luis Potos, he felt ill. The next day, still ill, Balderas Loredo went to the house of his godfather, Leopoldo Montes, who offered help and a bed. Asked to explain his condition, Cornelio related that he had been working in the United States for a year when he was caught by an immigration agent in Texas. The INS held him in custody for seven days, while apprehending more *sin papeles;* then all the deportees were loaded on a bus heading for the states of Nuevo Leon. Upon arriving in Monterey, the agents ordered the passengers off the bus. Because he was suffering pain, Balderas Loredo remained in his seat. His godfather claimed that the two guards then attacked him, beating his head and body with karate chops and kicks. Sometime later they put him off the bus.

Balderas Loredo's condition worsened while he told his story to his uncle. When he lost consciousness soon after,

Montes took the injured man to the a hospital in Ciudad Valles where he died without waking from his coma. An autopsy revealed that Cornelio had suffered multiple fractures, several ruptured organs, and a cerebral hemorrhage. The incident sparked protests in the Mexican press, but no investigation ensued.

Even in cases where abuse of undocumented immigrants comes to light in a courtroom, the victim has no practical access to fair procedure because he is usually deported before he can appeal. For example, a *sin papeles* who was beaten and shot during apprehension by the INS, some months later was indicted for assaulting an officer with a deadly weapon. Although he was acquitted of that charge, the jury found him guilty of a lesser charge of which he had never been formally accused.

According to news reports, in September, 1977, a smuggler named El Chaluperro brought Trinidad Gardea Valenzuela across the Rio Grande in a canoe and dropped him near the tiny town of Redford, 16 miles south of Presidio, Texas. He was sitting in a *coyote's* pickup, gun in hand, when Border Patrol Agent Phillip Hondurick spotted him. Gardea tried to escape by sprinting back toward the river—with his pistol in his belt, prosecution witnesses said Hondurick ordered him to stop; but Gardea keep moving. So Hondurick shot the fleeing man in the foot and knee "in self-defense." The agent caught Gardea at the river, knocked the much smaller man unconscious with the butt of his pistol, and dunked him several times. Still, it was Hondurick, not Gardea, who filed the assault charge.

At the trial Hondurick maintained that the defendent had turned and pointed a pistol during the chase. Gardea admitted having a gun, but insisted that he had kept it in his belt. Prosecution witnesses would not corroborate the Border Patrol agent's story. One agreed with Gardea that the gun was in his belt, while another claimed it was lying on the ground near the truck. In a statement even the press found confusing, the jury announced the defendant not guilty of assaulting a federal officer with a deadly weapon, but it did convict him of the "lesser included offense" of forcibly assaulting an officer—apparently referring to some action *other* than the alleged gun-pointing.

Since the only evidence of assault was Hondurick's word that Gardea had threatened him with a pistol, the jury's verdict baffled both the defendant, his lawyer, and courtroom observers. Judge Dorwin Suttle proceeded to sentence the defendant to a 3-year jail term and a $5000 fine—a stiff penalty—but later commuted it to 5 years' probation and deportation. Had Gardea been a U.S. citizen, he would have been able to appeal, but since he was deported, that became practically impossible without the aid of American authorities.

According to Dale Swancutt, chief of the El Paso Sector of the Border Patrol, it is standard procedure to charge undocumented immigrants with assault when they are injured by an agent. Swancutt told the *El Paso Times* that "Once it's established that the officer was assaulted, it affords the officer protection (from being sued). Most federal agencies will do that. Otherwise the agent would be naked."

In May of 1977 twenty INS agents surrounded the Haggar Slacks Factory in Edinburg, Texas, blocked the exits and prevented workers from leaving at the end of a shift. The immigration officers showed the manager a warrent issued to search for property—which turned out to be undocumented workers. Nine hundred factory workers of Latin American descent were held for over an hour at the factory while the agents interrogated them. Those who could not prove legal immigration status were escorted to their homes to produce identification. Fourteen women admitted that they were Mexican citizens, but claimed to be in the country legally; they were arrested and taken to the Border Patrol Station in McAllen,Texas for interrogation. According to reports by the *Edinburg Daily Review* and the *Brownsville Herald*, at the station, Patrolmen ordered the women to strip for a weapons search.

At 6 a.m. on June 6, 1974 Mario Rene Amado Perez awoke in his Los Angles, California apartment to find INS agents in his bedroom asking for documents. Since he had no papers, the agents whisked him off to headquarters, fingerprinted him and instructed him to sign a document. Amado Perez asked to see an attorney but the agents told him that he had no right to a lawyer and would not be released on bail unless he signed the document. Then they locked him in a small room with twelve other detainees, some of them small children. That evening the agents sent the undocumented immigrants by bus to Chula Vista, California, where they waited for several hours. When Amado Perez attempted to sleep on the floor, an agent allegedly kicked him in the side and told him not to sleep. At 5 a.m. the next morning, when the deportees arrived at a detention center in El Centro, Amado Perez asked to make a phone call, but the agents refused his request. They jailed him with over a hundred *sin papeles*, but only a few beds. In the morning he and the others crowded onto a patio where a single spigot in a urinal was the only source of drinking water. That afternoon Amado Perez was released on bail in El Centro. With only a few dollars in his pocket he was left to find his way back to Los Angeles, some 200 miles to the north.

The foregoing examples present instances in which brutality against *sin papeles* is alleged. More common are the mundane ways in which undocumented immigrants are abused by American citizens, especially employers. For example, in February 1978, Ronnie Earle, district attorney in Austin, Texas, reported plans to prosecute six cases in which undocumented workers had allegedly been cheated of several months' wages by employers. According to Earle, two construction firms in Travis county repeatedly hired undocumented workers, gave them food and lodging, and a promise that full wages would be paid later on. When the builders no longer needed the workers, they allegedly refused to pay them. Earle told the Austin *American-Statesman* that the six instances involved over a hundred hours of labor and almost $11,000 in wages. Earle filed suit against the employers under state labor laws—which provide a maxium penalty of $50.

The Constitution contains no language that excludes the foreign-born from its guaranteed liberties, whether they have entered with or without the proper documents. Theoretically, the protections against "unreasonable searches and seizures" in the 4th Amendment and against prosecution without "due process of law" in the 5th Amendment extend to non-citizens. These decrees limit the power of the government, not of individuals. They say what the government cannot do to individuals, drawing no distinction between citizens and non-citizens. Civil libertarians argue that if the founding fathers had intended to make the distinction, they would have done so clearly, by choosing to use the word "citizen" rather than "people" in the Bill of Rights. For example, Article II of the Constitution declares, "No person except a natural-born citizen, or a citizen of the United States, at the time of adoption of this constitution, shall be eligible for the office of President." But the 4th Amendment of the Constitution states, "The right of the *people* to be secure in their persons, houses, papers, and effects, against unreasonable searches and seizures, shall not be violated, and no warrants shall issue, but upon probable cause, supported by Oath or affirmation, and particularly describing the place to be searched, and the persons or things to be seized."

Federal immigration legislation, INS procedures, and Supreme Court rulings have resulted in limiting the civil liberties of undocumented immigrants. But some court decisions have upheld the rights of aliens to constitutional protections. In the 1889 Yick Wo ruling, the Supreme Court declared unconstitional a San Francisco ordinance discriminating against the laundries of aliens as violating the Fourteenth Ammendment. The court held that the provisions of the amendment prohibiting states from denying equal protection under the law "are universal in their applications to all persons within the territorial jurisdiction, without regard to differences of race, of color, or of nationality." But since the Yick Wo ruling the courts have fallen short of the principle of giving full constitutional protections to non-citizens.

In 1892, Congress passed the Chinese Exclusion Act, which among other provisions, required the expulsion of all Chinese laborers unable to prove lawful residence with the testimony of "at least one credible white witness." The law excluded Chinese immigrants from due process because it required the accused to prove his innocence or be deported, rather than assuming him innocent until proven guilty. In 1893, the Supreme Court ruled that the statute was constitutional. The majority of the court stated that the right of Congress to deport aliens was "absolute" and "unqualified" based on the "inherent power of soverignity. . . . in accordance with ancient power of the international law of nation-states." And because deportation is a civil procedure rather than a punishment for a crime, the court ruled that immigrants facing expulsion were not entitled to the civil liberties provisions of the Constitution: that is, the right to trial by jury, freedom from unreasonable search and seisure, and cruel and unusual punishments.

The ruling upholding the Chinese Exclusion Act was not unanimous; Justice Brewer in a dissenting opinion critcized the doctrine of the "inherent power of sovereignty" as ambiguous and dangerous. "Deportation is punishment," he wrote. "Everyone knows that to be forcibly taken from home, friends, and business, and property, and sent across the ocean to a distant land, is punishment; and that oftentimes most severe and cruel." Therefore, he argued, in deportation proceedings immigrants must be accorded due process of law and entitled to the guarantees of the Fourth, Fifth, Sixth and Eighth Ammendments.

In 1952, Congress passed the Immigration and Nationality Act (McCarren-Walter Act), which codified existing immigration laws and procedures and laid down some new rules. The law listed as grounds for deportation unlawful entry, commission of crimes, subversive political activity and overstaying the length of a visa. Immigrants suspected of violating any of those grounds could be arrested and held in custody at the discretion of the INS, pending a deportation hearing. The act empowered immigration agents to question, without warrant, any person "believed to be an alien as to his right to be in the United States," and to arrest any undocumented immigrant "likely to escape before a warrant can be obtained." It also stated that "for the purpose of patrolling the border to prevent the illegal entry into the United States of aliens," federal agents could search any vehicle within a "reasonable distance" and search any private lands within twenty-five miles of a national border.

The Immigration and Nationality Act of 1952 provides the statutory basis for the current power of the INS. Courts have allowed Congress wide discretion in dealing with deportation procedures, and that discretion has in turn been delegated to the INS. For instance: legislation provides that immigration agents may search any vehicle within "reasonable distance" of the border, and the agency has interpreted that to mean 100 miles.

The most efficient means of taking in large hauls of *sin papeles* is what the INS calls "area control operations." In these dragnet-like searches, agents sweep areas they believe to have a high concentration of undocumented immigrants, stopping and questioning suspects at random and taking in custody those without papers. Such raids concentrate on Latino neighborhoods, but stops, restaurants, factories, hotels, and other businesses that employ low-paid workers.

In conducting these sweeping operations, the INS claims the right to question any person who "looks like an alien," as to his right to be in the country. Agents construe the look of an alien to include having Latino features, wearing foreign clothing, speaking Spanish, speaking English with an accent or appearing to be "nervous." These flexible grounds for questioning individuals raise an interesting constitutional question. Although courts have tended to exclude immigrants facing deportation from 4th Amendment protections, they have not yet denied those same protections to citizens who may have the appearance of being foreign, and therefore the INS may not have grounds to question anyone without probable cause.

In 1975, the Supreme Court handed down a ruling which denied Border Patrol officers the right to stop cars near the border, solely because its occupants appeared to be of Mexican descent. But the court allowed officers to consider Mexican descent a relevant factor, so long as other factors caused "reasonable suspicion" about a suspect's citizenship. Given the elastic grounds for suspicion commonly cited by the INS, the 1975 ruling has done little to prevent agents from stopping Chicanos and other Latinos at random.

About 95 per cent of those undocumented immigrants who are apprehended choose to leave the country rather than face official deportation hearings. The INS prefers these "voluntary departures" because they save the agency the trouble of paperwork for an administrative hearing, and the cost of housing prisoners. But even well-informed immigrants often agree to leave voluntarily, because if caught in the U.S., after having been officially deported, immigrants face possible prison sentence.

Those immigrants who refuse to leave upon request are given deportation trials with considerably fewer protections than those available ordinary criminal hearings.

The 6th Amendment of the Constitution states:

> In criminal prosecutions, the accused shall enjoy the right to a speedy and public trial, by an impartial jury. . . . and to be informed of the nature and cause of the accusation; to be confronted with the witnesses against him; to have compulsory process for obtaining witnesses in his favor, and to have the assistance of counsel for his defence."

But the Supreme Court, in the Chinese Exclusion Case, ruled that deportation proceedings are not criminal, and, therefore, do not require that the accused be granted due process of law as defined in the Fourth, Fifth and Sixth Amendments. For this reason, deportees do not have the right to trial by jury; they are tried by an immigration officer, who combines the functions of judge, jury and prosecutor. Nor do deportation proceedings require that an attorney provide counsel for the accused. The Immigration and Nationality Act states that undocumented immigrants have the right to seek counsel, but the act requires that counsel shall not be provided at government expense. So, for those *sin papeles* who cannot afford to hire a lawyer, the court will not provide a public defender.

As it stands today, undocumented immigrants enjoy a very limited range of civil liberties, considerably inferior to those of citizens. The American Civil Liberties Union believes that the protections set down in the Constitution should embrace all persons within our borders, not just citizens. But clearly the Supreme Court has not shared that view. It has taken the position that Congress, because of its "sovereign powers" in matters relating to deportation, should determine what the range of liberties for *sin papeles* shall be. Congress, however, is a political agency.

Putting the status of undocumented immigrants in the political arena imperils civil liberties. The Bill of Rights lays down a clear set of protections for the individual which can only be changed by Constitutional amendment, a procedure demanding a two-thirds majority from Congress and ratification by two-thirds of the states. When the legislative branches of the state and federal governments pass laws in conflict with these constitutional protections, judicial review can strike down the legislation. But undocumented immigrants are subject to the caprices of changing political moods and the whims of politicians and administrators. Furthermore, Congressional intrusion into the realm of individual liberties obscures the protections of law. To understand his rights, a citizen has merely to read the Bill of Rights, a simple, coherent document. To understand his rights, an immigrant has to sift through whole volumes of INS regulations.

PART IV

Case
Histories

CHAPTER 31

The Pollero Game

Sin papeles are sometimes lured to the United States by black market labor contractors whom they call *"coyotes"*. The *coyotes* in most cases arrange for the delivery of workers to U.S. jobs through smugglers who are called *"polleros"*, or chicken-men. The *sin papeles* who cross are called *"pollos"*, or chickens. In translation, the chicken goes with the chicken man to the place the coyote has designated. The series of slang terms creates a picture of the victimization and exploitation which is often the lot of *sin papeles*.

Polleros are usually paid in advance, though some will accept what amounts to payment on delivery. Some are paid by relatives of *sin papeles* or employers in the U.S., and others take their fee from the *pollos* themselves. A typical agreement with a *pollero* is that payment will be made before a crossing, but that if the crossing fails, the *pollero* will continue attempts until a successful crossing and trip to the interior are completed. Small-time smugglers ordinarily collect from their clients themselves. Organized smuggling chains, however, have agents from the interior of the U.S. down into the interior of Mexico, and the man who actually brings *pollos* across the border is only a "mule," or transportation agent, paid by his own superiors.

Coyotes and *polleros* solicit openly in most Mexican border towns. If a *sin papeles* wants a job or a guided border crossing, he need only register in certain hotels, which everyone knows are pick-up places for *polleros*—or he may merely sit down in the public plazas where crossing agents solicit. In California, the smuggling business is highly organized, and lucrative. The going rate for a trip from Tijuana to Los Angeles, for example, is about $250. In Texas, where small-time smuggling is more predominant, the trip to *el norte* is cheaper. A Mexican may go from Laredo to San Antonio for $150 to $200, or from El Paso to Chicago for $200 to $300.

Polleros rarely show a concern for anything but cash. Some are careless and even brutal with their charges. Each year, the Border Patrol finds abandoned rental trucks whose cargo compartments are filled with *sin papeles* who smothered for lack of ventilation. There have been instances in which *polleros* raped and murdered their clients, and instances in which they blackmail them after settling them in the U.S. are not uncommon. Nevertheless, most *polleros* are interested in maintaining an honest reputation in the communities to which they deliver their clients. They are not humanitarians, nor are they sadists. Like Tim Sanchez, most are simply quick-buck artists.

On Friday nights, after Timoteo Sanchez gets off his job as a warehouseman in San Diego, California, he buys a bus ticket for Tijuana, Baja California, a border town infamous for its vices. Co-workers and friends who have known Tim for months believe that the 40-year-old family man goes there for a spree in the city's bars and flesh houses.

But Timoteo, a native-born American, goes to Tijuana to make money, not to spend it. He is a *coyote*, a professional smuggler of illegal aliens.

When Tim arrives in Tijuana, he goes to a Mexican motel, taking a room reserved for him in advance. While he sleeps, men he has never seen park a van with California plates outside his room, leaving the keys for Tim at the motel desk.

Tim spends the next morning and afternoon eating at out-of-the-way restaurants, talking to waiters, cab drivers, and street vendors. He browses through the city's handi-

craft shops, sometimes picking up items that friends at
home have asked him to buy. He doesn't take a drink all
day, and hasn't seen Tijuana's red light district since he
took the *coyote* job.

At 9:00 p.m. each Saturday, Tim heads the van north
towards San Diego. Before leaving the motel, he reviews
registration papers provided with the vehicle. Although he
does not use the same van each week, the name on its
ownership certificate is invariably the same, that of a Mexican-American used car dealer in Los Angeles. Attached to
the registration papers is a recent bill of sale, saying that
Tim has made a down payment on the van, and that re-
registration of the vehicle is pending. For all Tim knows,
the registration papers and bill of sale are authentic; someone may indeed have made payments in his name on the
vans he operates.

Those who drop off the van for Tim also leave with it a
walkie-talkie. Sanchez crosses the checkpoint at San
Ysidro on the California-Mexico border, just as any weekend tourist would. He then turns on the walkie-talkie, taking care not to move its channel setting.

On the highway to San Diego, about ten miles from the
border, a car waits at the side of the road for Tim's van to
come into sight. When it does, a voice comes over the
walkie-talkie, telling Tim to follow a car which will pull
out ahead of him on the highway. Tim's guide introduces
himself over the walkie-talkie by a nickname only.

The auto guiding Tim soon turns off onto rural highways, then begins a series of turns across desert backroads.
The vehicles move westward, towards Imperial Beach. After a drive of about 20 minutes, and within miles of the
Pacific beach, Tim is told to park his van and to walk
back south towards the border. Somewhere along the way,
over a stretch of two miles or so, Tim encounters a group
of men who are walking northward in the dark. They are
the *pollos*.

By a flashlight signal Tim identifies himself to the north-
bound party, which then joins him. Tim leads the men to
his van, and without speaking, motions for them to board
it. Once they are inside, and again trailing the lead car, he
drives north towards San Diego.

"The main purpose of the lead car is to keep a lookout

for the Border Patrol. When we get onto the highway, the car goes a mile or two up ahead of me. If the lead man sees anything, he tells me by walkie-talkie. When that happens, and it used to happen pretty often because roadblocks were legal then, I pull off the road and tell the *pollos* to get out," the *pollero* says.

Tim drives the San Diego road nervously, for twice before he has been caught. His first seizure came as he was reloading a group of charges he had forced out of the van earlier the same night.

"I had unloaded them, out there in the desert, nine of them. I told them to walk on up north, and to keep walking at a distance from the highway until they saw me driving by, giving the flashlight sign," Tim recalls.

"When I made connections with them about an hour later, only seven guys showed up. They said that the two who were missing had gotten scared and started back for the border. Anyway, I had just gotten them back inside the van, when along comes the Border Patrol from my rear, and I was caught. The lead man was looking for a patrol car which had gone north. I guess there must have been two patrol cars in the area," he says.

The seven *pollos* were taken away by the Border Patrol, and were deported back to Mexico within hours. Tim was released after an interrogation that lasted less than an hour.

"I told them that these seven guys were just hitchhiking. They checked my record, and it was clean, so they let me off. I guess I thought about quitting then, but I didn't. The whole operation is too easy to give up just like that," he comments.

But the following week, Tim was picked up again. This time, arrest led to a 60-day federal jail term and a fine of $1,000. Tim blames the arrest on the man who drove the guide or "lead" car that night.

"Everything that went wrong that night was his fault. After I got the van, I went up the road as usual, and the lead car took me out to the desert, just like routine. That night there were 13 *pollos*. Seven of them were the same ones that had been caught with me the week before. They had been deported, but made connections pretty fast.

"Anyway, I went down in the desert and met the *pollos*,

THE PALLERO GAME 213

just like normal. Then when we were walking back north, I noticed that the lead car was gone. I called the driver on my walkie-talkie, but no one answered. I would have stopped the whole show right there, except that these seven *pollos* who had been with me before were pretty irritated and wanted to go on ahead.

"So I tried to take them in without the lead car. I had only been back on the highway for a few miles when the Border Patrol came up on my rear, and put on their red lights. I believe the lead man tipped them that I would be coming," he charges.

Tim swears that he would have gotten even with his former lead man, but he never knew so much as the man's name. In fact, Tim has never seen the faces of any of his lead men.

"The whole thing is organized like the Mafia. I only know one of the guys on the top of the operation in Mexico, because I met him down there, back when I was younger and used to spend weekends in Tijuana. But other than him, I've never known anyone else who was involved."

On his release from jail, Tim again sought out his Tijuana contact. He was welcomed back into the smuggling chain, because he had not denounced his superior, had paid his own fine, and had not set up a *coyote* operation of his own.

"The guy down there likes me, because he says I'm loyal," Tim notes with pride.

In discussions with his Tijuana contact, Tim brought up his distrust of the "lead man."

"The boss told me that the Border Patrol had come down the road where our cars were parked, and had gone off chasing my lead man. They didn't catch him, so they doubled back on me."

Tim still does not believe the tale, and his smarting skepticism is silenced only by a stronger desire to stay in the *coyote* chain.

"What I think happened was that they caught my lead man. He ratted on me, so they let him go," Tim grumbles.

In a dozen trips since his release from jail, Tim hasn't heard the walkie-talkie voice of the lead man who he suspects betrayed him. His absence indicates that the

Tijuana-San Diego link may involve several teams of *coyotes*, all working in an operation whose size is larger than Tim's knowledge of it.

"I believe that I'm just one guy out of five or six who makes a run every weekend. But it's not my business to know," he stresses.

Tim says his job ends at a "cover house" in San Diego, where he parks the van. Once the *pollos* have gone into the cover house, Timoteo walks home.

"Whenever I get to the cover house, the lights are off. But that doesn't mean anything. I've been told not to go inside it, and I never have. For all I know, there are twenty *pollos* in there every time I get in with a haul of my own."

He denies knowing what happens to the *pollos* once he drops them off at the cover house. Someone else picks them up, perhaps for the trip to Los Angeles.

"In this business, the less you know, the better," he points out.

CHAPTER 32

Y———— ⬥ ———— ◆ ———— ⬥ ————Y

Crossing the Bridge

Undocumented aliens also cross at checkpoints and over international bridges, though doing so requires the cooperation of family members or professional smugglers from the American side of the border. Border Patrolmen frequently discover undocumented aliens under the hoods of cars, beneath seats, in trucks, and even strapped to underbodies. Inspection of trucks and camper vehicles often turns up human contraband; in one example, Border Patrolmen in Laredo, Texas, in 1974 unloaded 124 undocumented aliens from a camper which forded the river at a secluded spot downstream from the international bridge. In another instance, undocumented aliens were loaded into the mixing tank of a cement truck for their bridge crossing. As it came upon the bridge, the operator of the truck turned on the mixing apparatus, throwing his passengers about as it rotated, and at the same time, dispelling the suspicions of immigration agents.

Border Patrol literature is replete with examples of exotic crossings. Such stories make headlines, and keep the public interested in "the illegal invasion of our borders by Mexican immigrants." But tales about bizarre or lucrative smuggling schemes do not point to what is true, namely, that most successful *sin papeles* come to the U.S. through friendship and family chains.

215

Thousands of Mexican nationals each year escape the hazards of river-wading and desert crossings, and the fees *coyotes* collect, by simply coming across border checkpoints in the company of relatives or close friends who are American citizens.

The practice of checkpoint smuggling is simplest and most often carried out by Americans who are border town residents, because immigration guards do not usually interrogate drivers of vehicles with local license tags.

The temptation to wave a friend through a boundary checkpoint is one which all guards face, and most succumb to. Other local residents who have daily business of a legal nature in Mexico, or those who maintain families across the border, also get the pass-through treatment.

Often, border guards ask only one question of drivers with local plates: "Are all of you U.S. citizens?" A simple yes will do, and the whole carload, including illegals, moves on north without detection.

The cursory crossing-point interrogation sometimes runs as far as a request for birth certificates, but rarely goes deeper. The demand for birth papers is easily met: before bringing illegals into the United States, their smuggler borrows birth certificates from citizen-friends who are the same age as the Mexicans he plans to bring in.

Penalties for those who are caught can be severe, but most check-point crossings are conducted by citizens who are importing relatives. Immigration officers are usually lenient with family offenders, because they are not *coyotes.* Not infrequently, citizens caught with a cargo of Mexican relatives are simply reprimanded.

Understandably, Border Patrolmen think the problem of relative-smuggling is more than they can handle. Family loyalties are too deep-seated to be suppressed by force of law.

Frank Pais, a meat cutter in Garden City, Kansas, and a native-born citizen, last spring brought relatives of his Mexican-born wife into America without any papers, and at minimum risk.

"Last January, I wrote my brother-in-law, Alfredo, and told him that if he'd like to move up here, he'd have to go from his hometown, Ciudad Victoria, up to Acuña, a little town on the border. I told him to call me when he got there, and I'd arrange the rest."

Frank picked Acuña as a crossing point because he had been raised at Del Rio, Texas, just across the river, and still had a friend in the community.

His friend, Jesus "Chuy" Cantú, was to play the central role in the planned crossing.

Chuy, now 35, has lived in Del Rio all his life, with the exception of four years spent at a state-supported residence university at Lubbock. Conchis, his wife, was born in northern Mexico, and has never been naturalized. A daughter of *sin papeles*, she spent most of her childhood in Texas, and graduated from a secretarial college in San Antonio.

Through friendships in the community, Conchis, and in turn, Chuy, have come to know several checkpoint guards, as well as some of their informants in Mexico. Though in an excellent position to carry on a illegal crossing business, the couple had never contemplated a crossing until Frank called them with his request.

"Chuy and I never thought about doing it before, even though I have relatives in Acuña. My relatives there aren't rich, but they have small businesses they wouldn't want to give up. Chuy's family all comes from the American side, so before this, it was never necessary to cross anybody," Conchis explains.

One Friday night in March, Frank's phone rang in Garden City. Alfredo called to report that he and his wife, Angela, had reached the border with their two sons, age three and eighteen months. The family had checked into a cheap Acuña hotel after making the two-day bus trip from Victoria.

"I told Alfredo to hang on there until Chuy came to see him. He seemed too tired from the trip to care what happened," Frank recalls.

The beef plant worker then telephoned Chuy, to make arrangements. By prior agreement between the two friends, Frank was to drive Alfredo's family across the bridge in a car loaned to him by Chuy. But previous plans didn't work out.

Chuy had traded his car, which had local tags, for a pickup registered in San Antonio. Further, Frank's usual

40-hour workweek schedule had been altered late Friday by an order to work until noon on Saturday on an overtime basis—a change which meant he wouldn't have time to reach Del Rio before dawn Sunday, when bridge traffic is lightest.

After a lengthy and somewhat delicate long distance discussion, Chuy volunteered to bring the family across the bridge and to meet Frank in Del Rio early Sunday. After the two hung up, Chuy drove across the bridge, located Alfredo and explained the plans to him. The crossing was set for about sundown Saturday night.

Despite his offer to help, Chuy dreaded the task ahead of him. His own job as a state employee would be jeopardized if he were caught, and he did not look forward to betraying the trust of border guards who were his friends. Despite a sympathy for illegal aliens, his basic feelings were that the whole problem would be better handled by someone else.

Chuy's plan had been to go alone, and to bring Angela and the children first, pretending they were his own. But arrangements did not work out again; Conchis, who had gone on errands, telephoned to say she would not be back by sundown. Chuy had no babysitter for their children. He decided to take them along. After he had crossed the river and reached the hotel, a new problem cropped up. An informer for the Customs Service and other bridge-related agencies was standing across the street from the hotel entrance, next to an Acuña policeman. Chuy did not notice them until he, Angela, and her two children were leaving the building.

He decided that bluffing was the best course of action. He walked directly up to the policeman with Angela and her children trailing behind.

"Officer, I want you to send this man away. He was staring at me when I went into the hotel, and when I came out. I have business to do here, and if I'm under surveillance, I'd like to know why, here and now," he blurted.

A part of his strategy was also to give the informer and cop a chance to demand a bribe from him. But no payment was demanded. The policeman, apparently startled, complied with Chuy's request.

"We were just chatting here. We mean you no harm.

Take it easy, we're moving along," he told Chuy, as if their roles were reversed.

Confident that he had laid one possible threat aside, Chuy boarded Angela and her children into his pickup, and left—not for the bridge, but for a liquor store on the same route.

His ploy was to provide an obvious reason for crossing the border that afternoon: to buy a bottle of American-label whisky at bargain Mexican rates. After making the purchase, he resumed his trip in the direction of the bridge.

On the Mexican side of the international bridge is a toll stop. After paying, Chuy moved ahead, but gave Angela a warning.

"If anybody questions us, I'm going to say that you and the kids approached me in Acuña for a ride across the bridge. My story is that as far as I know, you are citizens. I never saw you before this, and was just giving you a ride."

Angela wasn't worried by the warning. Looking back on the event, she explains why.

" I didn't know then that being a wetback was such a serious thing. I didn't think they could do much to him or to us for trying to come across, so I guess I was pretty calm."

The entry guard recognized Chuy and merely waved him on. Chuy stopped, however, at the post of a second bridge functionary whose duty is collecting import taxes. He showed the man the fifth of whisky, so that a tax seal could be affixed to it. Chuy knew the customs collector, too.

"Hey, Chuy, who's that you got with you?" the guard queried.

"Man, that's my wife, don't you know?" Chuy joked.

"Well, I'll be doggoned. I didn't know you had *four* kids," the customs inspector retorted.

"Well, you know sometimes I work weekends and my wife gets a little help from a few other guys," Chuy jibed.

The customs inspector saw the humor in Chuy's responses, and shrugged the whole thing off. He apparently didn't believe that Chuy would engage in smuggling.

By the time he had reached home, however, Chuy was

worried. His strategy had been altogether too bold, he decided, and could easily have raised a net which would snare him later that night, when he returned for Alfredo.

After showing Angela the house, Chuy began drinking the whisky he had brought. His wife came in shortly, much displeased by what she found.

Chuy's response was to leave the house for that of a friend, Gerardo. The two had been close since childhood; certainly Gerardo would aid and comfort him, Chuy believed.

The two men set the bottle of whisky between them, and in short order consumed what Chuy had not downed at home. Then they began draining Gerardo's stock of beer. It didn't take long for both to pass the limits of safety and reason.

Gerardo volunteered to make the crossing with Chuy. They loaded up into Chuy's pickup and weaved toward the bridge.

Since Angela had not brought over any of the family's belongings, the task had been left to her husband. Alfredo, for his part, had made matters worse by buying a grand felt painting of Pancho Villa, folk hero of the Mexican Revolution. Alfredo intended it as a gift for Frank. When Chuy caught sight of the huge canvas, he was enraged.

"Pancho Villa's dead anyway. Why the hell did you have to waste your money on such a damn thing?" he growled, forgetting in his near-stupor that a paper poster of Villa hung in his own living room.

Gerardo, no less pleased, was at least more thoughtful. The family's three suitcases were what frightened him.

"There's no way we can take all that across. There's no room in the front of the pickup, and if we put it in back, the guards will see it. Now, how are they going to believe that we were just carousing in Boys' Town if we're carrying suitcases? They're sharp enough to know a wetback when they run onto one," he explained.

Alfredo was irritated: couldn't the two Del Rio men go back and bring a car? The bags could be stashed in its trunk, he pleaded.

Neither of the two citizens had any desire to make extra trips across the border.

"In the condition we're in?" Chuy queried, putting an

end to the dispute. The three men left the baggage in Alfredo's room and went back to the pickup. Chuy wrestled the pickup down Acuña's backstreets, stopping three times to take Alfredo and Gerardo into neighborhood bars. Both his companions refused anything stronger than beer, but Chuy kept pouring whisky down. He could barely walk by the time he conceded that crossing-time had come. It was after midnight.

By then, guards at the bridge had changed shifts. As Chuy was driving across the bridge, nearly past the international marker at its mid-point, he realized that he didn't know who would be on duty when they pulled up at the guard station.

"Now look, if the guards ask questions, I'll do the answering. If they get technical, Gerardo and I don't know you. We picked you up by the toll station on the Mexican side. From then on, you'll have to answer for yourself," he told Alfredo, a little sobered by the danger in front of him.

Alfredo was stunned by the warning. He didn't know enough English to answer any questions which might come to him and felt sure Chuy's unstable driving would draw attention.

They were stopped by the immigration guard. Chuy didn't know him. "Are all of you citizens?" he asked, poking his head slightly into the pickup cab on Chuy's side.

Alfredo was mute. Gerardo answered: "Say, Willie, you know me don't you? Man, we've just been having a few drinks over there, you know. We'll get home all right."

The guard stared stiffly in the darkness, and recognizing Gerardo, drew his head back. "You boys be careful," he admonished, waving them on.

Shortly, Alfredo was sitting with Angela on the couch in Chuy's living room. Conchis, who had already gone to bed, rose and joined the newly-arrived family. Chuy drifted off to the bedroom and passed out, while Gerardo, who had not returned home, sat down on the front porch of the small house to compose himself. Before long, a pot of coffee was brewing in a kitchen percolator.

Frank and his wife, Alma, weren't long in arriving. Alfredo explained the problems he had encountered with his baggage and convinced the Kansas couple to try and retrieve it.

Alfredo called the hotel's desk clerk, to explain that relatives of his would be coming for the bags.

Using the address Alfredo provided for them, Frank and Alma crossed into Acuña in their Datsun. After startling the night clerk, they got the key to Alfredo's room and took out his belongings. But the clerk followed after them as they returned down the hall into the lobby.

Frank trembled.

"I was afraid that he had already called the bridge or the cops. The guy probably thought that there was heroin in those bags, and that we were smugglers."

Border towns are notorious for smuggling operations of all sorts, and also for informers. They are cities in which all too many people go out of their way for the dollar.

Frank pulled a five dollar bill from his wallet, and paid the night clerk off. He said nothing to him, knowing that his language was an international one, especially at the border. The night clerk silently fell back as the pair left the hotel.

But outside, right in front of their Datsun, a Mexican policeman had stationed himself. By now Frank was oiled-up for the inevitable.

"Another damn bribe," he whispered to Alma, taking two dollars more out of his wallet. This was given to the policeman, who tipped his hat and went off.

It was still possible, of course, that either the cop or the night clerk would call the bridge. Prices paid for information on heroin hauls are alluring.

Frank and Alma had hidden everything in the trunk of their auto. Rather than going straight to the bridge, they found an all-night café. Not wanting to pass up the moment, they both ordered Mexican delicacies.

"What a shame to see Mexico and have only a half an hour to do it," Frank complained as he began his meal.

Afterwards, they drove directly to the bridge. On the American side, they were questioned, because their car had out-of-town license plates.

Frank showed his driver's license, and Alma, her "green card" of legal residency. The couple said they had passed the day in Acuña and were now on their way home. Frank pointed to the huge Villa portrait in the car's back seat, his only purchase in Mexico, he said. The guard accepted their story, and let the two go on without further inspection.

Had he opened the trunk, the couple would probably have been in for a hard interrogation: there were children's clothes in the luggage, and they had no children with them. As they would later find out, all of Alfredo's Mexican identification papers were also inside.

Alfredo's first move when the pair arrived at the house was to review his baggage. It had been tampered with, he concluded. His papers had been shuffled, and one of them was found outside the small leather case in which he stored them. Very little of value had been in the bags, and nothing had been taken.

Frank and Petra assumed that the night clerk had riffled through the bags with the idea that he would find heroin. The policeman had probably been informed that something was in the air, and was waiting to see if indeed a smuggler had been trapped. Frank's bribes had probably sealed the couple in safety.

But the venture was not concluded yet. Frank and Alma had to get their charges back to Garden City, and the trip was not without potential hazards.

Frank shook Chuy back into consciousness to seek his advice.

The best road, which goes through San Antonio, would not do for the return, Chuy insisted. Border Patrol roadblocks were often set up along highways from the border into San Antonio, and one could not be sure which avenue was safe on any particular night.

In fact, all major highways in the region were heavily patrolled. One might miss a roadblock, but have a blowout: Highway Patrolmen in South Texas cooperate with the Border Patrol, and are inquisitive. Aid from them could bring tragedy.

After reviewing a map, the two men decided on a route leading across a block of territory which is perhaps the most sparsely populated in Texas. The 90-mile strip from Comstock, about 20 miles west of Del Rio, to Ozona, includes only one town, Juno, whose population is less than 30.

Frank offered Chuy the portrait of Villa; after all, it could not fit into the Datsun, which would be crowded with passengers. Chuy didn't want to accept it, and his reluctance was strengthened by liquor, the effects of which were still with him.

Conchis interceded, convinced Chuy to take the gift, and helped send off the whole party of *sin papeles* and their relatives.

"I don't really want the picture, because I didn't do this for reward," Chuy continued at the door of the Datsun. "But just do me one favor, please. Don't ask me to do it again."

The return trip was entirely uneventful. The Datsun's dawn passage through unfenced South Texas was interrupted only by herds of sheep and several deer who felt the highway was theirs, too. About sunup, the Datsun came into Lubbock, the point above which Border Patrol highway checks are nearly unknown.

It was about noon Monday before Frank pulled his car, emptied of its passengers, up to the beef packing plant at Garden City. His apologies at work were accepted, and he was told to come back on the job the next day.

CHAPTER 33

———◆◆——————◆◆———

River Jumpers

Whether in the California desert or Texas brushland, border jumping is only the beginning of peril. Undocumented immigrants frequently walk by night to cities where they believe they can find work. The journey can take a week or more. Food supplies are scarce along the way, and always, there is the danger of detection. The following is the true story of a pair of undocumented immigrants who made their way from the interior of Mexico to San Antonio, Texas.

It was nightfall and nearly June on the border. Ricardo paused before he slipped down into the river. He was worried that it wasn't dark enough to cross yet, that the Border Patrol plane might be somewhere on the edge of sight, that *La Migra's* green vans might be starting up on the American side. Pelón, whose daily job was outwitting the *gringos*, tapped Ricardo on the shoulder, urging him on. Ricardo looked back at Alberto, his comrade for the passage north. Alberto was ready to go.

From the first Alberto, 26, and four years senior to Ricardo, had shown no doubts. Less than 24 hours before, the two had been sharing a single bottle of beer in Rosita, mourning again the downturn in work at the mines, and in their own fortunes. There wasn't any food in Ricardo's house, not even an egg, and his sister and her kids had no

225

one else to turn to. Alberto, married and with two boys, had somehow always managed to buy rounds of beer, but last night, had spent his final pocket change.

Mario, Adolfo, Adán and Paco had come by the bar on their way to the train station, plastic bags stuffed with bread slung over the shoulders.

"Come on, go with us to Texas. I'll pay your way to the border," Adolfo offered.

Alberto in an instant rose to take the challenge, without consulting Ricardo. Ricardo could only follow. There was nothing in Rosita, and no jobs in Monterey, either; the last devaluation had cut low on demand for smelter products, and in turn, on the market for Rosita's coal. So Ricardo stood up, too. He trailed the others out to the train station, without so much as sending word to his sister. Her nerves were afflicted, and if she knew he was leaving, she'd only upset herself still more.

The six Mexicans were in Piedras Negras, on the border, before midnight. They slept in the train terminal. At sunup, they headed out over caliche footpaths to Pelón's shack on the edge of town and some 100 meters from the Rio Grande. Pelón agreed to "jump them," as it is said in Spanish, for 50 pesos each, half a day's wage in the mines.

"And if we don't have fifty pesos or even a *tostón*," Alberto demanded. "Are we still your countrymen, or are we animals?"

Pelón, who knew for himself what it means to be Mexican, agreed to "jump" the pair on credit.

"You pay me next time around," he cautioned.

But he insisted on giving the safest route across the river to the four paying customers.

"You guys go without money, so you take the biggest risks. If I were to jump everybody where it's best, *La Migra* might get you all."

Ricardo yanked off his sweaty shirt, his caliche-caked jeans, and his shoes, which had holes cut where his toes stuck out. He hoisted the cotton bundle to his shoulder, where it brushed against the baseball cap with upturned brim that he wore on his head. His hand grazed his cheek as he raised the wadded clothing into place, and he realized that he hadn't shaved before leaving Rosita, and wouldn't shave for days in the future. Alberto also began stripping down. Once naked, both men eased down the gritty bank one arm up on their bundle of clothing, the other outstretched for balance. Alberto splashed down just seconds after Ricardo's feet touched bottom.

The water was waist deep, and lukewarm. Along the river floor, Ricardo's feet moved on smooth rocks, large ones like shale, and smaller, rounded ones, maybe brought down from the Rio Grande's source a thousand miles upstream. Ricardo began wading out, feeling his way one foot at a time.

"Watch out, go a little to the left when you feel a slope," Pelón warned from the Mexican bank.

Ricardo sensed the drop-off and moved to the left about five meters. Then he moved out again, Alberto behind. Two steps later, the river bottom fell off, and sandy water swept around Ricardo's chest. The current gained force, nudging him downstream. Ricardo squeezed harder on the dry bundle next to his head, and kept moving.

"Get past that dip and you've got it made," Pelón's faint voice called out.

It was dark now, and Ricardo couldn't guess where Pelón was standing. Was he walking away, abandoning them to the river? Ricardo didn't turn his head; the current was so forceful now that any needless motion could tip his balance, delivering him to the downstream drag.

His sense of time slipped away, and so too, did his immediate love for Alberto, who hadn't spoken. Perhaps his *cuate* had fallen off in a hole and been carried away. Ricardo couldn't care. His only purpose now was getting past the current without drowning. Sixty men had died while crossing the river in this area the year before, the papers said. Ricardo didn't want to be next.

Maybe it was seconds later, maybe it was as long as ten minutes, Ricardo didn't know, but he reached the American bank and nearly kneeled as the moonlight struck the brass crucifix on his chest. Alberto came sloshing up behind him, whispering his own prayer as he lay out on firm ground. Both men broke silence to swear that they'd been lucky. In a minute, they were dressed again. Their dusty clothes stuck to their dripping bodies.

There were no headlights along the rutted road about 15 meters in front of them, which Immigration agents ride on river patrols. Both aliens had been told that *La Migra*'s men come with rifles for shooting rabbits along the route. Both had also heard reports from Mexicans who had dodged bullets along the road, like rabbits. The two immigrants crossed over the road and went into the brushland behind. Then they headed westward, ducking mesquite branches and trampling huisache underfoot. Thirty minutes ahead, Pelón had told them, they would run into an irrigation canal. They were to follow it until it came to a paved road, then they were to cross the road. After that, they would spot a series of radio towers with red lights to the northeast. They were to follow the lights to San Antonio, a walk about six nights long. They chose San Antonio, because Ricardo recalled an address on King William Street where a cousin of his lived.

If they tired along the back country trek, Pelón had told them, they should lie down underneath a ranch house lampost, or in a tree, up off the ground; otherwise, snakes might get them. If they were thirsty, they were to seek out one of the natural springs which pock-mark the desertland. If hunger made them dizzy, they were to strip the skin off cactus plants and eat the moist and meaty, but sometimes bitter, leaves. If they were in danger, they were to beg aid from ranch hands, who were mainly Mexicans without papers, anyway. But Pelón warned them not to stay more than a few minutes with anyone who did not offer on-the-spot jobs. Ranch hands, with and without immigration papers, had been known to win small favors from *La Migra* for turning in members of their own race.

The two Rosita miners, now chilled by the desert night, kept on walking past a half-dozen radio towers. As they approached the second one, they sighted the silhouettes of four other men, but they did not cry out; Pelón had told them that the Border Patrol sometimes disguises its own agents as Mexicans, to make arrests under the cover of friendship. Instead, Ricardo and Alberto angled off from the towers, always walking northward, but now, with the lights to the west, not straight ahead. They stumbled and cursed, they sat down, they asked the skies for guidance, they dozed off in the dust. Then they awoke, and moved on again. Three nights later, nearly sick from bad water and numbed by noon sun and midnight chills, they gave up at the first ranch house they reached.

"So you boys just can't make it any further," the *gringo* householder chuckled, speaking in Spanish.

He invited them to his kitchen, then went towards the phone. Ricardo's eyes flashed over at Alberto, who was nodding, already asleep. Ricardo slapped his fingers together with a whipping motion of his wrist; then he looked straight down.

"Don't you worry about *La Migra*," the rancher volunteered, "I'm finding you a job."

Ricardo glared up, his hostility unconcealed. How did he know *gringos* could be trusted? The rancher talked English to the telephone, then went off into another part of the house.

Before fifteen minutes had passed, someone knocked at the kitchen door. The rancher appeared and let the caller in, another *gringo* about 50 years old. Ricardo shook Alberto, and slapped him lightly across the cheek. Dazed but not dumb, Alberto accepted the *gringo's* offer: $5 a day for picking melons for a week. The harvest would provide them with money to get them into San Antonio, Alberto whispered to his companion. Terms agreed, the *gringo* drove them off in his pickup, and the two coal miners slept deeply in bunkhouse cots that night. At daybreak they began loading melon crates.

When Sunday came, a Chicano who had also worked the melon crop gave the two immigrants a ride to the fringes of San Antonio. But he would not take them to King William Street. Dealing with undocumented aliens was becoming a dangerous affair, he explained. Ordinary citizens and *coyotes*, professional smugglers of aliens, had been sentenced to 18-month terms for aiding men like Ricardo and Alberto, and San Antonio was crawling with *La Migra*. The Chicano wasn't about to go to jail for anybody, *paisano*, *raza* or whatever, because he, too, had a family to feed.

The Chicano dropped them off on the driveway of a service station. The attendant, also Chicano, showed the immigrants a map. "King William," the name squeaked foreign sounds no matter who said it, Ricardo thought. The attendant was muttering "King William" and moving his finger across the map when a light green car with dark green spots on the doors showed up. Two green-uniformed *gringos* leaped out and scrambled into the garage, where they cornered a mechanic on his way out.

"Are you Cornelio Jimenez? Do you have any papers?" they asked in polite Spanish. The attendant whispered *pericos*—parrots—and pointed Ricardo and Alberto towards a side door of the station's office. They husted out and got down the street.

"*Pericos, pericos!*—So that's what they call the Immigration," Ricardo exclaimed.

A few minutes later the two immigrants hired a cab, and paid nearly half the week's melon earnings to get to King William Street.

The house on King William didn't look like anyplace where Ricardo's cousin, Pablo, could possibly live. It was two stories high, and brick, and if Pablo owned the house, he would have planted the vast front yard in corn, Ricardo joked. But darkness was coming, and they had no place to sleep. Ricardo strode up to the canopied porch and pressed the doorbell, trembling but bold. A white lady answered, talking textbook Spanish. She took the miners around to a garage apartment in the back, where they found Pablo.

The next morning Pablo drove them down to a sausage processing plant in an adjacent neighborhood. The foreman said there was a job open, but only for one worker. Ricardo stared at Alberto and Alberto stared back. Neither man spoke for a moment, because dividing a friendship hurts, much more so when there are spoils involved.

"Look, *cuate*, it's you who's got the cousin in this damn country. Let me have the job," Alberto grumbled.

Ricardo crossed one hand over the other and looked down at his fists. Then he deferred. It's better to have a cousin here than to have nothing, he thought. The foreman promised Alberto $7 a day, plus a bed in a house trailer down the street.

Ten days later, when the letter came, Ricardo was still unemployed. The letter, from Pablo's father, said that Ricardo's sister was nearly hysterical, beyond advice and control. The newspapers said that six men had drowned in the Rio Grande the night after Ricardo and the others had

left Rosita. People in the neighborhood were afraid their
sons had been lost, and Ricardo's sister was certain that he
was dead. In the letter Pablo's father said that he had been
asked to go to Piedras Negras to identify the bodies, but
had not gone, since the family had no money to pay expenses. If Pablo had not seen Ricardo, he should send
money to the family to help with burial expenses, the letter said.

Pablo read Ricardo the letter, then touched his slumped
cousin on the shoulder.

"Go on, go on back home to comfort your sister. Then
come back again. This time I'll send you money to hire a
pollero with a car and everything. You won't have to wait
more than two weeks, I promise."

Ricardo squinted up at his cousin. He doubted that Pablo would send the money, as he promised. Going back to
Rosita would probably mean another trek through the
back country, maybe alone, maybe without bread again.
Besides, going back was only half the problem. There was
also the going home, defeated, with nothing to his name.
People do come home from *el norte* but not ashamed. The
man who leaves his family behind is called *pocho*, and
only new prosperity silences the disrespect and gossip.

"Look, Ricardo, I know you don't want to go home
empty-handed. People in Rosita believe that everything is
easy here, but that's not true. The only thing that's easy
here is a free ride home. *Gringolandia* gives you that, and
you might as well take it," Pablo continued.

The next morning, Ricardo, still in his cut-out shoes,
walked down to the busiest street he could find. He stood
on a curb for about twenty minutes, until he sighted a
light green car with dark green spots on the door, a car
with a *"perico"* at the wheel.

"Wetback! Wetback! Wetback!" he hollered, flailing his
arms like a man stung by bees. "Wetback!"—that and
"King William" were the only words he'd learned in English. The *perico* saw Ricardo's waving arms and pulled
over to the curb. Calmly he got out of the car, its motor
still running.

"You got any papers, wetback?"

The next morning, Ricardo was on a Border Patrol bus
for the border.

CHAPTER 34

Visa Jumper

Jaime Marenco, 21, who has been in California for about two years, is a native of El Salvador—one of five tiny Central American nations whose surplus workforce has joined the northward immigration stream.

Jaime is a visa jumper, like most Central Americans who are in America illegally. He entered the United States on a tourist visa with a 30-day expiration date; he simply overstayed his time. Since no method of checking on the whereabouts of foreign tourists is in force, Jaime is not sure that Immigration authorities even know that he is in the United States now.

"For all they know, I came here and then got run over by a streetcar. I haven't reported myself since the day I came in."

His entry into the United States followed the marriage of his sister Magda to an American citizen who was vacationing in San Salvador.

"Magda got married and came to the United States in early 1974. A few months after she got here, she sent me a two-way-plane ticket to San Francisco," Jaime says.

The Salvadorean youth did not want to leave his homeland. After two years of unemployment, he had landed a five-dollar-a-day job as a ship maintainance worker, a job which kept him at sea about half the time, but let him go home at least twice a month.

"The only way Magda got me to come to America was that she sent me a picture of this *gringa*, who she said would marry me so I could get American papers."

Like thousands of other Salvadoreans, Jaime wanted "American papers" to make himself a small businessman.

"Import taxes at home are about 100% on most things. A person can fly to the United States, buy a few suitcases full of costume jewelry, and fly back home. If you can get the goods you've bought past our customs agents, they'll sell for three and four times what they cost here."

There is another commercial benefit to legal access to the United States. Salvadoreans buy used autos in the United States, drive them back to Central America, then resell them at inflated prices. The business is fairly good, because import taxes on used vehicles are lighter than on new ones and can also be evaded through bribery. Like jewelry running, the auto importer profits most who has friends in the Salvadorean customs service.

Jaime came to America believing he would be back home within weeks.

"The story about having someone ready to marry me was just cooked up to get me here. The girl whose picture Magda sent me was already married. Magda just wanted to have some family here."

Once in the United States and aware of the deception, the youth faced a decision: should he stay or go back? He was undecided at first.

"I had never seen America before, and actually, I didn't like it that much. I had a girl back at home, and I knew I'd lose her if I stayed here."

Jaime stayed anyway. The urgings of his sister for family companionship prevailed. He cashed in his return plane ticket, and began to ask around the neighborhood— San Francisco's lower Mission District—for a job.

Jaime's first problem, getting a Social Security card, was easily resolved. On a business street in the Mission District there was a vendor who made facsimile Social Security cards of metal, presumably for genuine clients whose paper cards were lost or damaged.

Jaime presented himself to the vendor, handed the man

$2.00, and a slip of paper on which his name and a false Social Security number were written. Two minutes later he had a piece of identification which had an official appearance.

But a job still didn't come. For two months Jaime followed every lead he could get, and always came back empty-handed.

His brother-in-law, Leon, decided to take Jaime to the ranching area near the Nevada-California border where he had grown up.

There Jaime had no difficulty finding ranch work. Dozens of cattlemen needed cowboys, with or without experience, and Jaime was dropped off at the first place where Leon made inquiry. The wage agreement Leon made for Jaime, however, left much to be desired: $60.00 weekly plus a line camp shack to live in.

Jaime's boss was an older cowboy who had worked with non-English speaking illegals before. In a matter of days, the two men made friends, and Jaime began picking up the English necessary to his job. Since Jaime was required to drive a pickup, often to another area of ranchland some 30 miles away, his employer took him into the nearest town, and, by cajoling a local official, secured a driver's license for his employee. Jaime now had two documents which supported any claim he might make to legality.

The young Salvadorean had never seen snow, nor had he seen ponds freeze over, as he did when winter came. He braced himself for the new climate, and put up with ranch loneliness as well.

Each Saturday, he went into town and bought groceries for the week, an expense which ran about $15.00. The rest he saved for himself, or mailed back to his family in San Salvador.

By the time winter passed, Jaime had saved $400.00, and was tired of the 72-hour work schedule he usually kept. He wrote Magda and Leon, begging to be taken back to the city. In early spring, about ten days after they read his plea, the couple came to the ranch to get him.

Jaime began looking for work in San Francisco again. This time he had better luck. A fried chicken chain needed a meat cutter to work in its central kitchen, which served fifteen Bay Area outlets. They hired him after a brief interview.

"Everybody who worked at the kitchen was Latin. The only thing was, they paid the ones who were legal the minimum wage. The illegals didn't get that much.

"As for me, I showed them my driver's license and Social Security, so they thought I was legal. I felt comfortable enough to put my $400.00 down as the first payment on my car," he says, gesturing to a well-worn five-year-old Ford.

Jaime says that the central kitchen facility where he worked was a two-story building whose design concealed a partial third story, where a crew of illegals slept when not working. The third floor, he explains, was not visible from the street.

"There were five guys there, all illegal. They worked maybe twelve to sixteen hours a day, and got paid five dollars a day, cash. The owner let them sleep upstairs, and eat whatever they wanted from the kitchen. I got to know one of them, who had been there for about two months. He said he was just putting up with the situation until he could save up enough to get out."

One afternoon, just before his shift ended, Immigration agents came into the company's downstairs offices. An employee of the office came hastily upstairs to warn workers there.

The five illegals—part of a work force of about 30—scrambled up a ladder that led to the attic, which was the passageway to their humble penthouse. Frightened, Jaime followed them up, knowing that the act would probably tip his employer to his real immigration status.

First and second floor employees were all questioned, to no effect. No illegals were found among them, and the search party went away.

The following day, Jaime and the five illegals were transferred to night shift work, because Immigration raids in interior regions are very seldom made at night.

"After all that happened, one of the illegals offered to let me sleep up on the third floor, on the cots with them. But I turned him down, because the company was still paying me the minimum wage. I figured if I moved in with the wetbacks the owner might really get wise and cut me to five dollars a day."

His illegal status soon cost him dearly, however.

"A couple of weeks later, after I was on night shift, I was pulling a box down from a shelf that was a little too high for me. The box fell, hitting me right in the face. It hit so hard that it broke one of my front teeth.

"So I went to the foreman. He told me that the company had insurance, but not for broken teeth."

"I explained the situation to Leon, my brother-in-law. He said the foreman had to be lying, but there was nothing we could do. So he loaned me $300.00—that's what it took to fix the tooth—and I went back to work."

Ironically, Jaime's return was rewarded. He was given a wage raise of ten cents hourly, and permitted to work overtime whenever he wished. Nothing was said about his Immigration status for another five months.

"Then one day they called me downstairs. They said Social Security had told them my number wasn't right. They told me to get my Social Security number straight or not come back."

He didn't go back. By now his English had progressed, and he had developed friendships in the Mission District's Latin community. A young Salvadorean girl whom he had begun dating told him about an opening where she worked, and Jaime went to apply, using the same Social Security number. He's working there today.

"The place where I work is an envelope plant. Nobody works there but "Oakies," Latins, and Filipinos. But it's not bad, because I'm making $3.26 an hour. Pretty soon I'll have my car paid off, and then maybe I can save to buy a truck. If I could take a truck back to El Salvador, I could make a living in the hauling business there."

Meanwhile, he is not worried about using a false Social Security number a second time.

"Well, by then I may be able to buy a good number from a guy I know who's going back to El Salvador. I'll just explain at the plant that I made a mistake. If that doesn't work, well, I'll just look for another job."

Leon and Magda have urged Jaime to marry the Salvadorean girl co-worker, who is apparently a legal resident. But Jaime is reluctant:

"In the first place, I don't like her all that much. I wouldn't want to marry her just for residency after she's been so good to me. And in the second place, she says she's a resident, but I'm not so sure of it. She's never said anything to me about getting married, and I'll bet it's because she has to find a citizen to marry for herself."

Conclusion

———×◦×‹‹◦›×◦×———

The legal abuse of *sin papeles* can be halted by administrative means. The economic and political issues presented by undocumented immigration, however, are not susceptible to simple solutions, and indeed, no solutions worthy of the name have yet been proposed by Congress.

The chief impact of undocumented immigration is economic, as the Linton study points out. *Sin papeles* compete with *inmigrantes* and citizens for lower-end jobs. They are especially pitted against blacks and Hispanics, because widespread employment discrimination has assigned these minorities to the least rewarding jobs in the labor market. Because they are easy prey for exploiters, *sin papeles* are sometimes hired in *preference* to legal resident and citizen job applicants. And in the long run, their presence depresses wage levels, because it enlarges the pool of workers who are disposed to accept nearly any employment under nearly any conditions.

The AFL-CIO's exclusionist stance derives from this observation. The *Wall Street Journal*, the voice of American finance, editorialized in June 1976 that "the easiest, cheapest and fairest way to protect the labor market will be to legalize the immigrants, putting the law to work protecting them rather than persecuting them." The *Journal*'s endorsement of amnesty fell on deaf ears among laborites, who know that any population increase, whether from immigration, birth or labor import programs, intensifies job competition. Whatever its source, unemployment threatens the wage levels of employed workers, and the AFL-CIO represents employed workers.

However, *sin papeles* are an unknown quantity in economic calculations. No close estimate of their numbers exists, nor is one likely to be available in the future. As long as there is no clear evidence that *sin papeles* have a significant effect on wage levels, the charge that immigrants lower pay scales is valid only in theory, and need not be accepted as a guide for practical politics.

Beyond accepting the charge, the AFL-CIO has actually promoted it, without any apparent necessity. The underlying fear of many of its workers, especially in agriculture, is that they will one day be denied wage increases by employers who say, "We can always hire *sin papeles* to replace you." Yet in the absence of statistical proof that *sin papeles* have flooded the job market, the threat they pose can easily be viewed as just that—a threat, and an empty one. Outside of the agricultural sector, American workers probably need not fear significant competition from immigrants, legal or otherwise, and might gain more by denying that anything threatens them, than by admitting that an uncounted and uncontrollable factor does. If the AFL-CIO challenges inflated estimates of the number of undocumented workers—as some unions outside the fold have done—there is no compelling reason to believe that the immigration controversy would continue. Instead of taking this course, however, top AFL-CIO leaders continue to endorse exclusionary legislation of little practical value.

The AFL-CIO has also spurned the option urged on it by independent unions and progressive scholars, to crusade for a shortened work week, with no subsequent reduction in workers' pay. If the work week were reduced to 30 hours, for example, while salaries remained constant, more than 20 million jobs would open up, because employers would be forced to expand their payrolls by more than 25 per cent. This demand, called "30 for 40" inside the labor movement, would end domestic unemployment entirely if it were granted, either by Congress or employers. And it would create room for importing foreign workers, either as *braceros* or immigrants. It is worth noting that during America's century of massive immigration, from 1820 to

1920, the workweek was trimmed from 72 to 48 hours in most industries, a decrease of more than a third.

Because they favor cheap labor policies and population growth, business and financial interests are essentially disposed to support liberal immigration policies. Much of commerce depends on population size, not prosperity, and therefore the food industry is especially inclined to favor ending immigration restrictions. Spokesmen for business and finance may prefer that undocumented immigration be tolerated, or legalized, or may suggest that a new *bracero* program be enacted but these are only variations on a unifying theme, namely that immigration is economically desirable. Immigration is a substitute for population growth, and whether it provides *braceros, sin papeles,* or *inmigrantes* as workers and consumers, it performs the same function. The business community is therefore opposed to exclusionism, and also to the alternatives available to labor. Naturally, industry opposes shortening the workweek, for profits would carry the burden of paid leisure and national full employment.

The economic interests which underlie both AFL-CIO and business proposals for immigration reform are obvious. What is not so obvious, however, is what inherent interest the Chicano movement has in the issue. The movement's very origin in strike activity attests to the generally working class character of the Hispanic community, and the oulook of its leadership. The short-run interests of many Chicanos as workers, especially in agriculture, may well lie in smothering job competition. But the long-run interests of the Chicano community as a political movement are those of the open borders movement. Politics, family ties, and ethnic loyalties mitigate against a purely immediate economic interest.

In 1970, the Census Bureau counted some 10 million persons of Spanish surname in the United States. In 1975, it estimated that the figure had risen to 11.2 million, but at the same time conceded that its samplings were inadequate, and the total could be higher. The Bureau also reported that the fertility rate among Latinos is about three times higher than that of the population as a whole. Demographers translate this finding into a prediction that by the year 2000, the Hispanic population will reach or surpass the 30 million level; some estimates predict it will

rise to 75 million. It is generally agreed that early in the
next century, Hispanics will surpass blacks as the nation's
largest minority, and it is possible as well that in Texas,
California, Arizona and New Mexico, Chicanos could out-
number Anglos as well as blacks. Demographic projections
promise the Chicano community clout in the politics of
the near future. That share grows larger if immigration
continues, and even more so if amnesties are granted to
sin papeles.

The immigration issue has created strange bedfellows
both inside and outside the Chicano movement. The "open
borders" policy of radicals in CASA differs little in basic
perspective from that taken by the editors of the *Wall
Street Journal*. The cautious exclusionism of the United
Farm Workers Union is but a step away from that of the
AFL-CIO leadership, whose position is open to support
from Ku Klux Klansmen: for different reasons, all three
parties want to limit the inflow of Mexicans to the United
States. The Carter plan, rather than siding with either the
open-borders or exclusionist camp, divides its measures between them, and is justifiably criticized for not providing
any principle for judging the issue. The plan is in effect an
unprincipled compromise, not a sound approach to the
problem.

It is perhaps fitting that disputants in the immigration
debate should lose themselves in a maze of paradoxical al-
liances, because the issue is essentially a misplaced one.
The salient fact, not to be found in "open border" vs.
"closed border" debates, is that undocumented immigration cannot be halted by any measures the government
is likely to take. Only total military occupation of the
southern border can stop it, and that would be expensive,
domestically unpopular, and diplomatically suicidal. Immigration can also be halted by terror—that is the point the
Klan wished to make—but as the history of the Klan's
"border watch" showed, Chicano groups will not tolerate
unofficial terror along the border, and the government is
not likely to adopt cross-burning as a model policy or
practice.

Both Border Patrolmen and *sin papeles* insist that the
border cannot be sealed. Immigration, legal or otherwise,
will continue so long as the Mexican economy is troubled,
and economists say that no relief is in sight. Crackdown

measures are essentially unenforceable, and if enacted, will most probably increase wage competition by further exposing *sin papeles* to exploitation and Chicanos to discrimination. In this context, it is clear that indeed, "illegal aliens have emerged as a favorite whipping boy," as the *Wall Street Journal* says. Politicians have used *sin papeles* as scapegoats, without providing any noticeable solutions to the problems of unemployment and discrimination. Such scapegoating has already led to near-hysteria over immigration and Hispanic presence in general.

Popular wisdom says that Americans are, above all, practical. If that is indeed the case, we might begin looking for a solution to the problem of immigration with the only fact available: that it cannot be halted. Since it cannot, the future of the Southwest is the future already predicted by demographers. By the year 2000, the region will be one in which Hispanics command political hegemony, if not an absolute majority at the polls.

Already the consequences of this future have been foreseen. In November, 1975, the Mexican newspaper *Excelsior* made public a secret report sent by historian Arthur F. Corwin to then Secretary of State Henry Kissinger. In the report, Corwin pointed out that "half of Texas can be converted within two generations into a Chicano Quebec," under a politically separate system. Constitutional lawyers believe that Texas, which came into the United States as an independent republic, might have secession rights. Whether or not Texas or any other Southwestern state would actually consider secession is doubtful. But the notion is already popular in the Chicano movement, which has given the name Atzlán to the entity Corwin predicted.

As unlikely as Atzlán is, the idea's attractiveness to activists and intellectuals is indicative of a serious problem. Quebec, though it remains within the structure of the Canadian national government, is nevertheless a reminder that all is not well to the north of our border. Quebec's French-speaking majority is restless because it believes that it has suffered discrimination at the hands of officialdom and business interests, and it has showed its discontent more than once at the polls. It is not unreasonable that in this sense, the Southwest might become an American Quebec.

"Ethnic integrity," is the phrase spoken by candidate

Carter and Klansman David Duke alike. It describes the uneasiness of American Anglos over Latinization of the Southwest. It summarizes the reasons why the AFL-CIO, instead of urging alternatives to exclusion, has embarked on a futile campaign to half immigration. "Ethnic integrity," the defensiveness of a predominantly Anglo nation also describes the fears which send voters to the polls to elect politicians who speak in the name of state and federal Rodino bills. "Ethnic integrity" is a daily fact of life in the Southwest, where Anglos and Latins live on opposite sides of town, and usually, attend different schools. It is the reason why, in the Southwest, bilingualism is punished as often as it is rewarded: bilingual Anglos earn more than monolingual Anglos in comparative jobs, but bilingual Chicanos usually earn less. Spanish spoken with an English accent is somewhat prestigious while English spoken with a Spanish accent is not. In sum, "ethnic integrity" does not mean what the words say at all. It means "Anglo dominance," and Anglo dominance defies the inevitable facts of immigration and birth rate differentials. Anglo dominance is already doomed in demographic projections. If it is not sent to an early grave, the Southwest may face ethnic strife in the future.

When the Pilgrims came to Plymouth Rock, the Spanish already lived in the Southwest, and across the whole southern two-thirds of the continent. Like their Protestant counterparts, the Spanish subjugated the native population. Unlike the conquerors of the northern hemisphere, however, the Spanish also intermarried and imparted their culture to the natives. The result, in Mexican territory and to the south, was the creation of a new man, the *mestizo*. Despite regional differences in the racial and cultural pasts of Latin American nations, none—with the possible exception of Bolivia—have maintained the language and social barriers which still divide *mestizo* Americans from those of European lineage.

American attempts to implant Anglo dominance in the Southwest have been ill-advised from the beginning. It may, in fact, be impossible to isolate the region from the continent below it. In Brazil, where the official tongue is Portuguese, Spanish is increasingly the language of the workplace in Rio Grande province, which borders on relatively poor Argentina. Like the American Southwest, Brazil's Rio Grande province is a receiving point for undocumented immigrants, mostly Argentines and Paraguayans. Since Brazil is governed by a repressive dictatorship, it can, if it pleases, use terror to halt immigration and drive back undocumented immigrants already in the country. But the United States, if it is both to preserve democracy and avoid Quebec-style strife, will have to shelve the policy of Anglo dominance in its southern border states.

If steps are taken soon enough, bilingualism, if not biculturalism, could be a fact of Southwestern life before the year 2000. Procedurally, the change would be neither radical nor unsettling. State agencies in Texas, New Mexico, Arizona and California could require all new employees hired after a set date in the future to speak both English and Spanish, and federal agencies could make a similar stipulation for personnel assigned to work in the region. Legislatures and Congress could require public institutions to provide intensive Spanish-language training to all students, and could order the school day divided into English and Spanish-language periods of instruction; if necessary, hours of instruction could be lengthened to assure mastery of both languages. The federal government could order electronic media to broadcast bilingually in the Southwest almost by fiat. Though adherence to the law has been lax, California statutes have for a century mandated that state documents be printed in both English and Spanish. Already, federal voting rights legislation has required Southwestern states to print ballots and publish election notices in both languages. Fundamental to any successful program of bilingualism would be a statuatory freeze on job promotions for those who, after a fixed date in the future, fall below a stipulated age but are still monolingual. For example, Congress could require that any Southwestern employee under 25 years of age in the year 2000 could not be promoted in public or private employment until he or she could pass written bilingual exams. While the constitutionality of such requirements appears doubtful at first glance, courts have upheld the legality of loyalty oaths and wage freezes, both of which limit the right of free contract in the workplace.

Bilingualism is an important reform for a variety of reasons. It would provide an atmosphere in which the assimilation of immigrants can occur with less trauma and more speed than happens now. It would also open the doors of public agencies to immigrants who wish to complain about Border Patrol abuse, exploitation by employers—or simply, to explain medical problems. Furthermore, a bilingual policy would win back prestige already lost in Latin America by American exclusionist policies, and the whole "alien invasion" debate. But most of all, it would break the back of Anglo chauvinism and racial prejudice, creating a grounds on which the Southwest could work out an equitable and peaceful ethnic coexistence.

Today, Southwestern racists believe that Spanish is an inferior language, possessing only crude concepts. Many believe that speaking Spanish leads to lying. Few are prepared to learn the language on their own, for they fear it would harm them. As a result, Chicanos, who are bilingual, know much about Anglo life and culture, if only from television and other public media, but Anglos know little about Mexican or Chicano lifestyles and attitudes. The result, in part, is "Mexicanophobia," fear of Latinos and their culture.

Bilingualism would make "ethnic integrity" a slogan of the past, not a possible hope for the future. It would remove Klan elements and Klan sentiments from the political picture, at least in part. More than anything else, it would provide a groundwork relatively free from prejudice on which the immigration issue could be resolved with the Mexican government. Unlike the U.S. government, the Mexican government could halt undocumented immigration, or drastically reduce it, by forcing it underground on the southern side of the border, where today, *coyotes* operate in the open. The Mexican government is currently struggling for its survival, and is unlikely to take measures to halt *sin papeles*, who provide desperately needed foreign exchange. But two decades from now, the Mexican government might well have nationalist leanings, and if does, bilingualism would serve as a signal that American proposals are motivated by neither racism nor a desire to exploit. Bilingualism would provide the posture of good faith which the United States cannot assume in Latin America today, for economic and political reasons dating back from the 1846 Mexican War up to the Ku Klux Klan's 1977 antics on the border.

Bilingualism is a frequent subject of Southwestern arm-chair debates. Already, it has become popular to declare that "culture cannot be legislated." This contention, though widespread, has already been defeated by history. Fifteen years ago, racists in Dixie argued that "morality cannot be legislated," yet the civil rights movement pro-vided that if morality could not be reformed, behavior cer-tainly could be. Segregation has disappeared from most sectors of public life in the South, and monolingualism could be subjected to a similar fate. Languages are not easily learned, it is true. But no institution in American so-ciety, besides slavery, has been as resistant to change as segregation, yet even segregation has been dealt severe blows.

The Dixie parallel, however, illustrates that bilingualism is not the whole solution to the problem of Anglo-Latin re-lations. In the South, both whites and blacks speak a com-mon language, but do not always share common concepts and meanings, because language is learned in private con-texts which carry economic, cultural and religious shades of difference into the words we use. Use of a common lan-guage aids the process of understanding, but does not guarantee it.

In the Southwest, bilingualism would open the door to a common culture, a truly Chicano culture, the culture of a new human type, neither *mestizo* nor Anglo, but hybrid of both. In at least one way, it would be more advantageous than suppression of either language, an alternative which international economics makes impossible. Bilingualism provides two different conceptual viewpoints: The bilingual person does not speak one base language and a translation of it, but rather two separate languages, each of which is riddled with its own historical contexts. A *"campesino"* is not a "farmer" as dictionaries tell us, because the American yeoman is unknown in Mexico, and the Mexican peasant, usually a poor person of Indian origins, is unknown in America. Likewise, different connotations and contexts ap-ply to abstract terms like "love," "honor" and "homeland." Bilingualism provides two separate paths to understanding any non-mathematical proposition. In fact, psycholinguists argue that the mere *sounds* of language influence the ways we conceptualize. Bilingualism would provide Chicanos and Anglos with dual inroads to linguistic-cultural understanding, where whites and blacks have only one.

Whether or not a bilingual Southwest would fit comfortably into the greater picture of American life and culture cannot be easily forseen. If Americans outside the region assumed "Mexicanophobic" attitudes towards the Southwest, the result would likely be an enlargement of conflict. On the other hand, we may with certainty know that failure to bilingualize spells strife inside the Southwest, where Chicanos are daily less patient with the second-class status accorded them. If America as a nation wants to head off turmoil over the notion of Atzlán, it has but one choice: to meet Atzlán half way.

Bilingualism would also provide a favorable atmosphere for resolving the immigration dispute internationally. By breaking the back of "Mexicanophobia," it would undermine its usefulness as a political rallying cry. Those spokesmen for business, labor and government whose actual motives are racist or demagogic would be discredited. In this atmosphere, the United States could consider undocumented immigration in its proper light, as an international economic issue. It could, as business urges, simply drop most restrictions to immigration. Or it could adopt a position which has already gained some support in the labor movement: repudiation of American foreign investment.

Since World War II, the export of capital has aggravated American unemployment. Whole industries, like electronics, have simply been transferred to foreign locations. Cheap foreign labor has undermined the garment and shoe industrics. Even agriculture, which deals in perishable goods, has suffered from imports of meats and vegetables, largely from Mexico and South America. Thousands of jobs once held by Americans are simply no longer available inside the country. Transnational corporations based in America derive most of the benefit of job exportation, for in other nations, wage levels are lower.

And yet government practices actually encourage American financial firms and manufacturers to invest overseas. If their holdings are nationalized by host countries, the U.S. government reimburses owners for their losses. The government currently insured more than $2.4 billion worth of such investments. U.S. taxpayers bear the risk. In December 1974, the government awarded $92.5 million to the International Telephone and Telegraph Company (ITT) after Chile nationalized its phone system.

Setting a moratorium on the foreign investment insurance program for all countries would slow the outflow of American capital. Cancellation need not be directed at investments in all countries. Because of its unique ties to Mexico, the United States might cancel investment insurance for that nation alone. Nationalization of American holdings in Mexico would cost taxpayers nothing without investment insurance. On the other hand, it might reduce Mexican immigration to a trickle within a few years' time.

The Mexican government has nationalized industries before. Petroleum, electricity, and the railroad and electric systems are already in government hands. But nationalized industries have been managed in such a way as to subsidize private industry, and in Mexico, *el norte* controls much of private industry. Today transnationals, mostly American-based, legally own nearly half of the stock in Mexico's top 290 corporations. An even greater percentage may actually belong to Americans through *sub rosa* channels; Mexicans in the business community frequently hold properties in their own names for foreign investors, whose activities are proscribed by law. Counting only legally-admitted holdings, however, foreign companies own a total 31 per cent of the value produced by Mexican industry. Nationalization would provide Mexico with new assets on which to borrow development funds.

Americans commonly refer to Mexico as a poor country, but the phrase describes only part of the truth. Mexico is indeed poor, but her poverty may be needless. Unlike other "underdeveloped" countries, Mexico produces petroleum, steel, coal and even uranium. Mexico builds and produces autos, trucks, medicines, and textiles. Nevertheless, foreigners own most of these industries, and participate as priviledged customers in buying products and services from nationalized industries. In early 1978, State Department officials negotiating a treaty to import Mexican natural gas for private American firms refused to offer the Mexicans more than $2.16 per thousand cubic feet of gas, a price 24 cents below the world market. The Mexican government had but two alternatives: to cancel construction of a pipeline to *el norte*, or to cave in to the cut-rate price offer. President Portillo chose the first alternative, because his people are weary of American high-handedness in economic affairs. But the gas deal was just one of literally hundreds of issues on which foreign interests have challenged Mexico, and generally Mexico has lost. Mexico, although it is capable of producing farm machinery, still imports tractors, and therefore, *must* export farm laborers to the U.S. When American agriculture was mechanized, the displaced farm population fled into industrial centers, where jobs were available. But much of the industry Mexico needs to provide jobs for its national economy is located in the U.S. The migration of rural Mexicans to Chicago and Detroit is as natural, in economic terms, as was the exodus 40 years ago of "Oakies," "Arkies," and "Hoosiers" to those manufacturing cities. What makes Mexican immigration different is the political reality of nationhood, the reality of borders.

The solution to the problem of undocumented Mexican immigration is not as simple as taking measures to legalize the *sin papeles*, though such measures would serve as a stopgap. Instead, the ultimate solution can only be one which grants Mexico an economic independence. Capital and the power to deploy it inside Mexico must be put in Mexican hands, for the benefit of the Mexican people, and not for transnational profit. The current status quo is one in which, to a great extent, Mexico's economy has been developed to serve the needs of transnational corporation, but not the Mexican nation. Until Mexico is allowed to declare economic independence, there are strong moral reasons for resisting exclusionist pressures in the U.S. If capital may be transnational within the confines of our morality, so too can labor. But beyond moral concerns, there are compelling practical reasons for refusing the exclusionist urge. If America will not control the export of her capital, Mexico is likely to refuse to control the exodus of her labor. Further, exclusionist campaigns intensify discrimination in the United States, whose history is already brimming with proof that racial and ethnic animosity is costly.

APPENDIX A

95TH CONGRESS
1ST SESSION

S. 2252

IN THE SENATE OF THE UNITED STATES

OCTOBER 28 (legislative day, OCTOBER 21) 1977

Mr. EASTLAND (for himself, Mr. KENNEDY, Mr. BENTSEN, and Mr. DECONCINI) introduced the following bill; which was read twice and referred to the Committee on the Judiciary

---

A BILL

To amend the Immigration and Nationality Act, and for other purposes.

Be it enacted by the Senate and House of Representatives of the United States of America in Congress assembled, That this Act may be cited as the "Alien Adjustment and Employment Act of 1977."

SEC. 2. (a) Section 249 of the Immigration and Nationality Act (8 U.S.C. 1259) is amended to read as follows:

"(a) A record of lawful admission for permanent residence may, in the discretion of the Attorney General and under such regulations as he may prescribe, be made in the case of any alien, as of the date of the approval of his application or, if entry occurred prior to July 1, 1924, as of the date of such entry, if no such record is otherwise available and such alien shall satisfy the Attorney General that he is not inadmissible under section 212 (a) insofar as it relates to criminals, procurers and other immoral persons, subversives, violators of the narcotic laws or smugglers of aliens, and he establishes that he—

251

"(1) entered the United States prior to January 1, 1970; and

"(2) has had his residence in the United States continuously since such entry.

"(b) This section shall not apply to any alien who has assisted in the persecution of any person on account of race, religion, nationality, membership in a particular social group, or political opinion."

(b) The title preceding section 249 of such Act is amended to read as follows: "RECORD OF ADMISSION FOR PERMANENT RESIDENCE IN THE CASE OF CERTAIN ALIENS WHO ENTERED THE UNITED STATES PRIOR TO JULY 1, 1924, OR JANUARY 1, 1970".

(c) The designation of section 249 in the table of contents (title II—Immigration, chapter) of such Act is amended to read as follows:

"Sec. 249. Record of admission for permanent residence in the case of certain aliens who entered the United States prior to July 1, 1924, or January 1, 1970."

SEC. 3. Section 201 (a) of the Immigration and Nationality Act (8 U.S.C. 1151 (a)) is amended to read as follows:

"(a) Exclusive of special immigrants defined in section 101 (a) (27), immediate relatives of United States citizens as specified in subsection (b) of this section, and of aliens in whose case a record of lawful admission for permanent residence is made pursuant to section 249, (1) the number of aliens born in any foreign state or dependent area located in the Eastern Hemisphere who may be issued immigrant visas or who may otherwise acquire the status of an alien lawfully admitted to the United States for permanent residence, or who may, pursuant to section 203 (a) (7), enter conditionally, shall not in any of the first three quarters of any fiscal year exceed a total of forty-five thousand and shall not in any fiscal year exceed a total of one hundred and seventy thousand; and (2) the number of aliens born in any foreign state of the Western Hemisphere or in the Canal Zone, or in a dependent area located in the Western Hemisphere, who may be issued immigrant visas or who may otherwise acquire the status of an alien lawfully admitted to the United States for permanent residence, or who may, pursuant to section 203 (a) (7), enter conditionally, shall not in any of the first three quarters of any fiscal year exceed a total of thirty-two thousand and shall not in any fiscal year exceed a total of one hundred and twenty thousand."

SEC. 4. (a) Notwithstanding any other provisions of law, any alien in the United States may, in the discretion of the Attorney General and under such regulations as he may prescribe, be permitted to reside in the United States temporarily until five years from the effective date of this Act, if such alien applies for such status within one year of the effective date of this Act and establishes to the satisfaction of the Attorney General that he

(1) enter the United States on or before January 1, 1977;

(2) has had his residence in the United States continuously since such entry; and

(3) is not inadmissible under section 212 (a) insofar as it relates to criminals, procurers, and other immoral persons, subversives, violators of the narcotic laws, or smugglers of aliens.

(b) This section shall not apply to any alien who—

(1) on January 1, 1977, was a nonimmigrant whose authorized stay, including any extension of the period of original admission, had not expired; or

(2) immediately prior to losing lawful nonimmigrant status had the status of a nonimmigrant student; or

(3) was formerly a nonimmigrant exchange alien as defined in section 101 (a) (15) (J) of the Immigration and Nationality Act subject to the two-year foreign residence requirement of section 212 (e) of the Act and has not fulfilled that requirement or received a waiver thereof; or

(4) has assisted in the persecution of any person or group of persons because of race, religion, nationality, membership in a particular social group, or political opinion.

(c) An alien granted temporary resident alien status under this section shall be issued such documentation as the Attorney General may by regulation prescribe.

(d) The Attorney General shall authorize the employment of any alien who is granted temporary resident alien status under this section.

(e) Notwithstanding section 211 (a) and 21 (a) (20) of the Immigration and Nationality Act (8 U.S.C. 1181 (a) and 1182 (a) (20)), the Attorney General may in his discretion and under such regulations as he may prescribe, authorize the readmission into the United States of any alien who has temporary resident alien status pursuant to this section and who is returning to a residence in the United States from a temporary visit abroad, without requiring such alien to obtain a passport, immigrant visa, reentry permit, or other documentation. An alien who qualifies for readmission under this subparagraph shall not be subject to the requirements of section 212 (a) (14) of the Immigration and Nationality Act (8 U.S.C. 1182 (a) (14)).

(f) If at any time after a person has obtained temporary

resident alien status under this section, it shall appear to the satisfaction of the Attorney General that such person was not in fact eligible for such status, the Attorney General shall rescind the grant of temporary resident alien status to such person, and the person shall thereupon be subject to the provisions of the Immigration and Nationality Act to the same extent as if the grant of temporary resident alien status had never been made.

(g) Except as otherwise specifically provided in this section, nothing in this section shall be construed to give or confer upon an alien who is granted temporary resident alien status any privileges, rights, benefits, exemptions, or immunities under the Immigration and Nationality Act for which they would not otherwise be qualified.

(h) An alien who is granted temporary resident alien status under this section shall not be eligible to receive any benefits under any of the following provisions of law:

(1) grants to States for medical assistance programs under title XIX of the Social Security Act (42 U.S.C. 1396 et seq.);

(2) aid to families with dependent children under title IV, part A, of the Social Security Act (42 U.S.C. 601 et seq.);

(3) supplemental security income for the aged, blind, and disabled under title XVI of the Social Security Act (42 U.S.C. 1381 et seq.); and

(4) Food Stamp Act of 1964, as amended (7 U.S.C. 2011 et seq.).

SEC. 5. (a) Section 274 of the Immigration and Nationality Act (8 U.S.C. 1324) is amended—

(1) by inserting after subsection (b) the following new subsection:

"(c) (1) It shall be unlawful for any employer to employ aliens in the United States who have not been lawfully admitted to the United States for permanent residence, unless the employment of such aliens is authorized by the Attorney General.

"(2) Any employer who violates this subsection shall be subject to a civil penalty or not more than $1,000 for each such alien in the employ of the employer on the effective date of this subsection or who has thereafter been employed by the employer, except for such alien whose status was adjusted or application for adjustment was pending pursuant to the terms of section 2 or section 4 of the Alien Adjustment and Employment Act of 1977.

"(3) The United States district courts shall have jurisdiction to enjoin violations of this subsection.

"(4) Upon determination that cause exists to believe that an employer has engaged in a pattern or practice of employing aliens in violation of this subsection, the Attorney General shall bring actions for both civil penalty and injunctive relief in the United States district court in any district in which the employer is alleged to have violated this subsection, or in any district in which the employer is found or transacts business.

"(5) Proof by an employer with respect to any person employed by him that, prior to the person's employment, or, in the case of a person hired prior to the effective date of this subsection, as soon as practicable but in any event within ninety days of such effective date, he saw such documentary evidence of eligibility to work in the United States as the Attorney General has by regulation designated for that purpose shall give rise to a rebuttable presumption that the employer has not violated this subsection with respect to that particular person.";

(2) by inserting after new subsection (c) the following new subsection:

"(d) Any person who knowingly and for gain assists an alien who is not authorized to work in the United States to obtain or retain employment in the United States, or who knowingly enters into a contractual or other arrangement to facilitate, for gain, the employment in the United States of an alien not authorized to work in the United States, shall be guilty of a felony, and upon conviction thereof shall be punished by a fine not exceeding $2,000 or by imprisonment not exceeding five years, or both, for each alien in respect to whom a violation of this subsection occurs.";

(3) by inserting after new subsection (d) the following new subsection:

"(e) The provisions of this section are intended to preempt any State or local laws imposing civil or criminal sanctions upon those who employ, or facilitate the employment, of aliens not authorized to work in the United States.".

(b) The title preceding section 274 of such Act is amended to read as follows: "BRINGING IN AND HARBORING CERTAIN ALIENS; RESTRICTION OF EMPLOYMENT OF ALIENS".

(c) The designation of section 274 in the table of contents (title II—Immigration, chapter 8) of such Act is amended to read as follows:

"Sec. 274. Bringing in and harboring certain aliens; restricted of employment of aliens.".

Sec. 6. The provisions of this Act shall become effective sixty days after the date of its enactment.

Appendix B Immigration Counseling Groups

ARIZONA

Catholic Social Services of
  Phoenix
Immigration and Family Reu-
  nification
1818 South 16th St. Phoenix,
  Ariz. 85034

CALIFORNIA

Catholic Charities of the
  Archdiocese of San Fran-
  cisco
Immigration Counseling Cen-
  ter
P.O. Box 3382
Corner 2nd and Reed
San Jose, Calif. 95116

Catholic Community Agen-
  cies
Los Angeles Diocese of
  Orange
1612 N. Spurgeon St.
Santa Ana, Calif. 92707

Catholic Welfare Bureau
Archdiocese of Los Angeles
1400 West Ninth St.
Los Angeles, Calif. 90015

Center on Administration of
  Criminal Justice
University of California Law
  School
Davis, Calif. 95616

Community Legal Services
210 S. First St.
San Jose, Calif. 95110

IMPACT Servicios de Inmi-
  gracion
1789 National Avenue
San Diego, Calif. 92113

International Institute of Ala-
  meda County
297 Lee Street
Oakland, Calif. 94610

International Institute of Fresno, Inc.
847 Waterman Ave.
Fresno, Calif. 93706

International Institute of Los
  Angeles
435 South Boyle Ave.
Los Angeles, Calif. 90033

International Institute of San
  Francisco
2209 Van Nexx Ave.
San Francisco, Calif 94109

International Rescue Committee, Inc.
3600 Wilshire Blvd.
Los Angeles, Calif. 90010

Jewish Family Service of Los
  Angeles
6505 Wilshire Blvd., Suite
  608
Los Angeles, Calif. 90048

La Raza Centro Legal, Inc.
3716 24th St.
San Francisco, Calif 94110

Legal Aid Association of
  Ventura County
631 Cooper Road
Post Office Box 259
Oxnard, Calif. 93030

Legal Aid Foundation of
  Long Beach
4790 E. Pacific Coast Highway
Long Beach, Calif. 90804

Legal Aid Society of San Diego, Inc.
964 Fifth Ave.
San Diego, Calif. 92101

Legal Aid Society of Santa Clara County, Inc.
D.B.A. Community Legal Services
330 North Market Street
San Jose, Calif. 95110

Los Angeles Christian Service Center
1068 S. Robertson Blvd.
Los Angeles, Calif. 90035

Mission Community Legal Defense, Inc.
2922 Mission Street
San Francisco, Calif. 94110

Neighborhood Adult Participation Project, Inc.
2600 Randolph Street
Huntington Park, Calif. 90255

One Stop Immigration Center, Inc.
1441–43 Wright Street
Los Angeles, Calif. 90015

Sandigan, Inc., Filipino Newcomers Service Center
944 Market St.
San Francisco, Calif. 94102

San Francisco Neighborhood Legal Assistance Foundation
1095 Market Street
San Francisco, Calif. 94103

West Side Planning Group, Inc.
707 N. Fulton
Fresno, Calif. 93728

COLORADO

Denver Opportunity, Inc.
431 Grant Street
Denver, Col. 80203

CONNECTICUT

International Institute of Connecticut
480 E. Eashington Ave.
Bridgeport, Conn. 06608

Jerome N. Frank Legal Services Organization
Yale Law School
127 Wall Street
New Haven, Conn. 06520

Jewish Family Service of New Haven, Inc.
152 Temple St.
New Haven, Conn. 06510

DELAWARE

Service for Foreign Born
Delaware Technical and Community College
333 Shipley Street
Wilmington, Del. 19801

State Service Bureau for Foreign Born People
900-A West 8th Street
Wilmington, Delaware 19806

HAWAII

Legal Aid Society of Hawaii
Suite 1100, 1164 Bishop Street
Honolulu, Hawaii 96813

State Immigrant Service Center
567 South King Street
Honolulu, Hawaii 96813

ILLINOIS

Asian American Community
Legal Aid Clinic
1651 North Kedzie
Chicago, Ill. 60647

Legal Services for Immigrants
343 S. Dearborn St.
Chicago, Ill. 60604

MASSACHUSETTS

Chinese-American Civil Association, Inc.
Multi-Service Center
85A Tyler St.
Boston, Mass. 02111

Hebrew Immigrant Aid Society—Massachusetts
18 Tremont Street
Boston, Mass. 02108

International Institute of Boston
287 Commonwealth Ave.
Boston, Mass. 02115

Massachusetts Office of Immigration and Americanization
182 Tremont St.
Boston, Mass. 02111

National Council of Jewish Women
Boston Section
70 Franklin St.
Boston, Mass. 02110

National Council of Jewish Women
Worcester Section
633 Salisbury Street
Worcester, Mass. 01609

United States Catholic Conference

Migration and Refugee Services
1312 Massachusetts Ave., N.W.
Washington, D.C. 20005

NEW HAMPSHIRE

Family Service Society
456 Beech Street
Manchester, New Hampshire
03103

MICHIGAN

International Institute of Metropolitan Detroit, Inc.
111 East Kirby Ave.
Detroit, Mich. 48202

International Institute of Flint, Michigan, Inc.
514 Liberty St.
Flint, Michigan 48503

Legal Aid Bureau of Detroit
Room 106, 51 West Warren Ave.
Detroit, Mich. 48201

MINNESOTA

International Institute of Duluth
523 Lyceum Bldg.
Duluth, Minn. 55802

International Institute of Minnesota
1694 Como Ave.
St. Paul, Minn. 55108

NEW JERSEY

Acquaviva Delle Fonti Mutual Aid Society
1142 Puddingstone Road
Mountainside, N. J. 07092

International Institute of Jersey City
857 Bergen Ave.
Jersey City, N.J. 07306

Archdiocese of Newark (Roman Catholic)
Office of Immigration
One Summer Ave.
Newark, N.J. 07104

Jewish Counselling and Service Agency
161 Milburn Ave.
Milburn, N.J. 07041

NEW MEXICO

Southern New Mexico Legal Services, Inc.
413 West Griggs
Las Cruces, N.M. 88001

NEW YORK

Albany Jewish Social Service
291 State Ave.
Albany, N.Y. 12210

American Civic Association
131 Front Street
Binghamton, New York 13905

American Council for Nationalities Service
20 West 40th Street
New York, N.Y. 10018

Americanization League of Syracuse and Onondaga County
410 E. Willow St.
Syracuse, N.Y. 13203

ANGYRA, International Society for the Aid of Greek Seamen

25 South Street
New York, N.Y. 10004

Board of Home Missions of the Congregational and Christian Churches
287 Fourth Ave.
New York, N.Y. 10003

Board of Social Missions of the United Lutheran Church in America
231 Madison Ave.
New York, N.Y. 10016

Catholic Charities of Buffalo, New York, Inc.
525 Washington Street
Buffalo, N.Y. 14203

Church World Service
475 Riverside Drive
New York, N.Y. 10027

Common Council for American Unity
20 West 40th Street
New York, N.Y. 10018

Community Action for Legal Services, Inc.
Brooklyn Branch
186 Joralemon Street, Room 701
Brooklyn, N.Y. 11201

Free Europe Committee, Inc.
Two Park Avenue
New York, N.Y. 10016

United HIAS Service
200 Park Ave.
New York, N.Y. 10003

International Center and Girls Club of Niagara Falls, Inc.

357 Portage Road
Niagara Falls, N.Y. 14303

International Institute of Buffalo, New York, Inc.
864 Delaware Ave.
Buffalo, New York 14209

International Institute of New York City, Inc.
55 West 42nd St., Room 1102–A
New York, N.Y. 10036

International Rescue Committee, Inc.
386 Park Avenue South
New York, N.Y. 10016

MFY Legal Services, Inc.
320 East Third St.
New York, N.Y. 10009

Nassau County Hispanic Foundation, Inc.
105 Main Street
Hempstead, N.Y. 11550

National Association for the Advancement of Orthodox Judaism, Inc.
132 Nassau St.
New York, N.Y. 10038

National Council of Jewish Women
New York Section
15 Park Row
New York, N.Y. 10038

National Lutheran Council
Division of Welfare to Immigrants
15 East 26th St.
New York, N.Y. 10010

New York Protestant Episcopal City Mission Society
38 Bleecker St.
New York, N.Y. 10012

North Eastern Conference of Seventh-Day Adventists
560 West 150th St.
New York, N.Y. 10031

Polish and Slavic Center, Inc.
940 Manhattan Ave.
Brooklyn, N.Y. 11222

Polish Social Service Bureau
17 Irving Place
New York, N.Y. 10003

The Salvation Army
120 West 14th St.
New York, N.Y. 10011

Unidad Civica Hispano Americana de New York, Inc.
15 Deasy Lane
Glen Cove, N.Y. 11542

OHIO

Catholic Service League
138 Fir Hill
Akron, Ohio 44304

International Institute of Akron
207 East Tallmadge Ave.
Akron, Ohio 44310

International Institute of Greater Toledo, Inc.
2040 Scottwood Ave.
Toledo, Ohio 43620

International Institute of Youngstown, Ohio, Inc.
145 Lincoln Ave.
Youngstown, Ohio 44503

Jewish Community Council of Dayton, Ohio
184 Salem Ave.
Dayton, Ohio 45406

Nationalities Service Center
1001 Huron Road
Cleveland, Ohio 44115

OREGON

Marion–Polk Legal Aid
Services, Inc.
1244 State Street
Salem, Ore. 97301

Willamette Valley Immi-
gration Project
519 S.W. Third Ave. #418
Portland, Ore. 97214

PENNSYLVANIA

Hias and Council Migration
Service of Philadelphia
1913 Walnut Street
Philadelphia, Pa. 19103

International Institute of
Erie, Pennsylvania, Inc.
354 West Seventh St.
Erie, Pa. 16502

Jewish Counseling Service
60 South River St.
Wilkes-Barre, Penn. 18701

Lehigh County Americanization Bureau
455 Hamilton St.
Allentown, Pa. 18105

Nationalities Service Center
of Philadelphia
1300 Spruce St.
Philadelphia, Pa. 19107

RHODE ISLAND

International Institute of
Rhode Island, Inc.
104 Princeton Ave.
Providence, R.I. 02907

TEXAS

Asociacion Pro Servicios So-
ciales, Inc.
520 Garza St.
Laredo, Tex. 78040

Catholic Community Services
3915 Lemmon
Dallas, TX 75219

Catholic Services for Immigrants
1801 Durango
San Antonio, TX 78207

Ecumenical Institutional Services, Inc.
108 Elmview Place
San Antonio, TX 78209

Immigration Counseling Center, Inc.
2405 Navigation Blvd.
Houston, TX 77002

Texas Rural Legal Aid, Inc.
519 S. Texas
Weslaco, TX 76596

South Texas Immigration
Project
741 East Bowie Street
P.O. Box 547
Alamo, TX 78516

WASHINGTON

Seattle King County Spanish
Surnamed Community Ac-
tion Board, Inc.
501 Dexter Avenue North
Seattle, Washington 98109

WISCONSIN

International Institute of Milwaukee County, Inc.
2824 West Highland Blvd.
Milwaukee, Wisc. 53208

Illegal Aliens—Border Patrol Activities

No. 126. Estimates of Illegal Aliens, by Region and Employment Status: 1976

[In thousands. As of November. Comprises rough estimates made by U.S. Immigration and Naturalization Service district directors, based on apprehensions of illegal aliens and number of legal aliens known to be in their districts. Regions are as defined by U.S. Immigration and Naturalization Service]

REGION	Total	EMPLOYED		REGION	Total	EMPLOYED	
		Total	Percent of total			Total	Percent of total
United States......	6,037	3,817	63.2	Eastern..........	2,058	1,128	54.8
Northern............	669	449	67.1	Southern........	1,514	1,094	72.3
				Western..........	1,796	1,146	63.8

Source: U.S. Immigration and Naturalization Service, unpublished data.

From *Statistical Abstract of the United States,*
Bureau of Census, Oct. 1977

No. 127. Immigration Border Patrol Activities: 1965 to 1976

[In thousands, except as indicated. For years ending June 30, except as noted]

ITEM	1965	1970	1971	1972	1973	1974	1975	1976
Persons apprehended [2]	53.3	233.9	305.9	373.9	503.9	640.9	602.2	878.2
Deportable aliens located [3]	52.4	231.1	302.5	369.5	498.1	634.8	596.8	871.2
Mexican	44.2	219.3	290.2	355.1	480.6	616.6	579.4	848.2
Canadian	5.8	7.8	7.5	8.2	8.7	7.4	7.3	8.1
Other	2.5	4.1	4.9	6.2	8.9	10.8	10.1	14.9
Aliens smuggled into U.S.	1.8	18.7	19.8	24.9	41.6	83.1	80.4	105.5
Aliens located (previously expelled)	14.0	67.4	90.4	115.8	152.4	162.4	184.6	229.8
Aliens located (previous criminal records)	4.0	3.8	4.2	4.4	11.2	10.9	10.3	15.9
Conveyances examined	1,172	1,792	2,024	2,473	2,666	2,905	3,470	4,297
Automobiles	752	1,311	1,508	1,893	2,020	2,230	2,663	3,211
Persons questioned [4]	5,285	6,805	7,664	9,024	9,507	10,202	11,265	14,061
In automobiles	1,877	3,416	4,029	4,855	5,135	5,591	6,888	8,135
Pedestrians	2,065	1,661	1,752	1,982	2,145	2,243	2,056	2,874
Value of seizures $1,000	594	4,547	6,153	12,961	25,954	47,210	28,654	23,281
Narcotics $1,000	394	3,865	5,379	11,709	23,464	45,056	26,302	20,763

[1] For 15 months ending Sept. 30.   [2] Foreign nationals arrested because they entered U.S. illegally or were present in violation of terms of lawful admission.   [3] Foreign nationals who entered U.S. illegally at other than ports of entry or who were admitted at ports of entry but became deportable as result of violations of terms of their admission.   [4] Totals include types not shown separately.

Source: U.S. Immigration and Naturalization Service, *Annual Report*.

SELECTED EMPLOYMENT, OCCUPATIONAL AND ECONOMIC DATA FOR THE
FOREIGN-BORN POPULATION IMMIGRATING TO U.S. BETWEEN 1965 AND 1970,
BY COUNTRY OF BIRTH: 1970

Country of Birth	Percent unemployed males in civilian labor force, 16 yrs old and over	Percent employed males in prof. & manag. occupations, 16 yrs old and over	Median family income, 1969	Percent of families below poverty
All foreign-born	4.1%	27.5%	$ 8352	16.1%
United Kingdom	2.4%	58.3%	$12317	7.2%
Ireland	2.2%	38.7%	$11276	6.9%
Norway	0	70.6%	$12811	3.4%
Sweden	2.2%	85.2%	$12895	4.8%
Denmark	0	59.0%	$11285	7.4%
Netherlands	1.5%	57.5%	$11269	9.5%
France	3.5%	46.0%	$10119	16.0%
Germany	1.4%	45.8%	$10286	15.1%
Poland	5.8%	20.3%	$10281	6.7%
Czechoslovakia	2.9%	37.2%	$ 9306	16.5%

Austria	1.1%	53.6%	$11243	5.7%
Hungary	5.0%	33.7%	$10274	10.9%
Yugoslavia	2.8%	15.7%	$9207	13.3%
U.S.S.R.	1.8%	25.9%	$9407	11.5%
Lithuania	0	17.7%	...	...
Greece	4.7%	10.9%	$8448	10.3%
Italy	4.0%	5.9%	$8785	10.2%
China	3.7%	37.8%	$7372	21.3%
Japan	1.8%	59.1%	$9320	13.6%
Canada	4.0%	41.8%	$11281	7.1%
Mexico	6.3%	3.4%	$5354	32.3%
Cuba	5.1%	11.1%	$7047	22.3%
Other West Indies	4.3%	12.1%	$7653	13.0%
Other Central & So. Amer.	4.1%	20.0%	$7476	17.6%
All Other Countries	3.9%	43.8%	$9052	14.9%

SOURCE: U.S. Bureau of the Census, Census of Population, 1970. Subject Reports. Final Report PC(2)-1A, National Origin and Language. U.S. Government Printing Office, Washington, D.C., 1973; Table 18

Program Activity	Percentage of Respondent
Input	Participation
Social Security Taxes withheld	77.3
Federal income taxes withheld	73.2
Hospitalization payments withheld	44.0
Filed U.S. income tax returns	31.5

Output	
Used hospitals or clinics	27.4
Collected one or more weeks of unemployment insurance	3.9
Have children in U.S. schools	3.7
Participated in U.S.-funded job training programs	1.4
Secured food stamps	1.3
Secured welfare payments	0.5

Source: Linton & Company, Illegal Alien Study, 1975

Distributions of Occupation of Mexicans Apprehended Illegal Alien Respondents in Their Country of Origin and in Most Recent U.S. Job, by Region of Origin (as percents of group responding)

OCCUPATION GROUP	TOTAL		MEXICAN ILLEGALS	
	Country of Origin	U.S.	Country of Origin	U.S.
Professional, Technical & Kindred Workers	5.6	1.6	1.7	0.5
Owners, Managers, Administrators, except farm	2.9	1.3	0.2	-
Sales Workers	5.3	1.1	3.2	0.7
Clerical & Kindred Workers	3.8	1.4	1.7	-
Craft & Kindred Workers	14.8	15.3	15.0	14.3
Operatives, except Transport	13.5	24.5	8.4	21.9
Transport Equipment Operatives	4.1	0.6	4.4	0.7
Nonfarm Laborers	9.1	14.8	11.8	17.9
Farmers & Farm Managers[2]	0.3	-	0.2	-
Farm Laborers & Supervisors[3]	35.4	18.8	49.1	27.0
Service Workers, except Private Household	3.3	17.4	2.2	13.5
Private Household Workers	1.9	3.2	2.0	3.4
No. of Respondents	628	628	407	407
SUBTOTAL[4]	100.0	100.0	99.9	99.9
Don't Know/Refuse to Answer	2.1	2.1	2.1	2.1
Not in Country of Origin, 1970-75	18.7	18.7	13.3	13.3
Total No. of Respondents	793	793	481	481

Source: Linton & Company Illegal Alien Study, 1975.

[1] Data cover period from January 1970-June 1975 and report respondents' major occupation in country of origin.

[2] Respondents included only farmers.

[3] Respondents included one supervisor in country of origin.

[4] Percentages may not add to 100 due to roundoff.

Average Gross Hourly and Weekly Wage, and Weekly Hours,
of Apprehended Illegal Alien Respondents
in Their Most Recent U.S. Job and of U.S. Production or
Nonsupervisory Workers (PNW), by Industry in 1975

INDUSTRY DIVISION	AVG HOURLY WAGE	
	Illegals	U.S. PNW
Agriculture, Forestry & Fisheries	$2.07	*
Mining	2.00	$5.79
Contract Construction	2.98	7.15
Manufacturing	2.92	4.73
Transportation & Public Utilities	2.77	5.75
Trade: Wholesale & Retail	2.57	3.71
Finance, Real Estate & Insurance	3.32	4.08
Services, except Private Household	2.79	3.98
Private Household Services	1.63	*
All Industries (excluding Agriculture & Private Household)	2.66	4.47

Sources: Column 1, 3, 5, and 7, Linton & Company Illegal Alien
Study; columns 2, 4, and 6, U.S. Department of Labor, Employment
and Earnings, Volume 21, No. 12 (June 1975), Tables C-1, C-2.

[1]Data for 27 of the 793 respondents who were self-employed or
omitted industry, wage, or hours are excluded. For comparative
purposes, the toal number of illegals excludes 134 respondents
in agriculture and 23 in private households.

AVG WEEKLY WAGE		AVG WEEKLY HOURS		No. of Illegals[1]
Illegals	U.S. PNW	Illegals	U.S. PNW	
$110.57	*	53.6	*	134
120.00	$244.92	60.0	42.3	1
126.39	265.27	42.8	37.1	124
121.22	184.47	41.2	39.0	259
134.00	228.28	48.6	39.7	10
112.69	124.66	43.4	33.6	.152
117.00	148.10	36.0	36.3	6
121.75	134.13	45.0	33.7	57
66.30	*	42.4	*	23
117.03	160.47	44.5	35.9.	609

* Not Available

NOTE: Note that average hourly wage times average weekly hours may not equal average weekly wage. In fact, for these data, that product is consistently greater than the average weekly wage, indicating a tendency for respondents with lower wages to work longer hours.

Characteristics of Households in the U.S. and in Selected Latin-American Nations

Household Characteristics	United States	Mexico	El Salvador	Guatemala	Colombia	Ecuador
Average No. of Persons per Household	3.2 (1970)	5.7 (1970)	*	5.2 (1964)	*	5.1 (1962)
Average No. of Rooms per Dwelling	5.1 (1970)	2.3 (1970)	1.7 (1970)	2.0 (1964)	2.9 (1964)	5.1 (1962)
Percentage of Households With Running Water	97.5 (1970)	38.7 (1970)	26.0 (1970)	11.3 (1964)	41.3 (1964)	12.3 (1962)
Percentage of Households With Electricity	*	58.9 (1970)	34.0 (1970)	22.0 (1964)	47.4 (1964)	32.3 (1962)

Source: U.N. Statistical Yearbook, 1973, Table 198.

*Comparable data not available.

INDEX

AFL-CIO, birthrate of undocumented aliens, and, 136–37
bracero program and, 38–39, 59, 60–61
Eastland, James O., and, 92
effort to impugn undocumented aliens as tax evaders and welfare cheats, 117, 118
exclusionism and, 96–97, 145, 147, 239–242
exclusionist groups and revival of alliance with, during Cold War, 42
United Farm Workers and, 181–82
Agribusiness, preference for *bracero* or undocumented alien workers, 59
Unions and, 52, 53
Aliens, undocumented, *see* undocumented aliens
American Civil Liberties Union (ACLU), undocumented aliens rights and, 204
American Legion, exclusionism and, 91
Amnesty program, 150–52
Anti-alien hysteria and Leonard F. Chapman, 98–110
Arrests of undocumented aliens, 69–75
Asian immigrants, restrictions upon, 27–29
Atrocities during annexation of Texas, 2
Attorneys not provided for undocumented aliens, 204
Atzlan, 243–44

Bergland, Robert (Secretary of Agriculture), 149
Bilingualism in Southwest, 245–51
Birthrate, statistics regarding undocumented aliens and, 135–38
Border, methods of crossing the, 215–24
Border Patrol, 69–75
backgrounds of patrolmen, 185–86
brutality and racism in, 186–87, 195–205
Castillo, Leonel, and, 191–92
changing role of, 40
Chavez, Cesar on, 182

crackdown on brutality in, 190
creation of, 30–31
deaths of prisoners of, 3–4, 197–98
deportation procedures and, 69–75
employers cooperation with, 39–40
methods of spotting undocumented aliens and, 14, 183–84
morale in, 185, 193
off-the-job pressures on members of, 189
problems enforcing law, 86
profile of, 183–93
reform of proposed, 142
Vietnam war surplus and, 183–84
Bracero program, 33–40
AFL, and 38–39, 48, 59, 60–61
Berkeley study of, 51
earnings under, 50
economic conditions in Mexico made it preferrable, 52
humanitarian objections to, 48–49
Labor and, 52–55
living conditions and diet during, 49
opposition to, 47
opposition to renewal of from UFW, 182
stimulation of un..'`cumented immigration as `. result of, 35
strikebreaking and, 53–54
Braceros
closing the door on, 47–55
exposure to pesticides, 49
Bridges, Harry, attempted deportation of, 42
Brownell, Herbert Jr. (Attorney General), 43
Brutality and abuse of undocumented aliens, 3–4, 195–205

Camejo, Peter, 142
Cantu, Mario, 141, 142–44
Carter, (Jimmy) Plan for immigration (Senate Bill 2252 Feb. 1978), 142, 145–52, 253–57
European parallel and, 153–62

Castillo, Leonel (Commissioner INS). 142, 173–80
Border Patrol and, 178
exclusionists and, 179
Mexicanophobia and, 180
Census Bureau, and Latin-surnamed persons, 241–42
Centro de Accion Social Autonomo (CASA), 140–44, 242
Chapman, Leonard F. (Commissioner INS), 4, 90, 98, 99–102
balance of payments deficit, blames undocumented aliens for, 133–34
development of statistics by, to prove undocumented aliens held attractive jobs, 111–12
deportation of aliens as remedy for unemployment, 109–15
errors in citation of wages paid to undocumented aliens, 111–16
historical facts regarding immigration, ignorance of, 101–02
inflated estimates of immigrant population by, 103–08
racist remarks of, 100–02
tax evasion, charges undocumented aliens with, 118
Chavez, Cesar, 139–44, 181–82
Chicano movement, 139–44, 181–82, 234–45
Chinese Exclusion Act, 1892, 201–02, 204
Chinese immigration to US, 27–28, 31, 53
Congress, U.S., and undocumented aliens, 5, 41, 48, 49, 78, 90–98, 135, 142, 145–52, 253–57
Corona, Bert, 140
Crossing the border, methods of, 215–24
Crossing the Rio Grande, 225–31

Deportation, the procedures of, 69–75
Discrimination against Spanish-speaking people, 87

Eastland, James O. (U.S. Senator), and Food Lobby, 92, 93, 95, 145
Employers abuse of undocumented aliens, 200

False documents, traffic in, 75
Federationist on legal immigration (1973), 60
Food lobby and Carter plan, 152
Food stamps, 125

Gompers, Samuel and exclusionist movement, 28
Gutierrez, Jose Angel, 144

Hernandez, Silverio, Border Patrol and death of, 3–4
Hill, Joe, 29
Hoover, J. Edgar, Palmer raids and, 30
Hospitals and clinics used by undocumented aliens, 129–31

Immigrants, civil liberties and, 195–205
Immigration, agribusiness and, 53, 59, 89
closing the door on, 1968, 57–61
history of, 23–32
Immigration, "open door" policy and, 23
quotas, Cubans and, 61
restrictions, effects of 1965-68, 65–68
what it takes to achieve, 65–68
Immigration and Nationality Act, 1952 (McCarren-Walter), 202
Immigration and Naturalization Service, change in attitude under Commissioner Castillo, 177
headquarters, undocumented aliens employed at, 111
investigators and raiding of UFW picket lines, 140
statistics on Mexican undocumented aliens, 115–16
"voluntary departures," 20, 70–71
Internal Revenue Service, 119

Japanese immigration, 28, 53

Korean War, effect upon immigration, 41
Ku Klux Klan, 167–71, 242
    Border Patrol and, 167–71
    Immigration and Naturalization Service and, 168

La Torre, Chole, 140
League of United Latin American Citizens, 142
Lesko Report, 103–08
Linton Study of Undocumented Aliens, 7–9, 88, 107–08, 112–16, 118–19, 124, 125, 130, 133–34, 239

McCarthy era, deportations of aliens during, 42
McGovern, George, and bracero program, 48
McCulloch, William (Representative), 91–98
Mass deportations, see "Operation Wetback"
Medina, Jose, on state anti-alien laws, 165
Meiklejohn, Kenneth J. (AFL-CIO lobbyist), 96–97
Mexican children, high mortality amongst, 83
    citizens, illegality of leaving without passports, 37–38
    economic crises, 77–84
    government and undocumented aliens, 246
    government slaves in Texas and, 24–25
    immigrants, racism towards, 32
    immigration, 24–27, 32
        changing attitudes towards in U.S., 85–88
        bracero program, 33–40, 47, 48, 49, 50, 51, 52–55, 182
        Operation Wetback, 41–45
        reasons for, 77–84
        unknown in early 19th century, 24
        World War I and, 29
        World War II and, 33–34
"Mexican invasion," fears of, 5
    campaign leading to passage of state and municipal legislation, 163–65

oil industry, 79–80
passports only issued in Mexico city, 19
Mexicans and Ku Klux Klan, 167–71
Mexico, living conditions for peasants in, 12–13, 82–83
    poverty of peasants as incentive to emigration, 12–13
    transnational corporations and, 249–51
    violence in as cause of emigration, 82

National Council of Agricultural Employers, and bracero program, 95–96
National identity cards, libertarian and Chicano fears of, 5
    exclusionists and, 135–38, 147–49
    Zero Population Growth and, 122, 135
Naturalization, standards applied to applicants for, 23, 65–66
Nixon administration and attitudes on immigration, 4, 90, 98, 99–102, 103–08, 109–16, 118, 133–34

Operation Wetback, 41–45

Palmer Raids, 30
Pistoleros, 82
Polleros, 209–14
Protective Order of Elks, exclusionism and, 91
Public Law, 78, see Bracero program

Readers Digest, 102
Rio Grande, Crossing the, 225–31
Rodino, Peter Wallace, Jr. and immigration, 90–98, 135

Sacco and Vanzetti, 30
Schools, impact of undocumented aliens on minimal, 130
Scott, Winfield (General), 26
Sin Fronteras (CASA newspaper), 141

Smugglers (*coyotes*), 13–14, 41, 73, 75, 209–14
  generally unarmed, 190
Social Security Administration 15, 117, 119–25 and national ID card, 147–49
Spanish language, racist fears of, 246
States and undocumented aliens, 5, 163–65
Swing, Joseph May (General), 43–45, 98

Taylor, General Zachary, and invasion of Mexico, 26
Texas, annexation of, US atrocities against Mexicans during, 26
  racial attitudes and, 35–37
Tijerina, Reieses, 144

Undocumented aliens
  accurate figures not available on, 239
  apprehensions of, 69–75
  attorneys not provided for at government expense, 204
  Border Patrol and, 3–4, 14, 17, 19, 30–31, 39–40, 182, 183–84, 186–87, 190
  brutality and abuse of, 195–96
  Chapman, Leonard F. and, 4, 90, 98, 99–102, 109–16, 118, 133–34
  Chicanos and, 18, 139–44, 181–82, 239–51
  civil liberties and, 195–205
  Congress, U.S., and, 5, 41, 48, 49, 78, 90–98, 135, 142, 145–52, 253–57
  contributions to unemployment insurance systems, 127–28
  documents of, difficulty in tracing, 72
  eastward population movement of, 4
  employers abuse of, 200
  escape valve for Mexican economy, regarded as, 144
  estimates of population in U.S., 103–08, 135–38
  exploitation of in US, 85–88
  food stamps and, 125
  hospitals and clinics used by, 129–31
  ignorance of welfare programs, 118
  impact on schools minimal, 130
  interviewed in custody of Border Patrol, 11
  Ku Klux Klan and, 167–71
  methods of crossing border and, 215–224
  Mexican government and, 246
  Mexico, living conditions in, 12–13, 82–83
  polleros and, 13, 209–214
  population and, 122, 135–38
  profile of, 7–9
  reluctance of Mexicans to emigrate, 13
  Social Security and, 15, 117, 119–25, 147–49
  States and, 5, 163–65
  scapegoats for social ills, 89–90
  sex of, 137
Spanish-speaking community, object of dislike in, 5, 87, 88
  "voluntary departures" of, 20, 70–71
  U.S. Constitution and, 201
  wages below norm, 110–116
  "welfare users and tax evaders, not found to be, 117–25
Unemployment insurance systems, 127–28
United Farmworkers (UFW), 139–44, 181–82
U.S. Balance of payments and undocumented aliens, 133–34
U.S. Immigration, history of, 23–32
U.S., Latinization of, 5
  Tourist and student visas to, 67–68

Visa jumping, 233–38

Wall Street Journal, undocumented aliens and, 239
Welfare programs, undocumented aliens, ignorant of, 118

Xenophobia, 5, 42

Zero Population Growth (ZPG), 135–38